RESPONSIBILITY
AND
RESTORATION

RESPONSIBILITY
AND
RESTORATION

The Course
of the Book of Ezekiel

M.E. ANDREW

UNIVERSITY OF OTAGO PRESS

© Maurice Andrew

ISBN 0 908569 32 7

Published 1985 by the University of Otago Press, Box 56, Dunedin, New Zealand.

CONTENTS

INTRODUCTION

The Book of Ezekiel is now little known. Possibly some people remember the phrase "wheels within wheels" from chap.1, the watchman in chap.33 or the dry bones in chap.37, but not much more. It is probably not excessive to assume that modern readers would regard the book as something of a joke, or at least, would show no interest in it.

I wrote this book from the opposite experience, the realization that once one begins to understand the Book of Ezekiel, far from being a joke, it is both interesting and relevant today. But this is not something which will come about simply by dipping into it. We must see the substance of Ezekiel both as a whole and within the pattern of its own sequence. Rather than writing a monograph which selects certain themes for special treatment, I hope to contribute to the reading and understanding of the book of Ezekiel in sequence, showing that individual sections and themes of the book should not be considered alone, but as different parts of a related whole.

Nor is my book intended as a commentary in the usual sense, concentrating on all the linguistic, historical and literary details. Few people read commentaries right through, but since this is an aid to acquaintance with the book as a whole it would be desirable to do so here. I emphasize the content of the text itself rather than its many historical and literary problems, even though they cannot be separated. I wish to present the theology of the Book of Ezekiel in such a way that readers might understand it now. This may not always be obvious, since suggestions about how Ezekiel might be understood today must consider the theology of the book against its own background; and often this will have to be done at some length. Further, when an attempt is made to state what "it means now", readers may expect particular modern examples which are, however, helpful only within a narrow sphere. The last difficulty is that when the theology of a biblical book is expressed in modern terms, it may appear too simple and not sufficiently different to be significant.

HISTORICAL BACKGROUND

Since the historical and literary problems raised by the Book of Ezekiel itself affect our understanding of the theology I shall briefly summarize them(1).

There is a problem in the very first verse of the Book, which says that Ezekiel's vision was "In the thirtieth year" but does not say to what the thirtieth year refers. The next verse,

1

however, reveals it to be "in the fifth year of the exile of King Jehoiachin", a reference to a King of Judah who was taken into exile by the Babylonians in 597 B.C. The implication is that Ezekiel's call vision came about 593 B.C., which would place him towards the end of a period of conflict between the Babylonians and the Judaean kingdom. It is often thought that the "thirty" refers to the prophet's age and that, as a youth belonging to a priestly family, Ezekiel could have been impressed by the religious reforms carried out by King Josiah in 621 B.C. (2 Kings 22-23) (2). He who inspired so much hope, however, was killed by the Egyptian pharoah Neco in 609 B.C. at Megiddo (2 Kings 23:29). The Judaeans themselves made a younger son of Josiah, Jehoahaz, king, but Neco displaced him with his older brother Eliakim and changed his name to Jehoiakim (2 Kings 23:30-34; see also Ezekiel 19). After the Babylonians became the dominant power in the area Jehoiakim switched his allegiance to them, but in 602 B.C. he rebelled (2 Kings 24:1). Nebuchadrezzar, the king of the Babylonians, was slow to act decisively, but about 598 B.C. he besieged Jerusalem. Evidently Jehoiakim died about that time - in any case his eighteen-year-old son, Johoiachin, left in this appalling situation, and after a reign of only three months, gave himself up and was taken into exile with some others (2 Kings 24:6-17). It has usually been thought that Ezekiel was part of this first exile. The very last thing which the Books of Kings relate is that, in the 37th year of exile (561 B.C.), the then king of Babylon pardoned Jehoiachin and gave him a place in the royal household (2 Kings 25:27-30).

In the meantime, however, Nebuchadrezzar had made an uncle of Jehoiachin, Mattaniah, king and changed his name to Zedekiah. He reigned for the next eleven years (2 Kings 24:17-18). In other words, the Judaean state had not been completely destroyed either physically or constitutionally. For these political as well as religious and personal reasons, it is understandable that the exiles,loath to accept their condition as permanent, hoped for a quick return home. At home, many of the leaders who remained in Jerusalem, far from foreseeing the utter devastation which was to come, wanted to shake off the Babylonian yoke. Zedekiah vacillated between the pro-war party and the prophet Jeremiah who opposed any further rebellion (see, for example, Jeremiah 37). Ezekiel expresses the belief that Jerusalem would face further siege (chaps 4-5) and its inhabitants further exile (chap.12). Chapters 4-24 of Ezekiel are directed against the religious and political situation in Jerusalem between 597 and 587 B.C. Ezekiel sees Zedekiah's final rebellion against Babylon (2 Kings 24:20-25:1 - 589 B.C.) as an unpardonable breach of faith (chap.17). In any case, the rebellion led to a long siege which lasted until 587 B.C. When the Babylonians did at least breach the wall, Zedekiah escaped by night, but was caught and taken to Nebuchadrezzar at his headquarters at Riblah, north of Damascus. Before his eyes were put out the last thing he saw was the slaying of his sons, then he was taken in chains to Babylon where he no doubt died

(2 Kings 25:2-7; see also Ezekiel 12). In Jerusalem itself the temple was destroyed, the walls broken down and more people taken into exile, with only the poorest remaining (2 Kings 25:8-12).

The news of the fall of the city appears in the Book of Ezekiel in 33:21-22. It is the turning-point from what had been predominantly a proclamation of judgement against Jerusalem in 1-24 to what is predominantly a proclamation of restoration to the exiles in 33-48, for the most part in terms of a return to the land and the re-establishment of the temple. Evidently the exiles were settled in their own area by the Babylonians (1:1; 3:15), and were able to move about freely. Elders, for example, were able to approach Ezekiel (14:1; 20:1). They had houses and could talk together about matters of mutual interest (33:30). The latest date in the book is given in 29:17 as the 27th year, that is about 571 B.C. Together with 1:2 it indicates that the book presents Ezekiel's activities between 593 and 571 B.C., a span comprising the long and inconclusive siege of Tyre which the Babylonians undertook from about 585-572 B.C. Since there does not seem to be anything in the book which makes specific references to any event after 572 B.C., it apparently concludes well before the time of Cyrus the Persian who, in 538 B.C., conquered the Babylonians, issuing a decree which was to lead to the return of some Judaeans and eventually to the rebuilding of the temple.

LITERARY HISTORY

All this may seem comparatively straightforward, but as Walther Eichrodt points out "This picture of the historical situation suggested by the dates given in the book and by various statements by the author has in fact been questioned by many scholars, at any rate in the last few decades"(3). The reason for this is that much of the book concerns Jerusalem and its inhabitants without having any direct reference to the exiles. It can be argued that, at least in this final form, the intention is to say what is happening in Jerusalem and what is said about it is primarily of importance to the exiles. This would not necessarily mean, however, that the material was not originally composed in and for Jerusalem and only subsequently and editorially remoulded for the exiles.

Gustav Hoelscher made a sharp distinction between Ezekiel, whom he saw as a poet, and the Book of Ezekiel itself(4). For him the problem of the Book of Ezekiel resided in the fact that the picture of the authentic poet-prophet had been overlaid subsequently in prose. He was able to find authentic material only up to chap.32 and believed only 144 verses of the total 1273 to be genuine.

3

Volkmar Herntrich, critical of Hoelscher's work(5), emphasizes rather the location of the prophet's activity. Since many of Ezekiel's statements have him speaking directly to Jerusalem, Herntrich thinks he was a Jerusalem prophet. He wonders whether it was not until after 587 B.C that he went into exile, arguing that a member of the 597 exile revised the book and was responsible for the visionary transport of Ezekiel from Babylon to Jerusalem. Other scholars are not sure that an exilic location could altogether be denied to the prophet himself. William Oestereley and Theodore Robinson believe that Ezekiel was active in Jerusalem from 602-598 and continued his activity in exile(6). So many variations of these views exist that some scholars have seen the variety as indicative of a completely wrong approach. Eichrodt thinks that "This unsatisfactory fluctuation in the theories ... is the necessary result of all the difficulties encountered by any attempt to work out such a fundamental theory on the basis of a text which states the exact opposite"(7). But the text itself presents the problem whatever its explicit statements about the location might be. Keith W. Carley sums it up best: "For all the weaknesses that are now apparent in their theories, the more extreme critics brought to attention matters which still present difficulties in the book. So it is no longer possible to regard it as a straightforward composition by a single man"(8).

Zimmerli, although he makes some remarks about being on a false track, says that the impossibility of eliminating the apparent contradictions in the Book of Ezekiel is clearly indicated by the fact that some commentators have taken the extreme solution of denying the book to Ezekiel altogether, and see it as a pseudepigraph(9). Charles Torrey, for instance, tried to show that the Book of Ezekiel came from a time as late as about 230 B.C(10). He maintains that the work originated in Jerusalem and addresses the time of Manasseh in the 7th century: he thinks that the thirtieth year of 1:1 (as a year referring to Judaean kingship) can only refer to the long reign of a king such as Manasseh (687-642 B.C.). James Smith, however, takes a different view(11). He believes that Ezekiel himself was a 7th century northern Israelite and that the corruption described in Ezekiel referred to Jerusalem in Manasseh's time. A latter redactor, he thinks, transferred the book into the work of a Judaean exile. Other scholars, however, take the dating down to the 4th and 3rd centuries B.C.

Georg Fohrer is typical of the inevitable reaction, in the early fifties(12). While not assuming that the book can be thought of as a complete literary unit from the hand of Ezekiel, he maintains that Ezekiel expressed himself more than once on some questions so that work on the book can begin from its own statements about the time and place of Ezekiel's actions. Most of the more recent comentaries have been founded on this principle; for example, those of Eichrodt, John W.Weavers(13) and Zimmerli. Zimmerli's commentary is particularly notable for its definition and exposition of the

nature and importance of the forms of speech used in Ezekiel.
Konrad von Rabenau has also done work in this sphere and thinks
that the book was based on an autobiographical narrative
composed by the prophet himself(14). Zimmerli himself (as will
be seen in the course of this book as I discuss specific
passages) particularly investigated various forms such as a
Word of Demonstration (of God's efficacy), and reports on
visions and symbolic actions. He also emphasizes the
significance of introductory and concluding formulae such as
"The word of the Lord came to me" and "then you will know that
I am the Lord". He does not however view these as fixed forms,
often seeing them undergo a process of growth. For this he
thinks that a particular Ezekielian school was responsible,
though the prophet himself may also have been involved to some
extent. He speaks of "The Phenomenon of `Fortschreibung' in
the Book of Ezekiel" in a later article which concerns the wqy
in which a textual unit was taken up again, especially when new
historical experiences gave rise to the rewriting of units
which had already been composed (e.g. 12:1-16) (15).

During the many years (1955-1969) in which Zimmerli was
engaged in writing both his long commentary and many other
specialized treatments(16), further work also appeared. John
Wolf Miller investigates the relationship between Jeremiah and
Ezekiel, arguing that Ezekiel had heard Jeremiah in Jerusalem,
as well as having a written form of some of Jeremiah's words
before him(17). For his part, Henning Graf Reventlow
investigates relations between Ezekiel and the Holiness Code, a
collection of sacral traditions in Leviticus 17-26 with a
setting in the Israelite cult, from which Reventlow concludes
that the prophet was the bearer of an office in the cult(18).

The first clear sign the consensus on Book of Ezekiel was
about to be broken came in 1965 with the book of Siegfried
Herrmann on prophetic expectations of salvation(19). In the
words of salvation in Ezekiel he finds a threefold pattern of
theme, exposition and exhortation not dissimilar to
deuteronomic-deuteronomistic preaching(20). While this has
some influence in Ezekiel there is also a priestly stream in
the composition of the book. For Herrmann this double and
thorough-going process of tradition leads to problems regarding
the historical Ezekiel which he sees as comparable to the
problem of the historical Jesus in the Fourth Gospel. As for
the expectation of salvation in the Book of Ezekiel, Herrmann
thinks it probable that none can be attributed to the exilic
prophet Ezekiel.

Hermann Schulz takes matters a stage futher - in what
Zimmerli calls "a perspicacious form-critical analysis"(21) -
when he postulates a regular deutero-Ezekielian stream of
editing in 3:17-21; 14:1-20; 22:1-16; 33:1-20 (22). He
finds here a particular form, the "sacral-legal word of
declaration" (sakralrechtliches Deklarationswort; for example
18:5-9: "If a man is righteous...if he does not oppress
anyone...he shall surely live"), which belongs in the tradition
of the "death law" (Todesrecht; for example, Exodus 21:12:

5

"Whoever strikes a man so that he dies shall be put to death").
Its history can be traced from the Book of the Covenant in
Exodus 20-23 through Leviticus 18-20 to the deutero-Ezekielian
stream. Since this consists of theological-legal
interpretation, rather than legal literature proper, it belongs
to a later post-exilic period, and is not something which could
be covered by different periods of creativity by Ezekiel
himself. Zimmerli devotes much discussion to this work, first
in a detailed review where he claims that it must be treated
very seriously(23). He does not deny that there are passages
using legal material with a specific vocabulary, but neither
does he think that they can be characterized as "legal
systematics" because he believes they all bear the accent of
the prophetic call to repentance. The question then inevitably
arises as to whether it does not relate to the situation of the
prophet directly after 587 B.C. Zimmerli argues against a
theory of "Deutero-Ezekiel" doing justice to all the factors
involved in the Book of Ezekiel. Later in an article on
"Deutero-Ezekiel"(24), Zimmerli points out that Schulz's work
reminds one of the much earlier work of Hoelscher, and supposes
that the reason for its relative lack of influence was an
excessively narrow literary-critical method. Although Schulz
works not only with the literary-critical method but also with
form criticism and tradition history, Zimmerli still maintains
that he does not give adequate consideration to the historical
and intellectual context for the texts attributed to
Deutero-Ezekiel ; also that he does not consider seriously
enough the possibility that they are best accommodated in the
time of Ezekiel himself. He then outlines how closely
Ezekiel's proclamation of judgement (and even the oracles
against the nations) concentrates on the destruction of
Jerusalem, and asks whether it is likely (contrary to what is
said in 33:21-22 after all) that the prophet would have been
silent after this event. He doubts further whether words of
such deep resignation as in 37:11 could have their setting
anywhere but soon after the fall of Jerusalem. He also thinks
that passages like chap.18 are characterized more by the call
to repentance than by systematic doctrine, and that the
different vocabulary used (as compared with the proclamations
of judgement) is explained by the cataclysmic situation after
the destruction of Jerusalem. An exclusively literary or
form-critical analysis does not do this justice. Zimmerli does
not deny however that passages like chaps 18 and 33 have a
certain stereotyped expression, and he thinks that the
proclamation of Ezekiel may have been handed on through the
medium of a "school", although not in later historically
obscure times(25).

Zimmerli does make certain concessions and leaves some
aspects of the questions open. It is therefore not suprising
that Schulz's work has been taken even further by Joerg
Garscha, who introduces another method, that of studying the
history of the redaction of the Book of Ezekiel(26). This
approach, examining the editorial processes leading to the

final form of a biblical book, is done by Garscha under the influence of Otto Kaiser. The latter goes so far as to establish the principle that every text is to be considered as a redactional formation until the opposite is proved(27). Garscha is not impressed by Zimmerli's historical arguments and bases his approach on theological premises rather than historical ones. The contribution of the redaction has to be clarified before the origin of individual traditions. Garscha is confident that only this procedure will lead to reliable results. In connection with remarks about Zimmerli's criticism of Schulz from the historical and intellectual-historical point of view, he states it as his intention to give a comprehensive view of Ezekiel which will overcome this. Garscha comes to conclusions even more radical than those of Hoelscher: to Ezekiel himself there can be attributed only a preliminary form of the fable of the vine in 17:1-10 and the basis of the allegory of the two girls in chap.23. After this comes material such as the lament over the kingship in 19:1-9 or the work song in 24:1-14 which is from a later "author of the prophetic book" (not Ezekiel). This "author" is responsible for the basic structure of the Book of Ezekiel and is to be placed in the period 485-460 B.C. Then follows a "Deutero-Ezekielian editing" (though it has to be noted that Garscha sees this as different from Schulz's "Deutero-Ezekiel"). Such material (e.g. 5-6; 20; 36:16-32) is characterized by a sharp polemic against the "inhabitants of these ruins" (33:24) and supports the claim of the exiles to the land. One of its emphases is on the knowledge of Yahweh; and it originated between 400 and 350. Some 50 years later the "sacral law stream" arose. This corresponds (with some modifications) to Schulz's "Deutero-Ezekiel". It is characterized by a strong individualizing tendency - thus, according to Garscha, 3:17-21; 14:1-20 and 33:1-20 concern themselves with the task of the prophet and his responsibility for the individual. There are also other special traditions which cannot be fitted into any of the three main categories.

Garscha thinks the process in the formation of the Book of Ezekiel was completed by about 200 B.C. and that therefore there was a period of about 370 years in which Ezekiel, the "author", "Deutero-Ezekiel" "Sacral Ezekiel" and other editors were active. Garscha himself admits, however, that any dating he is able to make after the time-span provided by the Book of Ezekiel itself is uncertain. Thus his confidence that he would overcome Zimmerli's criticisms of Schulz cannot be said to be justified. Zimmerli points out too that Garscha leaves chaps 40-48 out of consideration and this is relevant for the dating. Zimmerli thinks the method is in itself significant but has been used in a one-sided way. He maintains that the basis of all literary critical work (to which redaction belongs) must first be to take the text seriously rather than mistrust in principle what the text itself proposes.

Not only work of a redactional-critical nature has been in progress since Zimmerli's commentary. Zimmerli mentions in the foreword to his second edition that, as well as the investigations of Herrmann (mentioned above), those of Ruediger Liwak and Winfried Thiel on Jeremiah, Ezekiel and the Holiness Code keep alive the question of deuteronomistic influence on Ezekiel(28). There is also the work which has been done by Horacio Simian and Frank Hossfeld using the method of linguistic analysis(29). Simian also shows great confidence in the linguistic method which he has taken over from Wolfgang Richter. He recognises the problems which can arise in transferring the method from narrative to prophetic texts. However, he still thinks that in contrast to previous work it allows him to work without presuppositions. He outlines his method as 1. the definition of the "small units" and their division from one another; 2. the investigation of the form, including syntactic and stylistic characteristics, leading on to the structure and aim; 3. vocabulary and literary sphere; 4. pre-history of theological ideas (tradition criticism), leading to a history of the units up to the present text. He then applies this method to chaps 6, 35 and 36 only, with the aim of drawing out the connections of the literary units within these three chapters to one another and to other texts. He finds the oldest and most basic text in 36:1-11 and sets it in the 4th century B.C. It is then impossible to ascribe chaps 35-36 and probably 6 as well to Ezekiel.

Hossfeld thinks that arguments for a late post-exilic dating of redactional stages are very vague when it comes to defining their localization. He works on a broader basis than Simian, investigating eight different passages (17:11-24; 22:1-16; 28:1-10; 30:1-19; 34:1-31; 36:16-38; 37:1-14; 38:1-39:29); and while using basically the same method as Simian, he examines more closely the difference between narrative and prophetic texts, investigating the formulae characteristic of prophetic speech. He comes to the conclusion that he can make five points about the activity of the exilic prophet Ezekiel: 1. An exilic prophet Ezekiel is still the most plausible hypothesis because there is still substantial agreement between basic Ezekiel texts and comparable authentic proclamation of prophets from Amos to Jeremiah. There is both 2., a diachronic double aspect in his preaching which consists of judgement and salvation as the consequences of his specific historical situation, and 3., a synchronic double aspect in the preaching to the exiles and to those who remained in the land. 4. Since in pre-exilic Israel there were three main institutions, the kingship, the priesthood and the prophets, and since in exile only the latter remained, Ezekiel was a person of great interest. This is confirmed by the elders appearing before him (8:1; 14:1; 20:1 - see also 33:30-33. But 5., this does not mean that he was taken completely seriously, and like no other prophet Ezekiel is concerned for the effectivenesss of the prophetic word.

This means that, though his part in the texts is diminished, the personality of Ezekiel and his activity are not dissolved in the immense editorial work of the book. The subsequent work is also concerned with a balanced theological expression. The redaction is characterized by multifariousness, however, and Hossfeld believes he can recognize six stages in it. Though it is not possible to say from the Book of Ezekiel when these various stages took place, Hossfeld thinks that it was probably a fairly rapid succession and that the 6th century B.C. was one of the most productive literary epochs of Old Testament times. He does not find any evidence that Ezekiel himself was involved in the literary editing of his work.

Hossfeld, who has investigated only a selection of texts, feels that the selection does not allow him to say anything definite about the first two stages, so that the question arises as to how certain one can be about his six stages. Zimmerli says, that since Hossfeld's work is on a broader basis than others and he is working with more appropriate criteria, the method does give useful results. But it also has the danger of not recognizing the flexibililty of living speech, and one might add that it takes up considerable and sometimes wearisome space without achieving much.

Finally, two works should be mentioned which are not primarily interested in these questions, and which were published either before some of the works discussed, or before the latter had properly surfaced. Keith W. Carley(30) examines the relation between Ezekiel and other major streams of Old Testament tradition. He discerns a primary tradition which has been elaborated by later hands, possibly by certain elders of Israel (14:1). He thinks, however, that Ezekiel himself used earlier forms of expression to authenticate his prophetic activities, and that his work is best understood in the context of Israelite faith and thought. Thomas M. Raitt is mainly conserned to trace in Jeremiah's and Ezekiel's messages a development from judgement with calls to repentance, through a transition phase of the failure of repentance, to a radical and unqualified message of salvation(31). Of fifteen salvation oracles in Ezekiel, he believes eleven are authentic, taken on a majority count of Eichrodt, Fohrer, Pfeiffer and Zimmerli (thus he does not take into consideration the dissenting writings which I have mentioned). He sees certain trademarks in Ezekiel's promises: a concern for the disgrace Judah has brought on God; God acting for the sake of his name; the imagery of uncleanness, and forgiveness by cleaning; the stress on repossession of Jerusalem, the Davidic kingship and the restoration to the land.

It is impossible to reach firm conclusions in the face of all this variety of method and opinion concerning the Book of Ezekiel. So many scholars confident of their method and results meet with disagreement in the next critical work which is presented; and it is possible only to glean what one can from all of them, but not to opt wholeheartedly for any one of them. I am inclined to accept the view (as presented by

Zimmerli for example) that essentially the book comprises the work of an exilic prophet Ezekiel, and that this was then elaborated in a number of stages. To be more precise about the latter is difficult, though I believe that Hossfeld's work may form the best basis for future progress. This is not to say that views argued in detail (say by Garscha) do not make much more sense in their own context than might appear from my brief survey. In any case, those scholars whose views diverge widely from Zimmerli's would certainly agree that in the second half of this century he has given an incomparable renewed stimulus to the study of this remarkable book.

Brevard S.Childs agrees that critical scholarship could never return to a pre-Zimmerli stage in evaluating the book(32), but believes that, as Zimmerli bases his interpretation on a critically reconstructed pre-canonical form of the book, he has not correctly assessed the canonical shape of the book. He argues that that which distinguishes Ezekiel from other prophets is the much closer relation between the original function of the oracles and the long canonical process: "...the development was one of the closest continuity between the various stages of the literature". He sees the dominant feature of the book as its radical theocentric perspective. This means that temporal moorings are relinquished so that Babylon and Jerusalem become relativized in the divine perspective of the people of God as one entity. Ezekiel also used forms (sacral-legal, allegories etc.) which address the future as well as the present.

How can the close continuity which Childs sees really be balanced against the many signs of editing in the book itself, which Childs himself remarks upon? Although one might agree in principle with Child's attempts to understand the subsequent growth of the book positively, one wonders whether he would not find a justification for any apparent irregularity.

Disagreement about method and results in literary-historical matters, however, provides no excuse for postponing the interpretation of the book for people today - it only makes it the more urgent. Even my brief survey makes it clear that if one were to wait for firm results, the delay would be long. It is clear that the Book of Ezekiel presents a prophet convinced both of his responsibility for his people and the necessity of their response, and since that is so, the most urgent question is whether that responsibility affects us now. Every academic means is not only legitimate but essential to the task, but the appropriate academic means should increase the understanding of people now. Most of the work I have mentioned is concerned in one way or another with analysis, dividing the text up. Necessary as this is, it has to be remembered that the Israelites put it together into the whole which we now have, and (as I show in what follows) there is a pattern and purpose behind this whole. Interpreting the parts within the whole is particularly important at a time when knowledge of each biblical book in its sequence is weak. I hope what I write may be of profit to ministers and to students, to theologians of disciplines other than Old Testament studies, and of course to Old Testament scholars who are concerned for the continuing theological interpretation of Old Testament texts. I think however I would be happiest if it were found to be of value for educated people in general, for they are the ones often overlooked. There is a lack of studies in Old Testament scholarship which are suitable for such readers.

In the process of publication a number of works have appeared which could not be considered above. I mention especially:

Moshe Greenberg, Ezekiel 1-20, The Anchor Bible 22, Doubleday, Garden City, 1983;

T.W.D. Mettinger, The Dethronement of Sabaoth. Studies in the Shem and Kabod Theologies, Gleerup, Lund, 1982.

One or two explanations are necessary. The translations from Ezekiel in the course of this book use the signs <> to indicate when an alteration has been made to the standard Hebrew text (Masoretic text). Square brackets [] indicate that the material inside them is considered not to belong to the original text but was added later; and round brackets () indicate material which is not to be found in the Hebrew text but which is considered necessary for a clear English translation. A question mark means simply that I am not certain whether or not the translation is correct.

I THE SOURCE OF RESPONSIBILITY: 1 - 3

1. WHAT HAPPENS FIRST - GOD AND THE PROPHET: 1:1-28

The Book of Ezekiel begins with an extraordinary event:

> Now it happened in the thirtieth year in the fourth
> month, on the fifth day of the month, when I was
> among the exiles by the river Chebar, that the
> heavens were opened and I saw divine visions (1:1)

The visions, though remarkable, are not disconnected from the
times and the places of this world. Ezekiel names his
companions, the exiles, and his location, Chebar, and the date
places the vision in actual time. The thirtieth year (of what
?) is a puzzle(1). Evidently an explanation was already
thought necessary by the editors of the book, since in 1:2 they
say it was in the fifth year of Jehoiachin's exile, that is
about 593 B.C. Chebar is a canal near Babylon connecting parts
of the river Euphrates where the Judaean exiles were living.
 Rather than extolling himself and his visions as such,
Ezekiel clearly wants to connect them with an actual time and
place, as well as with the people in a particular condition of
distress.
 The significance of an event in Ezekiel then is not to be
gauged from its occurrence merely, but by means of the response
which people make to it, as the first three verses show. In
v.1, speaking in the first person Ezekiel says, "I saw divine
visions". But vv. 2-3 use the third person speaking about
Ezekiel(2), saying that what happened in the fifth year of
Jehoiachin's exile was that the word of Yahweh (the proper name
of Israel's God) came to Ezekiel and the hand of Yahweh was
upon him. The word and hand of Yahweh may be expressions which
Ezekiel himself uses as part of the description of his vision
later, but they are not exactly the same expressions as "divine
visions". It seems that others are expressing their
apprehension of Ezekiel's visions in their own particular way.
That they also stipulate the time and the place in almost
exactly the same way as Ezekiel emphasizes again the vital
importance of the connection between what is happening and this
world. The passage concludes by saying "... the hand of
Yahweh was upon him there", that is in Babylon. The point is
that Israel's God Yahweh would not ordinarily have been
expected to have had anything to do with Babylon so the visions
and the word and hand of Yahweh imply that something unique in
the exilic circumstances is about to take place.

The narrative proceeds in the first person to give the particular circumstances of the vision: "I looked and there was a stormy wind coming from the north ..." (1:4). Along with this wind Ezekiel sees flashing fire and, in the middle of it, what look like four living creatures. Thus begins the strange, indeed bizarre vision for which Ezekiel is known(3). There is no doubt that the vision is individual to him - there was certainly never anyone else who experienced anything quite like it - but for that very reason it is significant that his apprehension of the vision also contains within it elements of past tradition. Other Old Testament passages make reference to cloud, fire and brightness as heralds of the coming Yahweh (e.g. Exodus 19:16 ff; Habakkuk 3:4), which shows that there was such a tradition. But each presentation of the tradition with its particular details has its own thrust. Ezekiel 1:4, for example, speaks of the wind coming from the north, a traditional reference (c.f. Psalm 48:2), but for Ezekiel in exile in Babylon to see God coming from the north (which was the direction from which any approach from Jerususalem to Babylon would have been made) implies that Yahweh is not confined to Jerusalem, but can make himself known in an "unclean land". It means a great deal for Israel's present plight that their traditional resources reach backwards as well as forwards: the past coming into the present means much that is new for the present plight. The importance of this specification of the heading in 1:1-3 is hard to overestimate in the history of religion.

Exiles can now logically conclude that their situation might actually be changed despite a realistic knowledge of the obstacles which stand in the way. The God connected with Jerusalem, and of course Israel, makes himself known in a foreign country, implying that the old traditions can take on renewed creative life. To see God coming from an old environment to a new accompanied by intense brightness (1:4) denotes an awesome apprehension that something quite beyond the ordinary is going to happen.

The likeness of four living creatures having the appearance of men, yet having four wings (1:5-6) (4), are on the one hand traditional concepts of heavenly beings accompanying and extending the manifestation of Yahweh, but on the other an expression of totality appropriate to this particular situation. When Ezekiel sees the storm wind, the continual movement of the fire (1:4), and the likeness of four living creatures approaching (1:5-6), the totality of the vision, far from being static, is being borne dramatically in upon him. The straight, undeviating movement of the four creatures, is described later in 1:12, so that 1:7-11, which gives details of the parts of the bodies of the four creatures, may be a latter explanatory addition(5). The expansion may hold up the main movement of the passage, but it still contributes to the powerful totality of what Ezekiel sees. It is vital to remember something which is easy to forget in the grotesqueness of the vision, that Ezekiel sees it among the exiles in the land of the Babylonians, not just for himself. And despite the bizarre quality of the vision, the connection between the vision and people is shown by the fact that these curious creatures possess human features in addition to their awesome and powerful aspects. It is possibly the intention of 1:7, which states that their legs are straight, to indicate that these limbs are as much human as animal(6), even though they have hooves like a calf which sparkle dazzingly. Certainly they have wings, but under their wings are human hands (1:8). It is said in connection with their wings that they go straight forward, presumably towards Ezekiel (1:9). Each has four faces(7), a lion's, an ox's and an eagle's, but the first to be mentioned is that of a man (1:10). The final verse (1:11) leads into the statement about their going straight forward. The intention of the addition may be to present the vision as humanly recognizable and yet founded on the combined powers of a man and beast(8).

That even more is being borne unswervingly upon Ezekiel, is made abundantly clear:

> Each (living creature) was going straight forward,
> wherever the spirit would go, they went, not
> changing direction as they went (1:12).

The living creatures apparently have little will of their own, being the agents of a higher purpose. The tradition of the past directly affects the present situation; seeing the vision, Ezekiel has no reason to assume that the present situation is hopeless. In fact, he has real reason for being confident that a completely new impetus can arise, an idea expressed in visual terms (1:13-14) with fire and lightning moving continually among the creatures themselves, darting to and fro like lightning. The usual idea of a vision as something static within which a person is absorbed could hardly be further removed from the characteristics of this vision, for it is one of dynamic energy proceeding towards a person who is among other people.

In 1:15-21, however, it would not be going too far to say that the interest here in the technique of movement actually slows it down. The concern of the basic vision is only that the creatures moved, not how they moved. It seems likely, therefore, that vv.15-21 are a later addition(9). It is to be noted that this is the well-known passage about "wheels" and "wheels within wheels"(10), which has made Ezekiel's vision into something of a joke, so the most pedantic and complicated elements of the vision probably come from additions.

The wheels do, however, add two elements which were not present in the original description: when it is said in 1:17 that the wheels go in each of their four directions, the intention is surely to express the all-pervasive nature of the movement. Then, in 1:18, when it is said that the rims of the wheels are full of eyes all around, the all-seeing is added to that which is all-pervasive: Ezekiel's vision becomes not only something which he sees, but it is also something which "sees" him. In the vision the subject observes an object, but the subject also knows himself to be under scrutiny. The seer cannot make himself the centre of importance since he is himself seen. He is the medium of what is seen, but not himself the source of it.

The description of the original vision recurs in 1:22. Over the heads of the living creatures there is something similar to a plate beaten out like a sheet and glittering like frost. This extension of the moving brightness indicates that, with such a plate as foundation, something more is to come above it; the creatures are merely bearers of the vision's principal content. (This being so, such progression towards the climax is once again delayed in 1:23-25 where Ezekiel sees the creatures' straight wings and hears their confusing, rather meaningless sound which at this point has no effect on him.) (11)

The climax clearly comes in 1:26: it is nothing less than a vision of Yahweh himself though expressed in terms of extreme reticence. A literal translation makes this even clearer:

> Above the plate which was over their heads, there was something like the appearance of sapphire, the likeness of a throne, amd above the likeness of the throne there was a likenesss something like the appearance of man.

The first impression is of a tortured sentence, a tentativeness which shows Ezekiel seeing something recognizable, yet indefinable. The words for "appearance" (mar'ēh) and above all for "likeness" (demût) have been used before (1:5, 10, 13, 14, 16, 22), so that when the terms accumulate in this unique manner in 1:26, it reveals a preoccupation not so much with exact details as with visual impressions ultimately incomprehensible in themselves. The point is that it is not their actual nature which is important but the way in which they are seen and understood. I said before that it is not through a happening in itself that significance occurs, but rather through people's appreciation of it. The essential theological implication of Ezekiel's vision is that even in a vision of Yahweh, the human being is the medium. What he sees gives the lead:

> I saw from what had the appearance of his loins and upwards from there something like gleaming stone (?) (12) like the appearance of fire enclosed within it round about, and from what had the appearance of his loins and downwards I saw something like the appearance of fire; there was indeed brightness all about him (1:27).

The vision, while recognizable, is obviously so dazzling that its otherness is the overwhelming aspect of it, a shimmering glimpse of what is meant by the first verse that "Ezekiel saw divine visions"(13). By this awesome, shattering experience, he knows that he is not alone, not thrown entirely on his own resources, and also that he, though human, is confronted with visible otherness which he knows will shortly address him in his particular situation and for a particular purpose. It is shattering enough that this vision has a divine source; it is even more shattering that the source has a medium, and that he is it. With hindsight we can see that the image of the rainbow announcing rain has an implication not yet realized:

> Like the appearance of the bow which is in the cloud on the day of rain, so was the appearance of the brightness round about (1:28).

Such brightness all around, merging and shimmering and yet clearly distinct from other things, represents that which is still present for Ezekiel and his people in the place of exile, and which will transform their condition. Up till now Babylon was decisive in Babylon for the Israelites; now Ezekiel knows that Israel can determine Babylon for the Israelites in Babylon. The imposed regime of a foreign power cannot drown the reforming power of past tradition when it is given new vigour. Thus the vision of Yahweh, of which a human being is the medium, can transform the life of the people.

"Such was the appearance of the likenesss of the glory of Yahweh" (1:28): "the glory of Yahweh" sums up all the otherness which has gone before in the vision. But since this otherness is that which is decisive in the exiles' present situation in Babylon and which can change that situation, it also leads on to the next stage. This may be all Ezekiel sees but the matter is far from finished. How could it be so when "all" he sees is "the appearance of the likeness" of the glory of Yahweh, not confined to a sanctuary in Jerusalem, and not just any divine glory? And yet it is unmistakably the glory of Yahweh, the God of Israel, appearing to him in Babylon. Before this glory, Ezekiel can only be overwhelmed - until he realizes that it is personally directed towards him and talks to him. It is necessary now to return to the beginning, remembering that the vision also has a goal. The effect of this first part of the book is to show that what happens first is channelled through the medium towards a goal. There could be no more essential beginning than to link the source, the medium and the goal: God, prophet and people. Nothing of significance happens unless there is a continual integration of these three. No one of these makes sense without the others.

2. THE MEDIUM OF WHAT HAPPENS AND ITS GOAL - THE PROPHET AND THE PEOPLE: 1:28 - 3:15

When Ezekiel sees the vision, the glory of Yahweh, his reaction is to fall on his face and hear a voice speaking(1), 1:28 (2). Deuteronomy 4:12 provides an illuminating comparision: "Yahweh spoke to you out of the midst of the fire; you heard the sound of words, but you did not see a form; there was nothing except a voice". Ezekiel has at least seen something like a form, but he still hears a voice; indeed it can be said that this is the only matter which will bring events a stage further forward. The connection of the vision with the human now finds its continuing expression in personal address.

As is usual in the Old Testament, the word predominates over form: one only has to think of the prohibition of images. Has the form any importance at all(3)? There is no doubt that the word becomes more important, but prophets including those earlier than Ezekiel, do "see things". While Jeremiah in chap.1 is directly addressed by the word, he sees visions of a rod of almond and a boiling pot. The most famous call of all, that of Isaiah in chap.6 is in the form of a vision of the heavenly court. There is thus every reason to think that the vision of a form has its own importance. After all it is only when Ezekiel sees the vision that he hears the voice speaking. It is the combination that matters in 1:28, where the two parts of the experience are strongly linked: "Such was the appearance of the likeness of the glory of Yawheh and when I saw it I fell on my face and <u>heard a voice speaking.</u>" For Ezekiel the vision of the form culminates in spoken words. Something essential would be lost if this connection were ignored.

The connection remains valid even though the seeing of a form is expressed in vague terms, and though the vision of the form does not have significance in itself but only as the source of the speech. Some modern artists, by contrast, claim to see significance in the form of a work of art without reference to the content. The difference is that Ezekiel's vision connects with people in a particular time and place, but what it does imply, is that it is not possible to express everything in words. The whole point of the vision of the form is that it expresses that which cannot be entirely expressed in words, even though the most important implications for the human situation can and must be so expressed. Ezekiel has to express the significance of the vision to his people in words, but since the words have their source in the form, this verbal expression does not exhaust the total experience. Ezekiel never tells the people about his vision; it is primarily a personal source which he needs to inspire him to communicate with the people. And yet the very fact that something of the form is inexpressible means that Ezekiel must apply what he has seen to the present situation in words. There can be no

17

significance in the source and its medium unless they have a goal.

To apply the vision to the present human situation one must distinguish between the form and the meaningful human, communal content. Ezekiel's hearing a voice speaking from the vision means that it must have been significant for the particular people of his time and place. It is genuine only if he can communicate with the people where they are. In this way his vision differs from the visions of many people today who tend to use them for an otherworldly emphasis, people who, having visions, often seem to think that the visions make them "special" in a merely self-directed way. The means of the revelation becomes important in itself. It is appropriate here to quote Jeremiah who has only one word - "lies" - about those who put all the emphasis on the means of the revelation when they say, inflating their own importance, "I have dreamed, I have dreamed"; and he draws a contrast between "the dreams" and the word of Yahweh unfavourable to the dream (Jeremiah 23:25, 28).

The vision today frequently leads to a different place as well. Many visions, according to the recipient, establish something so completely different from and beyond this world that they reveal an extreme reluctance to accept this world as it is. The whole point of the vision in Ezekiel, however, is that it culminates in a verbal content for the particular situation of exile in which Ezekiel and his people find themselves. Out of imperfectly conceived form come the words necessary to apply it: "Such was the appearance of the likeness of the glory of Yahweh ... and he said to me, `Son of man, stand upon your feet and I will speak with you" (1:28 - 2:1). The vision results in an address to him. This simple statement gives concrete reference. The amazing fact that a vision of such sublimity should be addressed to him is taken in a very matter-of-fact way, as if to say, what else could a vision of Yahweh do but speak to the one who saw him!

The one addressed by this vision is not thereby singled out of humankind, but is called "son of man"(4). The expression is applied to Ezekiel some 90 times, of which more than 20 have the addition "and you". These two words emphasize that he really is the one at whom the communication is directed. (The phrase does not refer in Ezekiel to heavenly figures, but is an idiomatic Hebrew way of stating that the one addressed belongs to the human order.) The vision of the first part of the book expressing the apprehension of a source different from the human, yet still connected with it, is now given a specific mediating focus in the very form of address applied to Ezekiel. The son of man addressed by the word of Yahweh does not belong to the divine order: he is one individual member of the human order, the order of creatures. This mere created being, however, is the very one who can be sent to his fellows (2:3). The creature both recognizes his status as a creature and exercises his own kind of creativity by accepting an address for his people. He knows he is a creature since he knows his limitations for the task. He knows at the same time that it is possible for him to realize his creativity simply because he is the one who is addressed. He is temporarily singled out, sent to tell the others what they are; and the only reason that this is possible is that he belongs to them. He is, as he has been named, "son of man".

Though fallen on his face, he is told to stand on his feet: "Son of man, stand upon your feet for I will speak to you". Morever, he is given the power to make an active response: "Then the spirit entered me as he spoke to me and set me upon my feet so that I heard him speaking to me" (2:2). The "spirit" here means the difference between the man remaining prostrate before the glorious vision and his realizing of his own positive and creative response. Obviously the vision by itself is not enough - the man has to react. A great responsibility consequently falls upon him: "He said to me, Son of man, I am sending you to the <house> of Israel [to nations], those rebels who have rebelled against me, they and their fathers [have transgressed against me](5) to this very day" (2:3).

The human prophet as the medium of the vision now has to involve the people. In vv.3-5 occurs a pattern, "I send ... you say ... they will know", that is, Ezekiel's commission as medium is to provoke a reaction, an acknowledgement from the people. Their reactions must accord with the harsh realities of the situation, for the people to whom Ezekiel is to go are his own people, and they are rebels. They have rebelled in the past, they are rebelling in the present. Rebellion is characteristic of them. There are no concessions and qualifications - there is no side-stepping the issue by saying that things would be otherwise if only certain conditions were different. The way is open therefore to do something, for these rebels may be brought to know a different kind of existence (2:5). He must speak to them not as they ought to be but as they are now: "They are insolent and stubborn people to whom I am sending you, and you shall say to them, Thus says Lord Yahweh" (2:4).

The second part of the necessary pattern "I send ... you say ... they will know", reveals that the people's insolence and stubbornness have to be abruptly contradicted by Ezekiel's address. The important matter first is the fact of this address rather than its particular content. All that Ezekiel is to say to them is "Thus says Yahweh". For the first time the speech Ezekiel has heard is applied to the people, suggesting that, with the people in a desperate state, an alternative exists. Their state is desperate, but not hopeless, for the address "Thus says Lord Yahweh" means that their insolence and stubbornness can be changed.

None of this would be possible, however, without the medium of the prophet: "Whether they listen or not - for they are a rebellious house - they will know that there has been a prophet among them" (2:5). If he speaks and gives the opportunity of hearing, the people will know a prophet has been present, and

19

that the chance of change has been offered to them whether they respond to it or not. There are no illusions that the people will listen automatically - indeed the house of Israel is given a new name, the "house of rebellion". But even this does not necessarily mean that they will not listen. All that is necessary, whatever their attitude, is that they be given the opportunity. In any case they will come to the realization later that Yahweh had spoken, that they had been addressed by a source capable of transforming even them, and that this had been communicated through one of their own kind, the son of man.

But the task of transformation will be difficult as we see from Yahweh's words to the son of man:

> But you, son of man, do not be afraid of them, do not fear their words though briars and thorns are with you and you sit on scorpions, do not be afraid at what they say or dismayed at how they look for they are a rebellious house (2:6).

There is so little illusion about the state of the people that this man has to be given a special assurance(6). Rather than be discouraged altogether or go on blindly, he is to proceed both realistically and with hope. Having such a foundation there is some point in speaking "My words to them whether they hear or not", even to a rebellious house (2:7).

Under these circumstances his resources need to be as complete as possible:

> Now you, son of man, hear what I am about to say to you: do not be rebellious like the house of rebellion - open your mouth and eat what I am about to give you (2:8).

The prophet is to be given something to <u>eat</u> as well(7). He is to have nothing less than that inner <u>substance</u> which will be necessary to meet the rebels: a written scroll, further indicating the importance of words, is held out to him (2:9). These words must become part of his very own substance if he is to communicate them.

Before he eats the scroll, Ezekiel must see how it is written and what is written on it: "He spread it out before me and it was written front and back with lamentations, groaning and woe" (2:10). This is no ordinary scroll. Scrolls were usually written on one side only, so that the specific mention of writing on both sides probably means that this one is a completely adequate source. But it further stresses that the effect of Ezekiel's communication will not be one of rejoicing; on the contrary, it will be one of lamentation.

The next command shows that <u>eating</u> in this vision reinforces <u>saying</u>: "He said to me, Son of man, eat what is offered to <u>you</u>, eat this scroll, then go speak to the house of Israel" (3:1). What is happening to Ezekiel is to be transferred to

20

the people. Having eaten, he must speak; what becomes part of him must be communicated. Ezekiel understands that what comes from the outside must become completely part of himself; it is not only a case of eye and ear, but also of taste and consumption. "He said to me, Son of man, you shall feed yourself and fill your stomach with this scroll which I give to you" (3:3). Ezekiel's reaction to this seemingly ridiculous command is one of whole-hearted acceptance: "So I ate. And in my mouth it was as sweet as honey" (3:3). It is sweet not because he looks forward to the people's reaction of lamentation, but because he knows that what he must say is right, the only thing to be said.

Yahweh's next words demonstrate that Ezekiel must speak to the Isrealites themselves, not, for example to the leaders of Israel's oppressors: "He said to me, Son of man, go to the house of Israel and speak my words to them" (3:4). This would have been all the harder to accept, since the Israelites were used to the tradition of the Exodus where the words bringing lamentation came upon the Egyptians, not upon themselves. At first it sounds more promising. Many languages were no doubt spoken by many different nationalities in Babylon, and it would seem easier to address the Israelites:

> For you are not sent to a people of unintelligible speech and difficult language [to the house of Israel](8) not to many peoples of unintelligible speech and difficult language whose words you do not understand ... (3:5-6).

but all this is working up to the main, climactic point - "if I did send you to them, they would listen to you!" So a response would come where least expected - from foreigners, and not from Israelites! In his task of bringing the Israelites to react in acknowledgement, Ezekiel is faced with the greatest possible difficulties. His commission is completely different from that of Moses at the time of Exodus: to use the language of that tradition, it is the Israelites who have hardened their hearts and not Pharaoh.

> But the house of Israel do not want to listen to you because they do not want to listen to me, for all the house of Israel are obstinate and stubborn (3:7).

One further obstacle to be circumvented is that the Israelites do not even want to hear. The speaking of Yahweh the source and Ezekiel the medium are drawn closely together, in that the people do not want to listen to Ezekiel because they do not want to listen to Yahweh. Being obstinate and stubborn, they do not want to listen to the medium for the source which might change their present situation.

Not to listen to the source, however, is almost to admit that
there is an agency which could change things. To admit that
means recognizing one's present state, which is resisted with
the greatest of tenacity: "...all the house of Israel are
obstinate and stubborn" (3:7). Ezekiel, one of the people
himself, feels the whole weight of their nature. They stand in
complete opposition to the thrust of his vision. One is "the
glory of Yahweh" and the other is "a rebellious house", and
what he has to say must create a link between these two
opposites. Ezekiel must be prepared for the stubbornness of
the rebellious house which stands in the way, and this is why
his face and forehead are made hard, harder than flint (3:8-9).
It is not hard against hard, however, the one eliminating the
other; rather Ezekiel must be completely unafraid to evoke a
response in the face of rejection.

Ezekiel is equipped by becoming one substance with what is
said:

> He said to me, son of man, take into your heart and
> hear with your ears all my words which I will speak
> to you, and go to the exiles, the members of your
> people, and speak to them saying, Thus says Lord
> Yahweh, whether they listen or not (3:10-11).

It is particularly important that Ezekiel is told to go to the
exiles, because the first part of the message in chaps. 1-24
is mainly about Jerusalem. This has seemed a puzzle to many
scholars(9): how is it that a prophet in Babylon is so
preoccupied with Jerusalem and often appears to be actually
there? But it is of the greatest significance to the exiles
that they hear what is said about Jerusalem. That people in
one place are told continually what is happening in another
place makes it quite clear that he is not merely predicting
what will occur, but that the people themselves must take
responsibility for their future in the place where they now
live.

At the conclusion of the vision Ezekiel is taken explicitly
to the exiles:

> Then the spirit lifted me up, and I heard behind me
> a loud noise as the glory of Yahweh <rose> (10)
> from its place, the noise of the living creatures
> touching each other, the noise of the wheels
> alongside them, a very loud noise. The spirit
> lifted me up and took me away and I went [bitter]
> (11) with my own spirit greatly excited, the hand
> of Yahweh being heavy upon me. So I came to the
> exiles at Tel-abib [who dwelt by the river of
> Chebar] (12) the place where they were dwelling,
> and I sat among them dumbfounded for seven days
> (3:12-15).

That the spirit takes Ezekiel to where the exiles are living shows that everything which he has experienced is still intended to connect him with them. The loud noise behind him, the glory, the creatures and the wheels (all features of the vision) give perhaps the clearest impression yet of the force driving Ezekiel onwards.

Just how involved he, the human medium, is in spite of the outside source, is shown by the expression "going with his spirit greatly excited". The word mar, "bitter", eliminated here as secondary from the Hebrew text, is retained in the Revised Standard Version which reads, "I went in bitterness in the heat of my spirit". Such a reading, however, gives the impression that Ezekiel is angry, either because he must go at all, or because of the people to whom he has to go. The word hēmā, "heat", can mean "anger"; possibly the word "bitter" (which is missing in the ancient Greek and Syriac translations) was added in an attempt to provide an understanding of the unprecedented expression "in the heat of my spirit". But in context, I doubt whether this is correct. It is more likely that Ezekiel would be completely preoccupied with the vision moving him in troubled anticipation towards his goal, a preoccupation brought out by the expressions "the hand of Yahweh being heavy upon me" and "dumbfounded". Completely dazed among the exiles, who are never lost from view, he has been borne to them by the very matter which overwhelms him. (Ezekiel does what he has to do, and will be able to do for other people.)

The vision is not self-sufficient nor exclusively directed at its medium. Both vision and medium are needed in pressing towards the goal: Yahweh, the prophet and the people all belong together. Ezekiel left by his source for seven days dumbfounded among the exiles will reveal the potentiality of all this. It will burst forth. The consequences of the vision will not end with the vision itself.

3. THE MEDIUM - THE WATCHMAN: 3:16-21

In the visionary first part of the book (1:1-28), Yahweh is connected with the prophet and the people, with the main emphasis being on Yahweh himself. The function of the second part in 1:28 - 3:15 is to make the connection explicit, which it does in speech particularly directed to the exiled Israelites. The role of the medium in transmitting the vision by speech was so essential that a need was felt to insert a special passage about it. Even signs of secondary insertion play their part in drawing attention to the desire to emphasize the medium's role. The clause, "It happened at the end end of seven days", in 3:16a, fits together in the Hebrew more smoothly with v.22 than it does with v.16b. In addition,

23

3:17-19 are virtually identical with 33:7-9, and I shall argue
when I consider chap.33 that the subject matter belonged
originally there rather than in chap.3.

Why then insert the passage here? Ezekiel's role as the
exiles' watchman was thought to be essential right from the
beginning, especially in applying the meaning of the vision to
people(1). The prophet's function here is given a special
definition as the watchman: the insertion provides nothing
less than an interpretation of his activity. The
coming of the word of Yahweh is now seen for the first time as
the source of what the prophet is to do for the people. Up to
now communication has only been a voice in a vision, whereas
the formula "the word of Yahweh came to me", addresses a
particular content to a particular people. It comes forcefully
to them through one of their own kind who has a special
commission. The address is to him first, indicating that, if
Ezekiel does not speak to warn the wicked, no one else will.
It is nothing less than a choice between life and death, not
only for the wicked, but above all for himself. The watchman,
to be effective, must first watch himself. The word of Yahweh
challenges the people to rise above their exilic mentality and
Ezekiel to take the risk of telling them they can rise above
it.

The significant formula "the word of Yahweh came to me"
stresses some forty times in the Book of Ezekiel that the word
of Yahweh is not heard but comes. Thus it is also something
which happens. This "word-event formula", as it has been
called(2), connecting "word" with "event", typically introduces
a new section, and shows the prophet experiencing the word of
Yahweh as an event occurring at a particular time. "The word
of Yahweh coming to me" means that one person, cognizant of the
potentialities both for good and evil in the situation in which
he finds himself, realizes what can be done for the people and
their situation. Struck by the conviction that he of all
people is the only one who is obliged to initiate something, he
feels neither totally adequate nor abjectly inferior. He is
the recipient of an address:

> Son of man, I have made you watchman for the house
> of Israel: whenever you hear a word from my mouth,
> you shall give them warning from me. If I say to
> the wicked man, You are condemned to death, and you
> do not warn him from his wicked way in order to
> save his life, that wicked man will die in his
> iniquity, but I will hold you responsible for him
> (3:17-18).

Yahweh warns here that to misapply the possibilities of life
is so serious that the watchman who does not give warning is
just as much to blame as those who live a misapplied life; a
life, for example, which allows exile to become the only
factor, deadening every other consideration. It means that
Ezekiel, the medium between the source and the goal, must act

with total responsibility. Such responsibility means sole accountability. (The words at the end which I have translated, "I will hold you responsible for him", run literally, "I will require his blood at your hand".) So serious is the responsibility that, if it is not exercised, the source does not reach the goal and everything fails.

The son of man does not receive anything for himself; as watchman he is commissioned to function for Israel. His responsibility is the key factor in carrying what happens to the prophet over to the people. His commission, "Son of man, I have made you watchman for the house of Israel ..." cannot be separated from what he is to do for the people: "...whenever you hear a word from my mouth, you shall give warning from me ..." He is uniquely aware that his people do not live blameless lives, and that he must offer them an alternative to their present life. By comparing the emptiness of their life to the traditional life with Yahweh, he knows that the Yahweh of the past is speaking to him in the present. That is, the address of Yahweh depends both on the present and the past, but in the combination of the two their medium knows an address that is at once part of him and yet separate from him. He does not claim to be his own authority but examines the present situation of his people in the light of traditions which have made them what they are: "The word of Yahweh came to me : Son of man, I have made you watchman for the house of Israel".

It is in this context that the apparently negative statement about the wicked and death is to be seen: in his concern for the fuller life the watchman is to say to the wicked "You are condemned to death". The "wicked" are not bad people always doing bad things, as the English translation suggests; far more seriously, they are completely out of touch with the possibilities of Yahweh's life ("godless" might be a better translation). Since there is no indication that the exiles were ever in any danger of being literally put to death, to be condemned to death probably means being condemned to no more than what exists already(3) "Godless" people are no longer aware of the distinction between source, medium and goal, since all three are now absorbed within themselves and their dead situation. If he does not respond, the godless person will certainly die, but the watchman, since he gave no warning, will be held responsible. The narrative emphasizes Ezekiel's responsibility, not that of the godless even though the watchman himself is not godless.

That the responsibility of the watchman is paramount is borne out by what follows: "But if you do warn the godless, and he does not turn from his godlessness and his wicked way, he will die in his iniquity, but you have saved your life" (3:19). What the watchman has to do is so important that he can succeed even as he fails! As long as he exercises his responsibility towards the godless, even if the latter pays no heed, the watchman has done what he must and saved his own life. He offers a renewal of life to people who may pay no heed if they wish, but the attempt has to be made.

The warning must be given to a person once righteous but now turned away:

> When a righteous man turns from his righteousness and does wrong and I set a stumbling-block before him , he will die in his sin and his righteous deeds which he has done will not be remembered, but I will hold you responsible for him. But if you do warn the righteous man not to sin [righteous](4) and he does not, he will certainly live because he took warning, and you have saved your own life (3:20-21).

Righteousness is not something to be saved up. Righteousness implies a relationship with others, and such a relationship is either present or not. Contemporary readers might see an objection in saying directly that God sets a stumbling-block before a person. But it is to prevent the assumption that former righteous deeds will license later wickedness, that this tangible conception is used. The responsibility of the watchman is so important and extends so far that no one is without need of it.

The unit as a whole ends on a doubly positive note, as it should. It is after all possible both that the watchman will exercise his reponsibility and that the righteous will react positively, so that, in this double response, they will both live. It is appropriate then that, immediately after the medium is shown to connect source and goal, there should be a special passage on the medium as a watchman with ultimate responsibility.

4. THE GOAL - THE PEOPLE: 3:22-27

The prophet is not the only one to have a passage to himself · - so do the people. The material in 3:16a, 22-27 is often linked with what follows, the prophetic symbolic actions in chaps 4-5, because 3:25-26 is thought to present a symbolic action of the prophet bound with cords and made dumb(1). But other elements in this section clearly refer back to Yahweh's call: in 3:22-23 where Ezekiel is told to go to the plain and sees again the glory of Yahweh, he is evidently meant to be temporarily summoned away from the exiles to repeat the experience of his first vision(2). The repetition of the phrase "rebellious house" (3:26-27) and of the matter of hearing and refusing to hear clearly refers back to the call in 2:4-5, 7-8; and 3:11.

Here another aspect of the link between God, prophet and people is presented. Ezekiel's responsibility to this people has not ended since the people themselves still have the freedom and responsibility to hear or refuse to hear. At the end of seven days (3:16a), during which he remains in a trance-like state (3:15), Ezekiel feels the hand of Yahweh again, indicating a new development. Yahweh says to him:

> Arise, go out to the plain for there I will speak with you. So I arose and went out to the plain , and the glory of Yahweh was standing there like the glory which I had seen by the river Chebar; so I fell on my face (3:22-23).

The hand and the glory of Yahweh affirm that Ezekiel's trance is not just an endless musing, nor is its only issue the positive responsibility of the watchman. The otherness of the glory of Yahweh now entails its perplexing opposite. Ezekiel does see the same vision as before, with the same results: he falls on his face, and the spirit enters into him and sets him on his feet. This time though, instead of being told that he is to go to the exiles, he is given the opposite commission: "Go shut yourself up inside your house" (3:24). He is to be placed in a strange state, held so that he cannot go out among the people and speak to them:

> As for you, son of man, cords are placed on you and you are bound with them so that you cannot go out among them. I will make your tongue cleave to the roof of your mouth so that you will be dumb and unable to be their admonisher, for they are a rebellious house (3:25-26).

It seems curious that a man who has been expressly told to go to his people with a special responsibility to warn them, should now be told that he is to be bound and silenced so that he is unable to.

The probable explanation is that speaking cannot be taken for granted(3). The person who knows a special responsibility to speak also knows there is a time to be silent, that there are times when speaking can be prostituted. Speaking is one responsibility; listening is another. The reason is that the people's freedom to listen cannot be taken from them. No one can force things on them. A creative address cannot be taken for granted in a rebellious house, and if it is delivered and not listened to, it only trivializes such an address to persist with it heedlessly. If the emphasis had previously been placed on the responsibility of the watchman, it is now placed on that of the people. They will be addressed whether they listen or not, but their not listening is a factor which cannot be ignored. In fact it might be said that one aspect of a responsibility which is more than superficial is to see significance in the quality of the response from the people to whom it is directed. But there will also be times when the watchman must speak:

> But when I speak with you, I will open your mouth
> and you shall say to them, Thus says the Lord
> Yahweh. He who will hear, let him hear, and he who
> will not, let him not, for they are a rebellious
> house (3:27).

Against the background of being bound and struck dumb, this
final verse emphasizes the necessity of any address by the
prophet having its origin in his source.

The most important thing to note here, however, is that the
last sentence gives great freedom to the people. They are
ultimately free to listen or not to listen as they wish. If
the prophet has the responsibility to speak, the people have
their own responsibility to listen. It is their freedom which
is given the last say in this part of the book, before the
particulars in chaps.4-24. Yahweh is not a God to force
hearing, even though he represents everything which is other
and possible in contrast to their not-hearing and rebellion.
That the responsible medium must both speak and (because his
audience is free to listen or not) be silent, puts a peculiar
but profound emphasis on the integration of source, medium and
goal: Ezekiel would not have had the courage to handle these
opposites unless he had been aware of this integration. Such
integration can reconcile opposites, and thus bring about
change, in contrast with the uniformity of what is strictly
logical(4).

The passages on the watchman (3:16-21) and the prophet (3:22-27), which now follow the call, change the complexion of the commission to speak to the rebels. For 3:21 finishes with the warning being heeded and thus with the possibility of a response; 3:27, to be sure, still finishes on the note of Israel being a rebellious house, but with the difference that those being addressed can now hear. Since Ezekiel is sent to a rebellious house with the announcement "Thus says Yahweh", the implication is that he must speak judgement to them; but these additions interpret the whole Book of Ezekiel and the outcome of its message correctly: that proclaiming judgement to rebels can lead to restoration, and indeed that this is the ultimate aim of judgement.

To say this must not be taken as an excuse to tone down, far less ignore the judgement; on the contrary it implies that the watchman's basic responsibility is towards judgement, and that restoration is impossible without it. Further, part of the very nature of judgement is that it cannot be neatly apportioned; judgement on oneself may include seeing its necessity for those people and places which are dear, even when there is a vested interest in their being spared. This explains the curious matter already noted: that in 3:11 Ezekiel is told to go to the exiles, but then the bulk of what follows in a long section on judgement in chaps.4-24 is concerned with Jerusalem. After the first section (1-3) has shown who the source, medium and goal are and what in principle they have to do with each other, the function of this second main section is to stress how significant it is for the exiles to hear what is said about the judgement of Jerusalem.

The extraordinary thing is that the recipients of restoration are not to be those left in the place of tradition, but those who have been taken from it, the exiles! But there is also a point of resistance here: for what the exiles want to do is return to their former home as quickly as possible. What they least desire is restoration based on what is only further judgement on themselves, for, after all, they still imagine Jerusalem to be their only foundation and hope for the future. Thus, far from it being curious that Ezekiel in Babylon should be talking about Jerusalem, the point of the book is that it is necessary: the harsh condition demanded of the exiles is that they recognize that only by accepting the destruction of their only hope for the future can there be any possibility of restoration. Such then is their position as recipients of restoration, and this is delineated in the following chapters in overwhelming and inescapable variety of detail.

Since chaps.4-24 are concerned with what the exiles have to
hear about the judgement on Jerusalem, it is appropriate that
the first they hear of it is the Babylonians' renewed siege of
Jerusalem. After the Babylonians had first conquered Jerusalem
in 597 B.C. those taken into exile then would naturally have
hoped that this was the end of direct hostilities. But Ezekiel
was not convinced, and was thus determined to put an end to all
the exiles' expect- ations for the place on which they centred
their hopes. A startling address about the siege is taken up
without any introduction at the beginning of 4:1 in the form of
a direct command of Yahweh, which can only be taken with the
utmost seriousness.

The content of the command confirms it, for Ezekiel is told
not merely to speak but to act. The symbolic act which follows
demonstrates that what is about to happen is unavoidable: "Now
you, son of man, take a brick and lay it before you and scratch
a city on it [Jerusalem]"(1) (4:1). The brick of soft clay
baked in the sun was something recognizably Babylonian, the
usual building material(2). Ezekiel is therefore speaking in
Babylon to those very people who might be thought to have
sieges behind them. It is in Babylon, not from any refuge,
where they must observe that Ezekiel adds tangible, threatening
dimensions to his drawing. Siegeworks, set against the city,
are made unavoidably particular in the specifications:

> ..you shall place siegeworks against it, you shall
> build a siege-mound against it, throw up earthworks
> against it, and set camps and battering-rams
> against it all round (4:2).

Ezekiel is now commanded to take an iron plate and set it as an
iron wall between himself and the city (4:3). Such a plate
does not appear to play as natural a role in a siege as mounds,
earthworks and battering-rams, but rather shows Ezekiel's own
personal involvement. Since it is also said that he is to
direct his face against the city, the iron probably represents
the implacability of his stance against Jerusalem. Not only is
the inevitability of the siege expressed through Yahweh's
command, but Ezekiel himself is seen as a sign to Israel
through what he did without compromise.

The command of Yahweh, combined with its embodiment in
Ezekiel, works in two directions. Ezekiel does as it instructs
and reacts to it himself. At the same time, the fact that it
is Yahweh's command makes it clear that Ezekiel is not acting
out of individual authoritarianism; the portrayal of the siege
is not Ezekiel's own whim for tormenting the exiles, who have
already suffered siege. To act at the command of Yahweh is to
act in responsibility _for_ and not capriciously _against._ This
is true even of responsibility for judgement. It is the

opposite of the failure to face up to the inevitable, merely because people think they have suffered enough.

The action beginning in 4:4 involves Ezekiel even more in his own person. It is not introduced like the others with "take!" which denotes an external object, but with the more personal verb "lie!"(3) He is told to lie on his left side. He is given a more elaborate interpretation than before, and for the first time an action is spoken of which is not visible:

> Now then lie upon your left side and set the punishment of the house of Israel upon it; for the number of days you lie upon it, you shall bear their punishment (4:4).

The action of lying on his side can of course be seen (and it is significant that Ezekiel's involvement is visible), but setting the punishment of the house of Israel upon it cannot. This action is therefore different from what had gone before and from the other two actions introduced by the instruction "take" which are still to follow in 4:9-11 and 5:1-2. But what does "setting the punishment of the house of Israel on his side" mean? The end of the verse may help. The expression "bear punishment" (nāsā' cāwôn) is used elsewhere in the Old Testament (e.g. Leviticus 5:1, 17-19), probably to emphasize the seriousness of the guilt, and meaning that the people concerned have to shoulder their own responsibility and take the consequences. This is exactly what the exiles are not doing. What would ordinarily be taken for granted with respect to the recognition of their guilt and its consequences, Ezekiel has to do for them. He is not suffering as a representative for the people, but trying to show them through his own action that there is a punishment that they have to suffer. Ezekiel portrays an inevitable siege so that they may relate it to themselves. The siege is clearly not just an isolated event, but must provoke a reaction from the exiles if it is going to have its proper effect.

The words in 4:5 emphasize that Yahweh is the one who assigns the full extent of the punishment:

> For I assign to you the years (for which they have to bear) their punishment as a number of days: three hundred and ninety days for which you shall bear the punishment of the house of Israel.

The number, three hundred and ninety, with days representing years, may relate to the time elapsed since the reign of Solomon and the building of the temple. The forty years mentioned in the following verse comprise a traditional round figure for the time of Judah's exile and until the time of the building of the second temple(4). That Yahweh explicitly assigns the punishment emphasizes the terrible burden of guilt for which the exiles must take the consequences, even though they are already in exile. The Israelites must see the consequences of being a "rebellious house", their historical and their present characteristic. It is necessary to interpret the siege as a chance to realize the significance of the people's lives in connection with it. It happens to a specific people and can be used to confront them with their present condition. The judgement is not the event itself but the reaction to the event. The Judaeans, however, cannot think of the siege only as a matter for Northern Israelites:

> When you have finished these (i.e. the three hundred and ninety days for the house of Israel), you shall lie upon your right side for a second time and bear the punishment of the house of Judah; I have assigned to you forty days, a day for each year (4:6).

The passage is probably a later addition because Judah is not separated from Israel in the Book of Ezekiel, and the expression "house of Israel" usually means the whole of Israel(5). It shows that some people have come to understand the significance of the punishment laid upon them. The reaction to the event is beginning to take effect. It is more significant to hear this than that Ezekiel actually lay on his side for three hundred and ninety days plus another forty days, which is not likely despite the feats of yogis and fakirs(6). It is now becoming completely clear that the judgement is not merely the event but becomes such only when the event makes people react out of their present condition through the mediation of others; when they acknowledge the judgement for themselves.

It is difficult, however, to bring about acceptance even of the first stage of the inevitable, a difficulty recognized by 4:7, which re-introduces the siege theme: "Towards the siege of Jerusalem you shall set your face with bared arm, and you shall prophesy against it". Lying on one's side is a much too passive image for the siege; the energetic expression of this verse redirects attention to that original event. It is also the first time that Ezekiel is commanded to prophesy against the city. (All the preceding verses, whether original or later additions, were concerned with his reactions.) To be told to speak at this time (and only. in a formula) is premature before the series of symbolic actions has reached its climax(7), but 4:7 is a necessary link in returning to the main emphasis on the siege, and in integrating the punishment with the siege.

The integration is completed in 4:8 "Look, I am putting cords upon you so that you cannot turn from one side to another until you have completed the time of your siege". This image, taken up from 3:25, can be recognized as an addition because, while it repeats something said previously, it is now used with a different intent. In 3:25 the image of binding with cords expresses a necessary removal of the prophet from the people. In 4:8, however, putting cords on him so that he cannot turn from one side to the other until the time of the siege is complete suggests the key notion of responsibility once again.

It has been established that judgement is a combination of various factors; it can now be said that responsibility exercised for others and accepted by them is the integrating agent between the event and its acceptance as judgement. Responsibility implies the difference between assuming the event itself to be judgement, and realizing that the event has had to be presented through human intermediaries and its significance acknowledged by others, in order to become judgement.

Long before this is acknowledged by the people, it is necessary not just to say that the city is to be besieged, but to describe the consequences for the inhabitants themselves. This is what the second action prompted by the word "take", the original continuation of 4:1-2 (8), adds to the first:

> So now, take wheat and barley, beans, lentils, millet and emmer-wheat, put them in one vessel, and make them into your bread (4:9).

As well as acting out the siege itself, Ezekiel must show through his own diet the food the people will eat. A siege is not just something to observe, but something which involves the people in the harshest possible way. Their food is to be austere siege fare; the left-overs, reduced to what can be put into one vessel. Most serious of all, although Ezekiel is told to put these grains into one vessel, to make his "bread", they are to be mixed; and, at least as far as sowing seed was concerned, the law forbade such mixtures (Leviticus 19:19). Thus, probably, Yahweh himself commands Ezekiel to eat unclean food.

This painful aspect of Yahweh's command expresses the seriousness of the siege. To eat such food shows the state to which they have descended. It also makes Ezekiel's personal involvement in the siege all the more moving, for he was of course the most meticulous of priests. We see here too that Ezekiel's personal involvement expressed in his symbolic actions appears in this original part of the prophecy, so that the more elaborate interpretation of it in the addition of 4:4-8 does have a basis in the original. The second part of 4:9, which says that Ezekiel is to eat this kind of food for the three hundred and ninety days he lies upon his side, links the nutritional deficiencies of the siege with lying on his side. But the very improbability of eating such food for three hundred and ninety days brings out the extremely serious human consequences of the siege.

The food is not just scarce and unclean; it is rationed:

> Now you shall eat your food by weight; twenty shekels a day; you shall eat it at fixed intervals. Your water also you shall drink it by measure: the sixth part of a hin; you shall drink at fixed intervals (4:10-11).

The measurements add up to the meagre total of half a pound of food and one and three-quarter pints of liquid. It is rationed both in quantity and in time, since the Hebrew phrase "From time to time" indicates that it has to be eaten or drunk at fixed intervals(9). Rationing is also the theme of the last verses of the section, 16-17, which, since they speak of Yahweh breaking the staff of bread in Jerusalem and of the people eating bread by weight and drinking water by measure, are clearly based on 4:10-11 (10). But they are just as clearly a general comment on the effects of famine on the people in Jerusalem without any particular reference to Ezekiel's action and involvement. The people are to eat their bread with anxiety, and drink their water in horror. Yahweh is acting in order that there may be a shortage of bread and water, and that everyone will be desolate and waste away under their punishment. One almost detects here a satisfaction with the people's desolation. Most additions have their own understandable, and sometimes enriching, purpose. There is little to be said for this one, since it moralistically shifts attention away from the primary need (4:10-11) of soberly bringing before the people the fact of the siege and the nature of its human consequences. The main concern is not to insist on desolation for its own sake.

The other addition in 4:12-15, however, elaborates a particular consequence of the siege, one that concerns the uncleaness of the food. The provenance of this elaboration is shown in v.13: "Yahweh said, So shall the Israelites eat their bread unclean among the people whither I drive .them". This statement must relate not to the exiles under siege, but to the present plight of a state of uncleanness in exile. It is not about the siege at all. Verse 12 also refers back over v.11 to v.10: "You shall eat it as a barley cake, baking it before them on turds of human excrement", intensifying horribly the uncleanness of the food as already implied in v.9. For an Israelite, there could be no more shocking expression of the ultimately degrading consequences of the siege. Ezekiel responds with rare spontaneity, expressing his indignation(11):

I said, Ah Lord(12) Yahweh, I have never ever defiled myself; right from my youth till now I have never eaten carcasses of animals or those torn by beasts, and meat from an unclean sacrifice has never touched my lips (4:14).

This is the resentful reaction of a priest meticulous in his observance of ritual law. How far the consequences of the siege must go, is shown when a man replies indignantly to the holy God who is himself commanding the abomination!

The addition also shows how Ezekiel himself belongs to the human exiles. He is not one standing apart disinterestedly proclaiming the necessity of the siege, but is himself shocked by its consequences, some of which are totally unexpected even by himself. The acceptance and exercise of responsibility by his own person does not protect him from being painfully affected by it. For Yahweh himself to command the eating of unclean food, and in the crudest possible terms, is for Yahweh to go against his own being. The most serious consequence of the siege for humans is that it promotes their involvement (which in the meantime Ezekiel is demonstrating to the people) in a way which is not just physically uncomfortable, but which subverts every religious feeling they have. For Ezekiel that means the derangement of his whole being. Yahweh directing himself against himself, almost brutally removing Ezekiel from himself, gives expression to a most violent separation from the familiar supports of life.

The command of Yahweh does not simply mean that the siege will happen. It is a particularly pointed example of judgement residing not only in exterior happenings, but ultimately in the reaction of people to these happenings.

Ezekiel, who had addressed the God (4:14) who had repelled him (4:12), receives an answer, "But he said to me, All right, I will give you cow's dung instead of human turds so you can make your bread over them" (4:15), which is alleviation of a limited kind, for the cow's dung probably does not entirely remove the sense of uncleaness. In the original context, the statement may have meant that there would be some protection from uncleanness even in exile in an unclean land. Now it hints that the support which appeared to be lost still exists. The necessity of the siege and what that entails is not diminished, but for that very reason, the hint is that this support may be renewed through such judgement. What is to be is horrible; but those who respond positively can potentially receive restoration.

The climax of the original three-sign series is in 5:1-2. The first describes the various concrete facts of the siege; the second (4:9-11) adds, through Ezekiel's own diet, the effects on humans (which turn out to involve not only physical, but also spiritual suffering). The third is the destruction of the very persons of those besieged, expressed by a direct action on Ezekiel's body:

> So then, son of man, take a sharp sword and use it as a barber's razor and pass it over your head and your beard, and then take balances for weighing to divide (the hair). One third part you shall burn in the midst of the city when the time of the siege is finished; then you shall take another third part and strike it with the sword around about (the city); the final part you shall scatter to the wind and I shall unsheathe the sword after them (5:1-2).

Here the son of man's own person is once again directly involved, so it is clear that the interpretation of 4:4-8, involving the prophet's own person in symbolic action, has a basis in the original series. In a gripping and bizarre image,

Ezekiel shaves himself with a <u>sword</u>. The threefold division shows that there is no escape whatsoever from the destruction which will take place both in and around the city, even those who at first escape are destroyed. Shaving signifies humiliation, so that it is not only a question of destruction, but of shameful degradation. This is the lot of the city in which the exiles place their hope.

There can be little doubt that this was the original climax in the progression, siege, siege food, siege destruction - awaiting now only the necessary interpretation by word which follows in 5:5-6a, 8-9, 14-15 (13). What follows immediately in 5:3-4 introduces a new feature to contradict 5:1-2:

> You shall take from there (these hairs) a few in number, and bind them in the skirts of your garment. From them you shall take yet others and cast them into the fire and burn them up; from there shall go forth fire to the house of Israel.

Binding hairs in the skirts of the garment expresses intimate protection. It means that some survivors will be preserved, which cannot possibly be meant in vv.1-2. The extreme cautiousness of the statement about survival shows that there was some realization of the contradiction. Only a very small number will be saved, and v.4 goes on to say - acknowledging that this statement has been added - that even some of these are to be removed and thrown into the fire(14).

This addition was probably made in later exilic times when it was known that not everyone was destroyed in the Jerusalem siege. It represents the situation more comprehensively and realistically, and offers a more adequate understanding of God than the original. The God of preservation is placed after the God of judgement, indicating that to face the seriousness of a situation can lead one beyond it. The addition indicates that theology is never totally comprehensible in one period. It must be committed to a given situation, but should also be prepared to make revisions when circumstances change. It is realistic in refusing to see revision as something totally detached from that which it revises. Here it is clear that the God of preservation is not distinct from the God of judgement. That even some of the survivors are subjected again to the fire implies that the very assumption of preservation is a judgement in itself. This is developed by the last part of 5:4 where the fire is applied to the whole house of Israel. The judgement which seems to be necessary for there to be any future recipients of restoration is not of course a "fire of judgement" in any later sense. It is an image taken from the symbolic action in 5:2, and refers quite specifically to the Babylonian siege of Jerusalem.

In the original version, the demonstration of siege and destruction by means of symbolic action required a verbal interpretation. If the material defined above as secondary has been identified correctly, this is the first time that Ezekiel has spoken at all. The "messenger formula" which has not yet been used in this section confirms this:

> Thus says Lord Yahweh, This is Jerusalem: I have put her in the middle of the nations with other countries all around her, but she rebelled against my laws more godlessly than the nations and against my statutes than these countries which are round about her (5:5-6a).

Not only is this the first verbal interpretation, it is possibly the first explicit identification of the besieged city with Jerusalem. Difficult as it may be for present-day readers to imagine, it would have been possible for Judaean exiles watching Ezekiel's series of symbolic actions to fail to realize that he was actually referring to their only hope, their beloved Jerusalem. But now the terse sentence hits home: "This is Jerusalem". Ezekiel does not initially speak of judgement - indeed at first he does not speak at all - but presents happenings which only in their verbal interpretation lead him on to speak about judgement (5:8). The interpretation confirms conclusively what was said before, namely that for an event to become judgement there must be a reaction, which (in this case) leads to the acknowledgement that the besieged city is actually Jerusalem - "This is Jerusalem".

The unadorned sentences which give the reason for judgement are then expanded by contrasting Jerusalem with other peoples. If it is a shock for exiles from a defeated Jerusalem to hear that Jerusalem is to be besieged again, it can seem nothing short of incredible that this is because Israel has rebelled against Yahweh's laws more than other countries, the most provocative way possible of confronting Jerusalem with her guilt. The coming siege is all the more ruinous because of the high standing which Jerusalem once enjoyed: Jerusalem is said to have been set in the middle of nations and countries. The words used, gôyim and 'arāsôt place Jerusalem in the middle of the widest bounds of the people and places(15). Like other countries, Israel believed herself to be at the centre of things, "the navel of the earth ", its special position given a concrete expression by the geographical terms. But as the language of 5:5 makes clear - "I have put her in the middle of the nations" - Israel's pre-eminence is neither natural nor necessarily permanent, but is something given which could be taken away. Jerusalem's necessary judgement is in the realization that she must forfeit what she thinks she ought to be because of what she is. The siege means that what she in fact assumes will always be, is about to be nullified. The hateful actuality is that it is the Babylonians who are on the crest of the wave, who have still not finished what they are capable of, while the Judaeans by their attitude and conduct show that they still have not grasped this. How could improvement come about until they do?

Nothing new can happen yet, for 5:6 makes clear that Israel has herself, incredibly, rejected her special position. This is not general accusation, for the words used .for "laws and statutes", mišpātîm and ḥuqqôt, make concrete and comprehensive reference to all the detailed law which has been promulgated, and rejected by the people. Being the kind of people they are, they cannot change until there is the kind of judgement which makes them see the need for change. Verses 6b and 7 are rather repetitive; and it is most likely that the argument of vv.5-6a, which expresses accusation and the reason for it, is continued in the threat based on this reason uttered in vv.8-9 and vv.14-15:

> Therefore, thus says the Lord Yahweh, I, even I, am against you, and I shall execute judgement in your midst in the sight of nations. I shall do with you what I have never done before and shall never do again because of all your abominations (5:8-9).

The judgement is to be completely without precedent. The people are to be hurtled from a state of extreme privilege to one of unqualified rejection. The judgement is not only unique, but also shameful for being visible to others. The Babylonians are dominant and everyone else will recognize it, even if the Judaeans do not.

Such execution of unprecedented judgements would of course fit the fact of the siege and the siege alone very well, and the incomparable nature of the situation (Jerusalem again under siege after so short an interval) is made even more explicit in connection with the other nations in 5:14-15. It is likely, therefore, that the argument of vv. 5-6a, 8-9 was originally continued - and concluded - in v.14-15. That which intervenes tries first, in v.10, to express the unheard-of judgement in terms of a particular horror:

> Therefore fathers will eat sons in your midst and sons will eat their fathers; I shall execute judgements on you and scatter any of you left over to the winds.

This may be a memory of cannibalism during the siege, but there is no direct evidence. The unprecedented horror of this statement (there is no other reference in the Old Testament to people eating their parents) has the effect of diverting attention from the siege as a very sober reality.

This is also true of the other additional material in vv.11-13 and 16-17. It tries to expand on the judgement, giving the impression of exaggeration without necessarily being a very accurate interpretation. Verses 16-17 give particularly alarming details(16). The additional material is, in fact, a very good example of the later sense of "fire of judgement", as mentioned earlier - the term used for the accumulation of specific torments, but with the effect of directing the attention away from the heart of judgement. Thus though I have argued that most of the additions to the Book of Ezekiel have their own serious and necessary purposes, these are more like the uninspired elaborations on scripture of some modern preachers who, for want of proper exegesis, say more about their own religious preoccupations than about the Bible.

By contrast, however, the other additions draw even greater attention to the one serious purpose: that there was to be another siege, which the exiles should acknowledge as a judgement on themselves. Verses 14-15 provide the links with and the conclusion to vv.8-9:

> I will make you a desolation and a reproach among
> the nations about you, in the sight of all who will
> pass by. You shall be a reproach and a taunt, a
> warning and a horror to the nations around you when
> I execute judgements against you in anger, wrath
> and furious chastisements - I Yahweh have spoken.

There may be one or two additional items here too, but all the language is soberly and directly applicable to the siege itself, and also to the fact that the siege is visible to the other nations (v.8b). The emphasis at the end on Yahweh having spoken - the expression is also a concluding formula - removes by its open and frank address any possible hope of escape. It is appropriate that his part of the book, which begins with a command of Yahweh, ends with "I Yahweh have spoken".

The earlier verses 1:28-3-15 had expressed the fact of address. It is appropriate that the first application of this addresss (in 4-5) should concern the siege of Jerusalem, the threat to the object of the people's hope. Thus the material in 4-5, placed where it is, represents in the most unavoidable way the connection with their present situation. What happens in Jerusalem will not occur in an obscure corner, but in the centre of the world, with universal and exemplary significance. That is what Yahweh's pronouncement means: not something to grieve over in private, but something which brings public humiliation upon them in order to change them into different people. This is indeed the very grace of the judgement of God that it is to be found manifestly among those who have spurned him.

2. THE SUPPORTS OF RELIGION REMOVED: 6

Chapters 4-5 describe judgement against Jerusalem and its people. Chapter 6 extends this to the whole land and, while 4-5 include the religious feelings of the people, 6 concentrates on the destruction of religious places and the

39

security they represent. There is also a change of form. While 4-5 contain symbolic actions expressed as the command of Yahweh, 6 has expressive actions(1) in the framework of the word-event formula: "The word of Yahweh came to me" (6:1), "Son of man, set your face against Israel and prophesy against them" (6:2). The expressive action was originally based on the idea that a judgement directed against an object that could be seen was more effective than one directed against an object that could not be seen. The original sense is still present in Numbers 23:13 where Balak says to Balaam: "Come with me to another place from where you can see them ... then curse them for me from there". The expressive action in Ezekiel, rather than being meant literally, brings out the prophet's responsibility to concentrate totally on the place against which he is to prophesy with the whole will of Yahweh behind him. The introduction of the expressive action with the word-event formula also emphasizes its extent and solemnity.

The content confirms the extent and solemnity of what Ezekiel is to say: it is directed against nothing less than the mountains of Israel(2)! Since the mountains were the heartland of old Israel, the expression conveys significant totality. They had however also become the place of the illicit cult. For this reason, as well as because there had long been a close connection between people and land, to prophesy against the mountains of Israel is to prophesy against the people in their very religious foundations. "The mountains of Israel" were Yahweh's land and Israel's land, going back further, touching deeper than even Jerusalem herself. If there had been any thought of escape outside Jerusalem, it is now dispelled.

The prophecy against the mountains of Israel is explicit:

> You shall say, Mountain of Israel, hear the word of Lord Yahweh. Thus has Lord Yahweh spoken to the mountains, the hills, the gullies and the valleys, Look I am bringing a sword against you and I shall destroy your high places (6:3).

The repetition of formulae to do with Yahweh's word, and the comprehensive listing of all the parts of the mountains, clearly confirm the solemnity and extent of the prophecy. Not only will Jerusalem be besieged, every religious support will be destroyed. To state that Yahweh himself "brings a sword" implies that the very places where people think they are gaining religious security are the prime object of destruction. This is necessary if there is to be any true restoration and not just a renewed seeking of false security. The shame of the Israelites themselves - and here the close connection between mountains and people is evident - has to be brought upon them:

> Your altars will be destroyed and your cult places(3) broken down, and I shall cast your slain before your idols; [I shall place the corpses of the people of Israel before their idols](4) and I

40

shall scatter your bones round about your altars
(6:4-5).

The various types of altars are to be destroyed and the people
at the same time shamed, humiliated, polluted. Dead bodies
were considered unclean anywhere, but to place them around
altars was unthinkable. The image of Yahweh casting the slain
before their idols is shocking and demonstrates how far the
people have became distanced from their own source. They have
to be made responsible for Yahweh's and Israel's land. Rather
than being a gift enriching of life, the land becomes a place
for shameful death. The judgement means that there is no
support even in Yahweh's and Israel's land. Being removed from
the tried stays of life is expressed even more radically here
than in chap.4. For when the very land itself becomes
corrupted, all support is swept away.

What follows in 6:6-7 seeks to emphasize this(5), but the
original emphasis was made in the second expressive action in
vv.11-13a, "setting the face against", "clapping the hand and
stamping the foot", and saying,

> Alas for all the evil abominations of the house of
> Israel; they shall fall by the sword, by famine
> and by pestilence (6:11).

Such an expressive action may have been considered sufficiently
effective to eliminate the abominations, a view reinforced by
the classical triad of judgement (sword, famine and pestilence)
making clear that no one will escape:

> He who is far off will die by pestilence and he who
> is near will die by the sword, anyone who is left
> over at all will perish of famine. So I will spend
> my rage against them (6:12).

"He who is far and he who is near" means "everyone", and if
that were not explicit enough, any possibility of escape is
eliminated by the reference to anyone left over. The original
conclusion probably came with what has been called the formula
of recognition(6) in 6:13, "Then you will know that I am
Yahweh". The phrase, frequent in the Book of Ezekiel, is a
further indication of the reaction called for from the people.
The destruction comes about, and they must recognize Yahweh in
it. Many of those who continue to place their confidence in
manipulating religious activities, far from being automatically
protected, will be destroyed with them; the narrative
recognizes God in the bankruptcy of religion, and realizes that
greater efforts in that area will not improve matters at all.

The theme of no escape from the destruction of the religious
devices is reiterated in 6:1-5 and 6:11-13. That being so, a
section in 6:8-10 on those who escape seems in direct
contradiction, and must have been added later. But it does
show that those who did escape allowed the judgement to affect

41

them profoundly(7):

> .. they will remember me ... when I have broken
> their adulterous hearts which turned away from me
> and (blinded) their eyes which went wantonly after
> their idols;   they will be repelled at themselves
> for the evil they have done, for all their
> abominations (6:9).

The release is in the last statement, which seems to represent
the later experience when some did see the contrast between
their former religious practice and the truly beneficial, and
felt repugnance at themselves. This is a peculiar example of a
reaction to an event creating judgement: the people's own
feelings effect it.   The incident of the unclean food in chap.4
has already expressed the religious suffering caused by the
siege, but that came in the form of a command of Yahweh. Here
the repulsion originates from the people themselves.   6:8-10
shows, like 5:3-4, the reaction of people interpreting an event
to understand better what they are - and what they could be.
It demonstrates that the process of happening, reaction and
acknowledgement of judgement may require a number of
experiences over a period of time to be complete.

3. RESPONSIBILITY TO PROCLAIM THE END: 7

The responsibility expressed through the prophet's person
(4-5), and the responsibility of total concentration(6) now
lead inexorably to the responsibility not to shrink from
proclaiming the end of the very land:

> The word of Yahweh came to me, Now you son of man,
> thus says Lord Yahweh to the land of Israel, An end
> has come, the end over the four corners of the
> earth (7:1-2)

The theme of the end possibly elaborates what Amos (8:22) is
content to state quite baldly: "The end has come upon my
people Israel". Having spoken of the siege of Jerusalem and
its people, and of the destruction of the land and its
religious practices, to speak of the end brings this part of
the book to a radical conclusion. Addressing "the land of
Israel" about the end coming on the four corners of the earth
confirms that even Israel is not exempt from this comprehensive
judgement. In fact Ezekiel has his own special term for "the
land of Israel": 'admat yiśrā'ēl, used seventeen times in the
Book of Ezekiel and nowhere else(1). It is found only between
this place and chap.38, that is, before the great vision of the

renewed land, people and sanctuary in chaps.40-48;   so it is
possible that 'admat yiśrā'ēl refers to the land deserted by
Yahweh.

The end coming upon the land, made even more explicit, means
the end coming upon the people, those addressed:

> Now the end is upon you, I shall let loose my anger
> upon you;   I shall judge you; I shall judge you
> according to your own ways and bring upon you all
> your abominations. My eye will not spare you, I
> shall have no pity for I am bringing your own ways
> upon you so that your abominations will be obvious
> - then you will know that I am Yahweh (7:3-4).

The end comes ever closer. Yahweh and the people are closely
connected;   the pitiless Yahweh has to be seen together with
the judgement bringing their own ways upon them. There is only
one way forward: there can be no change until the people are
exposed to themselves as they are. They cannot complain that
Yahweh is imposing a judgement from outside on them; they can
only complain about themselves - which might at last make a
difference!   This is a much more direct expression of the
necessity of their reaction, involving themselves in the
judgement, than eating unclean siege food in chap.4. That
might offend their religious sensibilities, but all their
sensibilities are now about to be affected.

It indicates too the extent to which responsibility has to
go. Having to convince people of a further siege is hard
enough, but some people will not take any event too seriously
which is only foretold. Now the responsibility is to tell the
people not what will happen, but what is happening already in
their present condition. No doubt remains:

> Thus says the Lord Yahweh, Disaster <after>(2)
> disaster, see it comes: an end, the end has come,
> it has awakened against you (7:5-6a).

The end awakening against them suggests a revelation of the
people's own involvement with the end, a repetition which is
poetically effective since it leaves no doubt that they are a
disaster. (The repetitions of 7:6b-9 are not as effective)
(3).

A new theme appears, that of "the day", probably the same as
"the day of Yahweh" of which Amos had spoken, and which he said
was darkness and not light (Amos 5:18). "Behold the day, it is
coming, ... (?)(4) has come out, <injustice> (5) has bloomed,
arrogance sprouted. Violence has grown into a stem of
wickedness [?]"(6) (7:10-11a). The people evidently thought of
"the day" as a day of salvation for themselves: but for Amos
it means darkness. Isaiah (2:12) characteristically speaks of
Yahweh "having a day" against the proud and lofty, and here too
there is a unique interpretation, implicitly identifying "the
day" with "the end". So here we have the literal end of a

43

history of interpretation in which "the day" has changed from one of salvation to one of perdition. It is a powerful example of something beneficial turning against the very people for whom it is supposed to be beneficial. Ezekiel has the responsibility of saying that the people must see the coming of this day, this end, as the blooming of their own unrighteousness; they are thus brought into ever closer contact with the meaning. A metaphor of the people blooming, sprouting, growing, pictures the coming of the day. The coming of the day is to be found in their own actions: it has nothing to do with conquest by a foreign nation! The metaphors of growth are effective, because they paint for the people a picture of their own lives growing into this day. If in chaps 4-5 the first stage of the process of judgement was the siege, and the second in chap.6 the destruction of their religious support, the third is the people's own conduct.

There is no question of postponement:

> The time has come, the day has arrived, let not the buyer rejoice nor the seller mourn [for wrath comes over all its multitude], for the seller would not be able to return to what he has sold anyway [while their life remains among the living, for a vision comes, over all its multitude, it will not return], no one [in his guilt](7) will be able to hold on to his life (7:12-13).

The people are shown that all human activity will cease; normal feelings about business transactions, for instance, are no longer relevant. They must realize that they race towards the very opposite of normality. There is no escape whatsoever, as the image of battle makes clear: the horn has been blown (v.14), and if the sword is without, pestilence and famine are within (v.15); wherever the people are, the end is awaiting them. If any do escape to the mountains, they will <die>(8) there (v.16). They react despairingly to their own bodies, emotions, and material possessions. They lose bodily control: "All hands have become feeble and every knee runs with water" (v.17); their true nature is exposed in the signs of shame, sackcloth and baldness (v.18); and even the things in which people put their whole trust are of no use now - they throw away their money (v.19). They had used their wealth to make their abominable images; so it is appropriate that it should become plunder for foreigners (vv.20-21).

But this is nothing to what follows:

> I shall turn my face from them and they will profane my treasure, robbers will enter it and profane it; they will carry out slaughter, for the land is full of [commerce](9) blood, and the city is full of violence [I shall bring the worst of the nations and they will take possession of their houses]. I shall put an end to their proud

44

strength, and their sanctuaries will be profaned
(7:22-24).

The plundering of the temple constitutes a climax. Yahweh
turns his face from the people, and since "seeing Yahweh's
face" means visiting the temple, it is not likely that anything
other than the temple is meant when it is said that "they will
profane my treasure". When their own God allows his sanctuary
to be profaned the people are clearly at an end. The probable
addition at the beginning of v.24(10), "I shall bring the worst
of the nations and they will take possession of their houses",
means that the injury is meant to be an insult. Not just any
adversary carries it out, but those known as "the worst of the
nations". The end affects them in body, mind and in their
religion; no detail is spared. There will be no peace for
those who seek it; none of the traditional resources will
help:

> Anguish comes and they seek deliverance, but there
> is none; disaster on disaster comes, and rumour
> follows rumour - they seek a revelation from the
> prophet, but there will be no guidance at all from
> the priest and no counsel from the elders. [The
> King mourns and] (11) The prince is clothed with
> despair and the hands of the people are paralysed
> by terror. I shall deal with them according to
> their judgements - then they will know that I am
> Yahweh (7:25-27).

Thus the prophets, priests and elders cannot help the people;
the prince himself is in despair. The crisis is now
all-embracing.
   The first series of judgements in chaps 4-7 develops thus:
in 4-5 there is no hope in Jerusalem, in chap.6 no hope in
religion, and in chap.7 no hope in the people or in any human
authorities, including the political ones. Chapters 4-5 show
the siege resulting, after an initial reaction of indignation,
in an acceptance that there is punishment to bear. The purpose
of the punishment, however, is demonstrated more clearly in
chaps.6 and 7: the first concentrating on the religious
devices of the people, who then feel revulsion at themselves;
the second culminating in that direct confrontation where the
end is seen in the people's own ways, leading to a complete
loss of religious and social control. This is the judgement
which, as both chaps.6 and 7 show, proceeds to the recognition
of Yahweh himself in the very exposure of the people's own
bankruptcy, both in their religion and their leadership.
Whereas judgement had once been revealed as a happening, now it
is revealed in what the people do in their bankruptcy and
despair.

Why is it still necessary after the siege of Jerusalem to
present the great vision of idolatry in Jerusalem in
chaps.8-11? Because the image of "jealousy" (8:3) which
Ezekiel sees there is a particularly horrific example of the
conduct of the people and cannot be presented in any other way.
It is therefore of the greatest importance that the vision of
Jerusalem and its abominations originates not there but among
the people in exile:

> Now it happened in the sixth year, in the sixth
> month, on the fifth day of the month while I was
> sitting in my house with the elders of Judah before
> me, that the hand of [Lord] Yahweh fell upon me
> there (8:1).

It is there that the hand of Yahweh falls upon him, which
suggests a specific situation. The fact that the elders sit
before him probably means that they have come to consult him,
quite likely hoping for an authoritative word about the
imminent return home(1). The vision not only starts with the
exiles, but also ends with them in 11:25, when Ezekiel tells
them everything he had seen. What happens in the vision is not
self-referential, but is filled with significance for the
exilic situation.
  That "the hand of Yahweh fell on"(2) Ezekiel, indicates that
he will receive an authoritative message for the exiles. He
will become aware of the inadequacy of what the exiled elders
want and his visionary experiences confirms this conviction.
In it he is not alone: "I looked, and there was an appearance
as the likeness of a man(3), and below what looked like his
loins there was fire, and above an appearance of brightness
like the flashing of pale gold" (8:2). Such a figure is common
in visions, a guide to whom the visionary can relate and yet
who plainly represents an authority greater than his. What he
points out is noted very deliberately - the exiles will have
much to consider about Jerusalem before continuing to place
their hopes in that place. Here the description of the man has
probably been filled with details from Ezekiel's vision in
chap.1(4), with the intention of giving his visions of the
abominations in Jerusalem as much authority as that of the
source of his responsibility. Without such authority it would
be hard to believe that there were such abominations in
Jerusalem, so serious were they.
  In Jerusalem then, occurs an image of horror:

> He put out the form of a hand and grasped me by a
> lock of hair; the wind lifted me up between earth
> and heaven, bringing me to Jerusalem in divine
> visions to the entrance of the inner gate which

faces north where there was the seat of the image
of "jealousy" (?) [which makes jealous](5) (8:3).

That Ezekiel is grasped by a lock of hair indicates that what
he is describing is not experienced by him in the imagination
but as a fact. His levitation and translocation(6), commonly
experienced in visions, emphasize that his knowledge does
indeed come from Jerusalem and that what he describes is
happening there. Being grasped, lifted up and carried, shows
that Ezekiel did not seek out this experience for himself, but
has it forced upon him. No wonder - for what he sees is an
image and in Jerusalem. The meaning of the image of "jealousy"
is not clear, but it could be an image which makes (Yahweh)
jealous, possibly an image of Tammuz, the dying and rising God
so incompatible with Yahwism(7). Another suggestion is that
the word usually translated "jealous" (qin'â) means here
"passionate love", and so refers to an image of Asherah, the
goddess of love(8). Whatever the meaning, there can be no
point in the exiled elders questioning Ezekiel until what is
happening in Jerusalem is faced. (This would apply whether
they are enquiring about the return or about some practical
matter of life in exile.) The image clearly shows that events
in Jerusalem are so urgent that they take precedence over
everything else. No hope whatsoever can be placed in Jerusalem
in view of such an image. Urgency is also expressed in the
composition of the book as it now stands, which indicates first
an inflexible belief in the siege of Jerusalem, but then makes
clear that there is a particular justification for this - "the
image of jealousy", which needs a section all to itself. By
following after the first section (4-7) on the siege and the
collapse of all the people's religious and political supports,
the pernicious, all-pervading force of the image of jealousy is
given ample expression.
   A probable later addition, linking this vision with the
vision of the call, says in 8:4 that where the image of
jealousy is, there is also the glory of the God of Israel, like
the appearance Ezekiel saw on the plain(9). But it makes the
supplementary point that the God of Israel is the necessary
contrast to the hopeless abomination in Jerusalem. I said
before that the hand of Yahweh on Ezekiel among the exiles
represented the beginning of their knowledge that their
inadequacy can be overcome. This striking contrast confirms
it.
   From now on things gather momentum. Having seen the image,
Ezekiel is asked whether he notes the great abominations of the
people, which effectually remove Yahweh from his own sanctuary
(8:5-6). These might appear to be merely repetition of the
abominations of the altars mentioned in chap.6. But chap.8
elaborates the horror of the despicable cult as chap.6 had not
done. Indeed it appears that whatever is described is not
final: "... but you will see still greater abominations than
these" (8:6).

The man brings Ezekiel to the entrance of the court of the temple (8:7), telling him to go in and look at the abominations they perform (v.9). When he does so, he sees that all kinds of abominable images are scratched on the wall (v.10). A matter of central importance to the religion of Israel is being flouted, the prohibition of images. What is worse is that seventy elders of the house of Israel stand before these images, each burning his own incense to them (v.11)(10). The number "seventy" probably indicates a comprehensive representation from Israel. These important people are turning all their hopes and efforts in a direction totally at variance with Israel's rightful direction, completely disorientated by the events which caused the exile. How could the exiles look to them? The explanation is in the words of the elders: "Yahweh does not see (it)(11), Yahweh has forsaken the land" (8:12). Their apparent sincerity shows the hopelessness of their attitude. Since the Babylonians had conquered Judah, many Israelites could have believed that their God had forsaken them. This itself is an abomination, for it implies that Yahweh is related only to events, not to the sort of people they are, and their attitude to the events. But still this is not the end: "You will see still greater abominations than these they are doing" (8:13)

What comes now seems to involve the people even more personally. The man brings Ezekiel to the gate of the temple where there are women sitting and weeping for Tammuz (v.14)(12). It is perhaps significant that this is the only place in the Old Testament which has occasion, or can bring itself, to mention this deity by name. Tammuz was a Sumerian-Babylonian god of vegetation who died and rose again. He represented nature's death - hence the weeping. Their devotion to a god concerned with the dying and reanimation of vegetation indicates that Israelites no longer trust Yahweh's control over life. They are in a state where they are prepared to resort to alternatives, and in so doing, turn their backs on that which had been depended on before. This actually happens, for when the man brings Ezekiel to the inner court of the temple, he sees about twenty men at the door of the temple with their backs to it, turned towards the east and worshipping the sun (v.16). These men are possibly members of king Zedekiah's government(13), those who pressed him, after his appointment by the Babylonians in 597 B.C., to further revolt; they showed nothing but contempt for sensible political advice or, as is known from the Book of Jeremiah, for the theological admonitions offered by that prophet. They seek a substitute religion, so that their whole attitude could not be better characterized than by turning their backs on Yahweh's temple.

The man goes on to say to Ezekiel (v.17), that it is evidently too little a thing for the house of Judah that they perform the abominations they do here, since they also fill the land with violence. The cultic conduct of the people is therefore combined with misconduct towards other people, and an expression which follows demonstrates this. The usual translation "They are putting the branch to their nose" has never been satisfactorily explained, but it may mean "they are forcing their stink up my (God's) nostrils"(14), that is, a coarse expression for the behaviour of the people: they are farting in God's face! Abomination has been added to abomination(15), and surely it can go no further. But no one can be in any doubt about the abominations to be faced before moves in a new direction can be made. Nothing here can be lightly turned aside and "forgotten"; only the opposite is possible - the people suffering in detail for the details of their abominations: "So I too will act in anger; my eye will not spare, and I will show no pity" (8:18).

Chapter 9 elaborates on the judgement. The "man" who, at least by 8:18, appears to be identified with Yahweh, calls out in Ezekiel's hearing that the judgemental acts on the city are near at hand. Ezekiel sees seven men coming, six of them with weapons of destruction, and the other, clothed in linen, with materials for writing (9:1-2). An old tradition of seven deities or demons probably lies behind this; Ezekiel uses it to specific purpose, developing the seventh figure in a particular way(16). The linen clothes have priestly associations as well as those of a scribe, representing the god in ancient oriental mythologies who served as a scribe. The figure of the priest-scribe is appropriate, because he suggests the purity and accuracy of inevitable judgement. All seven together with their supernatural associations suggest that here is a judgement not only inevitable but irresistible, for no one could be anything but helpless against such a band. Likewise when they take up their stand by the altar, it means that the temple could not afford any protection against them. Judgement itself comes from the altar and under that authority they operate.

In 9:3 it is said that the glory of the God of Israel lifted itself up from the cherub (the winged figure above the ark) to the threshold of the temple. The departure of the glory of Yahweh is. a motif which appears later (11:23); so the fact that here it is called "the glory of the God of Israel"(17) suggests it is an addition which infers that the God of Israel could only have been absent from the temple during a judgement which starts at the temple itself. The God of Israel himself cannot stand in the way of judgement, so it <u>is</u> inevitable and necessary. Yahweh himself says to the scribe:

> Go through the city [in the midst of Jerusalem] (18) and make a mark on the foreheads of all men who sigh and groan over the abominations which are done in it.

Then to the other six he says, still in Ezekiel's hearing,

> Follow him through the city and strike; your eye shall not pity and you are not to spare anyone; you are to exterminate old and young, young girls,

children and women, except that you shall not touch
anyone on whom is the mark. You shall make a start
at my sanctuary (9:5-6).

One can only react in horror to a command in the name of God
not just to kill but to exterminate (the language is
deliberately strong); and the command to kill in the name of
God cannot be accepted without realizing that putting it in
this way leads to unacceptable implications. But we need not
believe literally in the existence of the seven, semi-divine
destroyers; it is a vision after all. The destruction was
thought to be Yahweh's but it was too horrific to attribute it
directly to Yahweh - and so a visionary metaphor is used.
Perhaps it expresses the difficulty of describing "Yahweh's
destruction" exactly, while at the same time not being able to
relinquish the idea. If Yahweh bringing a sword in 6:3
expresses the destruction of those religious places in which
people found security, and Yahweh casting the slain before the
idols (6:4-5) shows how far they have gone from their source,
then for Yahweh to command an extermination of all groups in
Jerusalem is to express the conviction that there is no
automatic security even in this place. How could there be when
chap.8 has shown, as 4-5 had not done, how the people of
Jerusalem are lost in their own conduct?
In the course of chaps 4-7 the behaviour of the people and
judgement develop progressively together. Chapters 4-5 present
first the external event of the siege; chap.6 begins with the
destruction of the high places. In chap.7, however, before
military images are used, the end is described in terms of the
sprouting and growing of the people's own arrogance and
wickedness. Chapter 8 adds realistic and detailed descriptions
of the actual abominations of the people of Jerusalem before
the destroyers are introduced in chap.9. The process of the
integration of judgement brings what happens into ever closer
connection with what the people themselves are doing. Their
continual exposure to judgement is the only way to bring about
a genuine reaction.
It is striking that destruction is not seen to be
comprehensive, for there are exceptions. This sounds like a
more acceptable attitude, but it has to be said that in the
destruction of cities, indiscriminate killing is more likely
than the selective saving of the guiltless(19). It is
certainly very unlikely that, when the destruction of Jerusalem
took place in 587 B.C., it was those who "sighed and groaned
over the abominations" who escaped. But if the seven
destroyers are not to be taken literally, why should the
details of this hope for deliverance be? For that is what this
is, a hope that there will be deliverance, and that the
deliverance will be seen in terms of the recognition of what
was wrong and what was right. To connect events with the kind
of people who are involved in them is to make this, not just an
escape or a deliverance, but a basis for restoration even as
destruction occurs. Restoration does not just mean that some

50

fortunate individuals escape, but it is an appreciation of the possibilities both for evil and good among the people involved. The insight here is that both "Yahweh's destruction" and the possibility of the restoration to follow connect with what was about to happen - the further destruction of Jerusalem by the Babylonians which took place in 587 B.C. (Ezekiel's vision is dated about 591).

Until this point the focus has been on the shift in emphasis from externally imposed events to what the people themselves do. This should not of course conceal the fact that other outward happenings were still taking place. That the people's conduct could be linked with these raises the question as to whether what is said here is meant to interpret what is happening. That is, it is not so much Yahweh causing the happenings as the happenings being interpreted in the light if what is known of God.

A watchman cannot see the destruction of Jerusalem divorced from the people who were living in Jerusalem at the time - and to see it in this way can only be done quite specifically, some might think brutally, in terms of men, women, and children. The terms are not simply confined to people, but extend to place. There is no question of appealing for automatic deliverance with words such as those heard earlier by Jeremiah (7:4), "the temple of Yahweh, the temple of Yahweh, the temple of Yahweh": the destruction actually begins at the temple (Ezekiel 9:6)(20). There is no refuge anywhere. Death is found in the very place of traditional refuge. And yet this situation is restorative for the very reason that it allows reality to be faced and inspires the willingness to act on it.

The destruction starts with the elders before the temple (9:6b), at the place and with the people who are especially close to Yahweh. Yahweh himself commands (the "man" recedes ever more into the background now), "Defile the temple and fill the courts with the slain" (9:7). Corpses were thought to be unclean, and here the temple itself, not only the altars outside, is made unclean at Yahweh's own command. The judgement consists of the overthrow of all that is most precious. The seriousness of this is confirmed and personalized by Ezekiel's state and reaction. He does not observe at a distance, satisfied that his predictions have been vindicated. While the destroyers strike, he is left alone, so that, unusually for him, he is forced to voice a question(21):

> I fell on my face, cried out and said, Ah Lord
> Yahweh will you destroy all that is left in Israel
> in pouring out your wrath against Jerusalem?
> (9:8).

His responsibility to describe what he sees conflicts with his personal inclinations. But the fact that there is at least one person who is concerned with what is happening shows that the destruction is not inevitably total. The seeds of restoration survive as long as one person cares. This is the counterpart to the guilt of the people:

> The guilt of the house of Israel [and Judah] (22)
> is boundless: the land is filled with blood and
> the city with the warping of justice, for they have
> said, Yahweh has forsaken the land and Yahweh sees
> nothing. So my eye will not spare and I will show
> no pity(23) - I shall bring their ways on their own
> heads (9:9-10).

They are completely responsible for their own conduct, as is
explained by their own words: they think Yahweh has gone, and
they expect no assistance from him. While this attitude lasts,
no mercy is possible either.

The man clothed in linen with the writing-case reports in
9:11 that he has done what he was commanded. Chapter 10:2 goes
on to report another order given to the man in linen. But
before this, in 10:1, appears a vision of something like a
throne on a metal plate, already familiar from the call vision
in chap.1(24) (The throne has no immediate connection with the
orders given to the man in linen.) In the course of chap.10,
much of the detail about cherubim and wheels is practically
identical with the material in the call vision, though
"cherubim" are now spoken of rather than living creatures. It
looks as though these are additions, to connect the destruction
of Jerusalem and the presence of Yahweh in Jerusalem with his
appearance to Ezekiel at his call; they are intended to
indicate that the shocking vision of the root and branch
destruction of Jerusalem is not an aberration, but proceeds
from the continuing national and personal authority of Ezekiel.
The original purpose, though, was to bring the commands to the
man in linen to fulfilment, and to register their consequences.

As if destruction by massacre were not enough, there is also
to be a conflagration: the man in linen is now commanded to go
and fill his hands with the burning coals from among the
cherubim(25) (10:2) - the semi-divine creatures over the ark,
the place of Yahweh's presence. The priestly function of the
man in linen now becomes clearer - no one else could have gone
in there to handle the means of conflagration which comes from
the very holiest source. A destructive conflagration added to
a destructive massacre appears at first to express an
insatiable lust for destruction. The narrative of Ezekiel's
vision however shows him either to be appalled at what he sees
(9:8), or coolly descriptive in order to convey its sheer
necessity. The man scattering burning coals is no more literal
than the six destroyers; he emphasizes the necessity of the
complete destruction of idolatrous conduct. That Yahweh
himself is connected with the punishment demonstrates it
further:

> The glory of Yahweh rose from the cherub to the
> threshold of the house, and the house was filled
> with smoke and the court with the brilliance of the

glory of Yahweh (10:4).

Ezekiel's call vision represents the glory of Yahweh, which is in total contrast to the state of the people in Jerusalem. The departure of the glory of Yahweh is a powerful statement of the terrible rightness of what is to be. People and places cannot be idolatrous, and assume that there will be no retribution. There is a visible removal of presence from those who desperately manipulate their own fate. The most meaningful connection in life begins to be severed. It is still seen, however, and an action evidently connected with purification now takes place:

> The cherub put out his hand [from between the cherubim](26) towards the fire which was between the cherubim, and he took some and put it in the hand of the man clothed in linen; he took it and went (10:7).

The fire is given to the man from the holiest of sources, which means the destruction it will bring is not wilful, but comes from the same source as the glory of Yahweh (10:4). Since this verse speaks of the glory of Yahweh going to the threshold of the house, it may well have been continued originally in parts of 10:18 and 19, where the glory of Yahweh departs from the house and stops at the door of the east gate. The glory, though, never completely recedes from Ezekiel's sight. It is clear confirmation from the highest authority of the destruction, but it is not the complete withdrawal of hope. Even when the glory of Yahweh goes up from the midst of the city, Ezekiel sees it stop on the mountain east of the city (11:23). Thus the source of restoration moves but does not disappear. The glory of Yahweh is still visible to Ezekiel, and on this note the vision ends. Despite everything, the memory persists of a manifest continuing presence.

The vision is concluded and he returns to the exiles; indeed, in 11:24, before he states that "The vision I had seen went up from me", it is said that the wind lifted him up and brought him back to Chaldea to the exiles. Here he tells the exiles of his vision: "Then I told the exiles all the things Yahweh had shown me" (11:25), for his vision of the image of jealousy, of worshipping the abominations, of the seven destroyers, and of the departure of the glory of Yahweh from the temple, was all for the benefit of the exiles. Everything which is to happen in Jerusalem, together with its implications for judgement and for ultimate restoration, has to be understood by the exiles in Babylon, the very people who (understandably) hope for a quick return to Jerusalem. The most horrifying example has shown that the only hope lies not with Jerusalem, but with themselves! The greatest task of responsibility is to convince the outcast and humiliated of this fact.

The two reports inserted into chap.11 confirm the reaction required of the exiles. Both reports (11:1-13 and 11:14-21) interrupt the narrative of the glory of Yahweh leaving the Jerusalem temple to demonstrate in two stages how hope moves continually further away from Jerusalem towards the exiles. In this chapter, as well as in chap.8, occurs another vision of the people in Jerusalem. If it were consistent with the vision traced through 8, a few verses in 10 and at the end of 11, then the people in this chapter should already have been destroyed, as reported in 9:11. Possibly it narrates a later vision of Ezekiel: 8:1 dates the initial vision c.591 B.C., while 11:3 probably indicates a time after 589, when the siege of Jerusalem had begun. This later vision shows a different people and attitude in Jerusalem, and shows there is no safeguard from destruction for them either. But the most important consideration for the book as a whole, in its final form, is that following this vision comes one of the clearest statements that the ultimate purpose of the destruction of Jerusalem is the restoration of the exiles.

The spirit once again brings Ezekiel to the temple where, at the gate, there are twenty-five men (two named) who are <u>rulers</u> of the people (11:1). The term used may mean that they are military commanders(27); at any rate, they are probably a group of high officials with power to influence affairs in Jerusalem. That individuals are named sharpens the matter into unavoidable specifics - the people about to be described really do exist. Ezekiel is left in no doubt as to what they are:

> Son of man, these are the men who are devising
> iniquity and counselling evil in this city; who
> say, ...?(28) It (the city) is the cooking-pot and
> we are the meat (11:2-3).

Once again the true nature of the people is revealed by what they say. The wickedness which they advise stems from their own attitude. They think that in the siege (which seems to be the meaning of the image concerning the meat in the cooking-pot), they are the choice people (the meat) who are protected by the inviolable city of Jerusalem (the cooking-pot). It may be that such cooking-pots were used to cook expensive food(29), which would mean that these men see themselves as an elite, in possible contrast to the exiles who have already been carried away. The misleading advice they give to the city, is not to worry about anything; they think they are themselves secure.

It is against such people who can only bring about catastrophe that the emphatic instruction to prophesy is directed:

> Therefore prophesy against them, prophesy son of
> man. Then the spirit of Yahweh fell upon me, and
> he said to me: Say, thus says Yahweh, so you have
> spoken, house of Israel - I know what has come into

54

your mind (11:5).

It is not said elsewhere that the spirit <u>fell</u> upon Ezekiel nor is the spirit ever connected elsewhere with the word of Yahweh(30). This might argue for the vision being a later addition, but the unusual expression draws attention to the nature of the men in Jerusalem, and contradicts the way they disport themselves in their superficial, self-directed security. "The spirit of Yahweh falling on Ezekiel" highlights the difference between taking for granted that these "responsible" people know what they are doing, and being convinced and equipped to contradict them totally. It should also be noted that the twenty-five men now represent the whole of Israel.

The self-satisfied security of some of them (rarely questioned but unable to stand examination), allows them apparently to murder each other in Jerusalem: "You multiply those you have slain in this city and you fill its streets with the slain" (11:6). There has been some controversy about the meaning of the word translated as "slain" (hālāl), which some say means only those slain in battle. But battles between Israelites in Jerusalem at this time do not seem likely, so others think that the reference is to victims of murder or executions(31). This seems probable in a city under a state of siege, and after what has been said in chap.9 on the massacre of the population of Jerusalem by the six destroyers, it is ironic that the people there are in fact murdering one another. They need protection, but from the "protected" elite! Thus, far from being a place of legitimate protection, Jerusalem herself must be destroyed - another variation on the theme of the necessity and inevitability of destruction. The opposite of what the self-satisfied believe about themselves will prevail:

> Therefore thus says Lord Yahweh, Those whom you have slain, who you have laid in the midst of (the city) - they are the flesh and it is the cooking pot, but you I shall bring out of it (11:7).

That is, those who think themselves protected are to be deprived of protection, and ironically it is the slain who are left protected. The very things against which the rulers of the people hope to be protected are brought upon them: "You have feared the sword and it is the sword I shall bring on you, says Lord Yahweh" (11:8). Yahweh shows that their unacceptable conduct can bring about a result contrary to their superficial expectations, one which will leave them with nothing but judgement.

With regard to what I said before about prophetic interpretation being given in connection with what is happening, it is to be noted that in this passage what Yahweh says is clearly linked with current events (11:5-6). Ezekiel does not hear the word of Yahweh in isolation from what is happening around him. The material in 11:9-11 speaks of Yahweh bringing the people out and handing them over to foreigners so that they fall by the sword right at the border of Israel, rather than being protected by the city. This probably anticipates what happened after the destruction of Jerusalem in 587 B.C. at Nebuchadrezzar's headquarters at Riblah(32) (2 kings 25). These verses thus form a later addition to show that exile and destruction did in fact occur - the city did not give automatic protection. The formula of recognition "You will know that I am Yahweh" (11:12), connecting with a statement that they did not walk in his statutes but acted according to the ordinances of the nations round about them, confirms that Yahweh is known in the present situation. He is not associated with a strange and contrary existence which bears no relation to the true life of Israel.

Ezekiel's attitude differs from that of the twenty-five men, as is shown in 11:13 where he sees a particular fate overtaking a particular person and is himself drawn into it with his own loud cry:

> While I was still prophesying Pelatiah, the son of Benaiah, died. I fell on my face and cried with a loud voice, Ah Lord Yahweh, are you going to put an end to the remnant of Israel?

Ezekiel is deeply committed to the effect of what he is prophesying, and concerned for the future of the people to whom he is prophesying destruction. This is the main point - rather than speculations about how Ezekiel was able to see such an event and what relationship it bore to Pelatiah's death. There is not enough evidence to make these any more than speculations(33), but what is said clarifies, right within the prophecy of judgement, Ezekiel's concern that there is to be some hope for the future.

Such a future however is not to be found among the Jerusalemites. They are given into the power of foreigners, the death of Pelatiah probably indicating the end of that influential group of Jerusalemites. When Ezekiel cries, "Are you going to put an end to the remnant of Israel?", the answer, in terms of the Jerusalemites, could only be "Yes!": a future could, by implication, only be found elsewhere.

Such an implication is made specific in 11:14-21, which is probably a further addition because it resumes with the word-event formula in 11:14 (34), and with the quotation from the Jerusalemites in v.15 expressing their ill-founded confidence in possessing the land while the exiles are far away. Probably therefore it comes after the destruction in 587 B.C. Although in 33:24 similar words are quoted directly after a report on the fall of the city, the words quoted in 11:3 indicate a time before this, during the siege. Thus the two sections of the chapter probably derive from different times, but their present place together only emphasizes all the more that talk of the judgement of Jerusalem is primarily for the recipients of restoration, the exiles.

Judgement, then, is not an end in itself, but creates a potential new beginning. A beginning which has to be achieved in the face of traditional attitudes. The inhabitants of Jerusalem are still assuming (even after the destruction of the city) that they are still the natural possessors of the land: "Son of man, your brothers [your brothers](35) your close relations (are those) of whom the inhabitants of Jerusalem(36) have said, They are far from Yahweh; the land has been given to us as a possession" (11:15). It is even likely that the exiles would have agreed with them, so strong was the tradition of Jerusalem. Ezekiel's responsibility is to bring the exiles to see that the hope lies with themselves.

The connection between the exiles and hope is perhaps clearer here than in any other part of the book. The language used reveals how Ezekiel stands with respect to what the Jerusalemites are saying: those called far from Yahweh, the exiles, are his brothers; indeed they are called those of the same clan, for whom he would have the responsibilities of a blood relation(37). This is not literally true, but shows how closely Ezekiel is identified with the exiles. And, contrary to what the Jerusalemites think, there is a hope for the exiles:

> Therefore say, Thus says Lord Yahweh, although I removed them among the nations and scattered them through the lands, yet I have become something of a sanctuary for them in the lands where they have come (11:16).

This is a striking statement about the eminent position which the exile now holds. Though the language is cautious (literally, "I have become for them a sanctuary a little"), it is striking that Yahweh himself is said to have become a sanctuary at all in exile, and not in Jerusalem(38), the glory of Yahweh having departed from the sanctuary in Jerusalem. The statement expresses a totally unexpected continuity in exile of their faith. It acknowledges the presence of Yahweh in places where they had not expected him to be, and turns out to be an answer to Ezekiel's cry about the end of the remnant in 11:13. It is also the most obvious confirmation of Ezekiel's experience in his call-vision that Yahweh is present in Babylon, not confined to Jerusalem. Even if it is qualified, to say that Yahweh has become a sanctuary for them there, is to say that Yahweh is anything but far from them; it transfers Ezekiel's experience to all the exiles within the context in which they live. The Jerusalem sanctuary is not unique; in the meantime at least it does not count as much as the exiles.

What the exiles have does not replace the sanctuary in Jerusalem - the statement itself indicates a time when such a sanctuary might be renewed - but exile is not a place of complete forsakenness, in contrast with Jerusalem in its present state. Therefore any future for Israel can only

realistically proceed from the exile, and the statement
expresses the conviction that the place of bondage can also
engender freedom. On this basis Ezekiel is now told:

> Therefore say, Thus says Lord Yahweh, I shall
> gather you from the peoples and assemble you from
> the lands where you have been scattered, and I
> shall give you the land of Israel. When they come
> there, they will remove all its detestable things
> and all its abominations from it (11:17-18).

The change in person from "they" to "you" between 11:16 and 17,
and then back to "they" again in v.18, as well as the somewhat
pedantic obviousness of the latter verse shared by v.21 (which
is also obscure in expression at the beginning), probably means
that vv.17,18,21 are later additions(39). However, v.17
follows on naturally from v.16: if the exiles are not
forsaken, then the logical consequence would be for them to be
brought back to their land.

This sort of promise, however, does interrupt the intimate
relation between Yahweh and the exiles expressed in the phrase
"sanctuary for them" in 11:16 and resumed in vv.19-20:

> I shall give them a <new>(40) heart and put a new
> spirit within them; I shall remove the heart of
> stone from inside them and give them a heart of
> flesh so that they may walk in my statutes, keep my
> ordinances and do them - they will be my people and
> I will be their God.

In vv.19-20, however, there is a purposeful development, which
is demonstrated in the turning of the people's nature towards
responsiveness. The exiles are not "far from Yahweh" at all;
there is great hope for them. In contrast to 11:2ff which
shows the Jerusalemites acting in a manner opposite to what
would be expected of them, 11:16ff shows Yahweh acting with the
exiles in a manner opposite to what would be expected in such a
place. How closely Yahweh is acting with the exiles is
revealed in the rather awkward expression, "I have become
something of a sanctuary for them" (11:16), formed in Hebrew
from the syntactically similar and more generally used phrase,
"I will be their God" (v.20).

Those whom Yahweh has not forsaken, the recipients of
restoration, do not cling to automatic guarantees but respond
in terms of their particular situation. For them the
destruction of Jerusalem is no longer so totally overwhelming.
In chaps.8-11, a clearly defined group of people, the
Jerusalemites, fail to show the involvement and reaction which
will enable them to accept judgement positively; this
contrasts with the reaction of Ezekiel which he was
endeavouring to hand on to the exiles. In chaps.4-7 we have
observed a change of emphasis from external events to the
people's own conduct. But a change can now be observed within

the people's own conduct. In chap.7 the people's conduct is described relevantly and effectively (though in a general way) as the blooming of unrighteousness. In chap.8 it is described in great detail as particular abominations. The abominations which Ezekiel sees are deeply offensive, and it is these which the exiles are obliged to see in their beloved Jerusalem. But from what they have been told of events in Jerusalem, the destruction of that city can no longer be so devastating to them. They are now the ones who, by reacting appropriately, can and must be the recipients of restoration.

5. THE EXILES FACED WITH STILL MORE EXILE: 12

Since chap.11 absorbs the destruction of Jerusalem into the hope given to the exiles, it might be thought that it was hardly necessary to continue. But as I suggested, the material in 11 which has just been considered was added later; from the standpoint of 8-9, the exile was still to come, so it was only possible to add the material in 11 after the bitter exile had been experienced. The result could not be taken for granted; it did not happen easily. Chapter 12 shows that the exiles did not always appreciate the potentialities of their situation, nor that they were prepared for more exile to be experienced by the inhabitants of Jerusalem.

At the beginning Ezekiel is said to be living with a rebellious house who have eyes to see but do not; he is therefore told to prepare an exile's baggage and go into exile by day so that they might see him. It may be that, from his symbolic action portraying exile, they would understand, even though they are a rebellious house (12:2-3). Clearly they are having great difficulties with accepting exile. The sequence of composition confirms it: following the call-vision in 1-3, what is going to happen is expressed in the symbolic acts of siege; in 8-11 correspondingly, following the vision of the abominations in Jerusalem, the consequences of siege are expressed in the symbolic act of exile. Since exile could apply only to the people left in Jerusalem, it means that the exiles have to appreciate once again what is going to happen to the Jerusalemites(1). The necessity of this comes to Ezekiel as the word of Yahweh (12:1) (2) which indicates the terrible truth that being in exile is not enough; it is no more an automatic guarantee of hope than being left in Jerusalem. That the exiles are having great difficulty in comprehending appears in the express mention of going into exile by day in their sight (12:3), a fact repeated in 12:4.

Ezekiel says he is going to take his final leave in the evening because it was usual to start a journey when it was cooler. An addition in vv.5-6 describes him digging through

the wall and going out with his exile's baggage on his shoulder
in the dark, with his face covered so as not to see the land.
Digging through the wall, going in the dark, and covering the
face as a disguise all indicate an attempt at escape rather
than going into exile, which makes little sense. Moreover
going in the dark contradicts the earlier emphasis on going by
day. The matter becomes clearer in the later description
(12:10 and 12) of the prince in Jerusalem going into exile, of
whom it is said that

> .. he will lift (his baggage) on his shoulder and
> go in the dark; they will dig through the wall to
> bring (the baggage) out that way. He will cover
> his face so that he might not <be> seen [he the
> land] (3).

That this difficult text has obviously been worked over
indicates some uncertainty about its place in the context. But
it seems to refer to something which had already happened when
it was written, and which is reported in 2 kings 25:4-7: when
the Babylonians breached the city, some made an escape by
night; but the Babylonians pursued and captured the king
(Zedekiah), and brought him to the king of Babylon at his
headquarters in Riblah where he was blinded and taken off into
exile. Thus the addition in 12:12 ("not seeing the land"), and
the similar enigmatic statement in v.6, almost certainly refer
to the blinding of Zedekiah. The information in 12:12 and 2
kings 25 does not correspond exactly, but it is close enough to
infer that whoever wrote it had some information about what
happened to Zedekiah. Since it is used as an interpretation of
Ezekiel's symbolic act, it shows how deeply the exiles felt
about Zedekiah's fate(4); it is part of the very substance of
the present text: the application has been made not only in
vv.10-13 but has also been projected back (vv.5-7) right into
the heart of it. And, though it introduces details additional
to the exile itself, it does emphasize, from a knowledge of
what actually happened, that the destruction of Jerusalem
leading to the exile did take place, involving even the
greatest of its inhabitants.

It might be thought that to mix a "prophecy" of an event
which has already taken place with an account of Ezekiel's
symbolic act is not entirely honest, but this is not the case.
It is a way of emphasizing that the substance of what Ezekiel
prophesied did take place, and indeed in some shocking
particulars which he had not foreseen. Combining present and
future in this way testifies to an understanding that prophecy
is closely connected with what actually happens to the people,
and is not mere words.

Something similar is apparent in 12:8-9:

> The word of Yahweh came to me in the morning
> saying, Has not the house of Israel, the house of
> rebellion, said to you, What are you doing?

Presumably this is the morning after Ezekiel has performed the symbolic act, and it is significant that the request of the people for an explanation is subsumed under the word of Yahweh. The connection I noted before between event prophetically interpreted and what Yahweh says is even more striking here(5). It may seem strange to say that at least part of the word of Yahweh is what Ezekiel would hear the people saying anyway, but the word of Yahweh himself is connected with what the prophet hears from others, and with his response to them. Ordinary discourse can be linked with the word of Yahweh, and with what did actually happen. In 12:8ff. the original narrative and the later application intertwine. In v.9 the people enquire about the act they have seen, followed in v.10 by what happened, the application to the prince in Jerusalem. The original application lay, however, in the direct answer to the question in v.9,

> What are you doing? - Say, I am a sign to you; as
> I have done, so will be done to them; they will go
> into exile, into captivity (12:11)

The original application can be recognized in the juxtaposition of the persons "you" and "them", which does not indicate secondary addition, since it fits in with the circumstances outlined at the beginning, of Ezekiel speaking about the Jerusalemites to the exiles. By "they will go into exile", he means the Jerusalemites, but it is this very matter which is a sign to the exiles ("you")(6). The original narrative was almost certainly concluded here, where the exiles must realize that there will be more exile.

This was the end of the original narrative, but not the end of the course of events. Just as the siege was not the end, but was followed by the exile, so the exile itself developed in distressing ways. The original end in 12:11 is now followed by the details already mentioned of what happened to Zedekiah (v.12). The capture and mutilation of Zedekiah was not the end either, but the prelude to his exile:

> I shall spread my net over him so that he will be
> caught in my hunting net. Then I shall bring him
> to Babylon, to the land of the Chaldeans which,
> however, he will not see, and there he will die
> (12:13).

The image of the net is used elsewhere (19:8) for capture and exile, and the information in 12:13, apart from the mention of Zedekiah's death, corresponds once again to 2 Kings 25:7. What actually happened later complements Ezekiel's symbolic action and its application, all of which comprises the word of Yahweh.

This chapter therefore strives particularly for the understanding of the people. In chaps.8-11, apart from the later addition from 11:14 on, the word-event formula had not occurred. Everything was expressed in terms of the vision, the hand of Yahweh and his spirit, recounting Ezekiel's experience and informing the exiles about the state of the Jerusalemites. But now, in chap.12, matters are again expressed in terms of the word of Yahweh: in fact, "the word of Yahweh came to me" occurs no less than five times. The judgement of exile is being addressed directly to the exiles and it is their part to understand. In 12:3, after Ezekiel is commanded to go into exile so that the exiles can see him, it is said that perhaps they will understand (see) though they are a rebellious house. It has been said before, with regard to Ezekiel's involvement in the siege (4:8), that his responsibility was the integrating agent between what happens and its acceptance as judgement. The people themselves now have a complementary part to play in the process of integration: in supplying understanding. The source of their understanding is the word addressed to them, which entails understanding in the sense of accepting that the second exile will take place despite their own exile. They must understand at the same time that they themselves are a rebellious house. In the complex relationship of happening (people's conduct), reaction, acknowledgement as judgement, the middle element (reaction) can be explained more precisely and significantly as responsibility and understanding.

The kind of acknowledgement to which this leads appears in further additions (12:14-16) (7) which describe generally the scattering and exile of those about Zedekiah. If these are later additions, the statement in v.15, "They will know that I am Yahweh when I scatter them among the nations...", expresses the belief that the exiles confirmed Ezekiel's understanding of Yahweh. They are acknowledging the exile to be right and are painfully aware, as 12:16 has it, that the reason a few of them escape into exile is to tell others of their abominations. This shows clearly that knowing God in changed circumstances is an admission of the kind of people they had been. As a sign for Israel (12:6 and 11), Ezekiel is an exile, not an escaper; the sign creates changed people capable of further changing.

The next three units in chap.12 in vv.17-20, 21-25 and 26-28 were originally independent of vv.1-16 and of each other(8). In their present position, however, they make the point that exile presupposes destruction and its accompanying fear, and that this is something which will come about, and without delay. It was inevitable that in speaking to the exiles of the Jerusalemites still facing exile, Ezekiel should oscillate between the two themes of exile and the destruction of Jerusalem it presupposed. It was all the more necessary, since the Judaeans could not conceive of the destruction of Jerusalem at all, particularly since there had been one exile from it already. Ezekiel must use various approaches to make them take the matter seriously. In chaps.8-9 and 12, the destruction and exile had been described as something merely to be observed. Ezekiel's personal involvement is quite clear but, in the original sections at least, that of the people is not. In the further symbolic action which follows in 12:17-20, the people's feelings of fear are represented by Ezekiel's action: "Son of man, you shall eat your bread with trembling and you shall drink water with agitation and anxiety" (12:18). It has been suggested that the word used for "trembling" (ra^{c}aš) is not usually applied to humans, so that this usage is especially emphatic(9). As the direct word of Yahweh, Ezekiel must tell the people that, when he speaks of eating bread in anxiety, and drinking with shuddering, he is referring to the inhabitants of Jerusalem. For the land is to be stripped of everything on account of the violence of all who live in the land (12:19). This will demonstrate that the consequences of violence are as serious as the violence itself. The destruction will be terrible, and far from being put out of mind, it will be felt with all its force. In linking the knowing of Yahweh with the destruction of the cities and the devastation of the land (12:20), God is known both in the people's appreciation of what they have been and of what is happening about them.

But whether Ezekiel speaks of destruction or exile or of their terrible effect, the people have various defences to erect against hearing. In the next two units he disputes directly with what the people say. The word of Yahweh conflicts with a popular saying: "Time goes on and every vision comes to nothing" (12:22). That is, the people are sceptical as to whether what Ezekiel predicts will happen at all. The word of God is in the responsibility Ezekiel feels about what the people believe and in his absolute certainty that they are wrong:

> Therefore say to them, thus says Lord Yahweh, I shall put an end to this saying, and they will not repeat it any longer in Israel. But say to them, the time is close when the vision will come true (12:23).

In a possible reference to the passage on false prophets to be found in the following chap.13, it is added that there will be no more unfulfilled visions or flattering divinations because Yahweh will do what he says without delay (12:25).

The theme of delay is taken up more exclusively in 12:26-28. The belief of the people to be disputed here is that "The vision which he sees is for many days in the future and he is prophesying for far-off times" (12:27). This is even more subtle and insidious than that quoted in the previous unit, because it does not deny that something will happen, only that it is not imminent, and therefore there is no cause for concern. The people delude themselves most of all with this kind of defence. It is contradicted utterly with "None of my words will be delayed. The word which I speak will be done, says Lord Yahweh" (12:28). The exiles are called on not only to accept the destruction coming on Jerusalem, but also to realize that there is no comfort in delay.

It is imperative that the people listen to Ezekiel, because
even those who, like the prophets, might be expected to be in
touch with reality are not. On the contrary, Ezekiel accuses
the prophets of Israel of prophesying only out of their own
imaginations (13:2-3). Their illusions contrast with the true
word of Yahweh which comes to Ezekiel (13:1). These prophets
may prophesy, but to them it must be said, "Hear the word of
Yahweh" (13:2). It has been suggested that, since they are
specially called "prophets of Israel" (and no one but Ezekiel,
who also talks of "the mountains of Israel" and "the land of
Israel", uses this phrase), there must be an allusion to a
particular "sort and condition of men"(1). They are foolish,
which, as the context makes clear, means not that they are
stupid(2), but rather that they are blindly confining
themselves to something totally inadequate. They are out of
touch, deprived of the word of Yahweh, since they only know
their own imaginings, and are ignorant of the circumstances and
the people. They are not the sort to call forth a genuine
reaction to what is really happening.

These prophets retain the form, but no longer possess the
true content. It is possible that 13:4, which is an address to
Israel about the prophets rather than a direct address to the
prophets themselves, is an addition(3); the significance of
comparing them to foxes in the ruins is uncertain(4).
Evidently, they are thought somehow to adapt themselves to the
ruins rather than setting about reconstruction. It may be that
Ezekiel is referring to the prophets' use of the defeat of
Jerusalem to make themselves important, when they impressed
people with their assurances that worse was not going to
happen. Out of touch with the true circumstances, they ignore
reality in the service of their own advantage. They are like
people of today at an accident, who know how it happened and
believe that it could not happen to them, but do nothing to
help. They are not the kind of people who, when the enemy has
made a breach in the walls, attempt to stop it getting wider
(13:5). The house might be collapsing about them, but they
remain inactive. So deluded are they that they expect Yahweh
to fulfil a word which he has not in fact sent them (13:6).
That Yahweh has not sent them means that what they say bears no
relation to the circumstances. Their falsity stands revealed
by the unrealistic nature of their expectations. It is the
exact opposite of Yahweh's word, for Yahweh's word is realized
in a determined adherence to the real situation.

A direct question to the prophets challenges them to admit
that they deal only in illusions (13:7). It may be that even
before 587 B.C. something had happened to show that their
optimism was badly founded(5). If so, it shows again the close
connection between Yahweh's word and what is plainly happening
in the world. Once again the responsibility is to take sober

cognizance of it. It is clear too that, as in chap.12, judgement applies the word to the circumstances of a special group in Israel. Since the prophets are the very people who should recognize the connection between the word and the circumstances, a specific address is needed to show that they are failing in this.

Ezekiel's attack on the prophets means that he is responsible enough to declare that a particular class of people, no matter how exalted, are neglecting their duty. Ezekiel shows that the consequences of the prophets being out of touch with the circumstances is that they are out of touch with both Yahweh and the people:

> Therefore, thus says Lord Yahweh, because you have given expression to illusions and seen deceptive visions, therefore I am against you, says Lord Yahweh, and my hand will be against the prophets who see deceptive things and give false oracles; they will not be found in the company of my people, nor will they be recorded in the registrar of the House of Israel or enter the Land of Israel - then they will know that I am [Lord] Yahweh (13:8-9).

That Yahweh should speak solemnly against them demonstrates the extent of their deceitfulness and falsity, as a result of which they will no longer have a place in the company of the people of Israel. Those not prepared to express God in terms of reality will soon find that they themselves are no longer part of that reality. It is significant that "the prophets of Israel" will not be recorded in "the house of Israel" or enter "the land of Israel". All these entities should belong together - making a harmonious and fruitful relationship - but the prophets have broken the connections.

Breaking the connections is particularly apt in relation to the word which Ezekiel uses for "company" (sôd), which implies an intimate meeting of people who have something in common, whether on social or religious occasions(6). Ezekiel brings this into a more comprehensive and official sphere by linking it with the "register", probably a list of citizens of particular distinction. Whether on an intimate or an official level, these prophets have lost their connections. It is possible that Ezekiel refers to the kind of prophet who is mentioned in Jeremiah's letter to the exiles (chap.29), who predicted a short stay in exile and a quick return home. These prophets above all are people uncommitted to the exile.

"...Then they will know that I am Yahweh", Ezekiel says. These prophets would have been discredited very quickly among their people; they would have known that the word which the prophets so confidently gave as Yahweh's was not his at all, for it merely separated the latter from those for whom they were supposed to be responsible. In the restoration there is no future for this kind of person, since restoration cannot be reconciled with superficial hope directed towards the glory which selected groups might gain from it. The consequences which are inflicted on the prophets arise simply from their lack of realism. The passage emphasizes this. The prophets have to be given reasons and have consequences drawn for them so that they will know that their work is only concealing a ruin on the point of collapse. Rather than giving true guidance, these prophets only mislead Yahweh's people, prophesying peace when there will be no peace.

Ezekiel now turns to the content of these prophets' message (13:10). In doing so, he uses a metaphor at once suitable to express deceit and also intimately connected with the imminent physical fall of Jerusalem. He speaks of a shoddily constructed wall, and in saying that the prophets come and daub it with whitewash so that its limitations are concealed, he exposes the prophets' deceitfulness. When the wall collapses in a storm people can only ask scornfully what has became of the whitewash (13:11-12). As clear as it is that whitewash will be ineffective in a storm, so it is clear that what the prophets say will be ineffective in the storm Ezekiel sees approaching Jerusalem. Ezekiel's imagery is incisive: the prophets are not merely irrelevant; they will be overwhelmed by the events to come.

But Ezekiel has not finished. He likes to develop a theme, exhausting it in all possible detail, so that he leaves no way for people to escape the issues involved(7). He therefore goes on to speak of female equivalents of the prophets:

> Now, you, son of man, set your face against the daughters of your people who set themselves to prophesy out of their own minds, and prophesy against them (13:17).

What these women are engaged in is evidently not so much prophecy as magic, though the exact meaning of their practices is not clear:

> You shall say, Thus says Lord Yahweh, Woe to those sewing magic bands for all wrists and making veils for heads of every size in order to hunt for lives. Do you wish to hunt down lives belonging to my people and keep others alive for your own profit? You have profaned me among my people with handfuls of barley and pieces of bread to put an end to lives which should not die and keep alive others which should not live [when you lied to my people who listened to lies](8) (13:18-19).

Among the suggestions made about the bands and veils is that they were used to bind down mediums at a seance to show that the mediums were controlled and therefore genuine(9). In any case these women have the reputation of being able to exercise control over the lives of others, possibly using spells to put an unnatural end to some lives, and to prolong the lives of others equally unnaturally. To say that they are profaning Yahweh probably means that they are using his name as an authority for their illicit spells. They are prepared to manipulate fellow human beings in this way for payment, apparently a rather pitiful one of barley and bread. But they manipulate other human lives for power and profit. Ezekiel believes that the fate of their victims, however few, is worth investigating.

What these women do bears no correspondence to reality:

> Because you have disheartened the heart of the innocent falsely - though I had not disheartened him - and encouraged the guilty with the result that he did not repent from his evil way to save his life ... (13:22).

Whereas Ezekiel expresses the conviction that those he calls innocent are indeed so, he also knows that given the right encouragement the guilty can change and live. This knowledge is so convincingly articulated that it most likely comes from his pastoral care of particular people. He speaks of what he knows. Unlike the false witnesses who stand in the way of genuine deliverance, Ezekiel does not regard the people as victims for his manipulation. His responsibility is to them and not to his own power and status.

7. THE POSITIVE COUNTERPART OF A NEGATIVE REALITY (THE ELDERS): 14:1-11

Ezekiel now introduces some of the elders, who come and sit before him (14:1); and it might sound as though his estimation of them is higher than that of the prophets. But when the word of Yahweh comes to him (14:2), this apparently placid scene is disturbed by the sober estimate of their true nature:

> These men have made their idols their dearest object of devotion, and they have set the stumbling-block of their iniquity before their own faces - am I really to be enquired of by them? (14:3).

The elders are not fulfilling what might be expected of them, any more than the prophets are. Without any hesitation it is said that they are idolaters. The phrase used runs literally, "They have put their idols onto their hearts", which may mean that this is something they do privately(1). If that is so, the elders are trying to have the best of both worlds. In public they enquire of Yahweh, but in private, they try any means to resolve their situation. Such a contradiction could only lead to the kind of inward turmoil which confounds them - they themselves have put the stumbling-block of their guilt before their own faces, as Ezekiel puts it so vividly. In other words, the very elders who come to enquire of Yahweh are out of touch with Yahweh. That people who try unorthodox methods of finding solutions should also turn to Yahweh means only that they will not find a solution anywhere. The impossibility of this is implied in Yahweh's question: "Am I really to be enquired of by them"?

Given the manner of their description, one would expect the elders to bring on themselves the same kind of negative consequences as the prophets. But the address to Ezekiel unexpectedly uses the description as a means, not of condemnation, but of instruction. The elders are addressed in terms of "any man":

> Any man from the house of Israel who makes his idols his devotion and who places himself before the stumbling-stone of his guilt, and then comes to the prophet, I Yahweh, am brought to answer him <myself>(2) because of his many idols, so that I may claim the devotion of the house of Israel which has estranged itself from me with all their idols (14:4-5).

The new emphasis in the change from what happens to an ever closer concern with the peoples's own conduct, is that this conduct can actually be turned to the benefit of others. A more literal rendering of the translation offered above would be, "he who sets his heart on idols is to be answered by Yahweh himself so that Yahweh may lay hold of the heart of the house of Israel". This last expression "to lay hold of the heart of" has been understood, to be sure, as an aggressive act(3), and it is true that the answer to the idolater is exclusion from God's people (v.8). That Yahweh himself answers could also imply, however, the radical conviction that the apparently comfortless punishment of the deceitful elder or any Israelite can be used to entirely change other idolaters. Such a positive interpretation is confirmed after the instruction of vv.4-5, which is not followed by judgement of the elders, or even an accusation, but by an exhortation to the house of Israel: "Repent and turn from your idols and turn your face away from all your abominations" (14:6).

Here is the nub of the whole passage(4). It shows an extraordinary shift of emphasis, proceeding from the exposure of the elders to an exhortation to the people who, even if they are not deceitful, behave basically as the elders do. Making such an exhortation presupposes that they are able to make a complete change: the negative state of the elders is being used to positively transform the people. Since everything proceeds from the situation of the elders gathered before

Ezekiel, it must be the exiles who are called on to make the appropriate reaction. Revulsion at themselves is not enough (6:9); they must react with positive behaviour. The present juxtaposition of the passages of the prophets and the elders probably directs the present reality of both prophets and elders towards the fulfilment of the potential reality of the people. Only those who do not proclaim peace when there is no peace, or who do not try to exploit both idols and Yahweh, are capable of it. Ezekiel demonstrates that the stark negative can make people realize not only the necessity but also the possibility of its positive counterpart.

Ezekiel has still not exhausted all the possible dimensions of the dialectic between the negative and the positive. At first 14:7 appears to be mere repetition of v.4: they both speak of any man of Israel who has made his idols the object of his devotion; both also have similar phrases concerning the stumbling-block of iniquity, and both say that if such a person comes to the prophet with an enquiry, Yahweh himself will be brought to answer him. Verse 7 differs, though: to any man from Israel, there is added "any of the strangers who reside in Israel". The addition may have come about in the first place because common legal formulations were being used, but the effect of its use is inevitably to state that what applies to an Israelite also applies to a stranger and so brings another class of person into the argument.

Another addition at the beginning of v.7, which is not to be found in the equivalent place in v.4, is a statement concerning either the Israelites or the stranger forsaking Yahweh for idolatry. This would seem to stress right from the beginning the separation of the idolaters and Yahweh, a reading confirmed by what follows in v.8, which says that Yahweh will set his face against them, make them into a sign and a byword and cut them off from his people. Rather than repeating v.4 it would seem now that these verses contradict vv.4-5 because there, when Yahweh answers himself, it leads to laying hold of the hearts of the house of Israel and to the positive exhortation in v.6. In v.8, however, Yahweh cuts the idolater off from his people, by which act "you know that I am Yahweh". Yahweh is known in the difference between - in fact the sheer incompatibility of - Yahweh and the idolater, which is made evident by the fact that the idolater becomes a sign and a byword. The essence of this argument continues in v.9 which, in addition to the Israelite and the stranger, introduces the striking case of a prophet who if deceived, has been deceived by Yahweh and Yahweh himself destroys him. It does not matter who they are, stranger, Israelite or even a member of one of the leading groups among the Israelites - they all "will bear their guilt: the guilt of the enquirer and the guilt of the prophet will be the same", as v.10 confirms. No change is possible for any of them. A very different end seems to have been reached than one might have envisaged from vv.5-6.

Verse 11 encompasses everything between vv.6-10, and shows that the exhortation in v.6 and the possibilities for change which it opens up are the crux not only for what comes before, but for what comes after. The consequence of the conduct of them all - stranger, Israelite and prophet alike - is - "that the house of Israel go astray from me no more, that they no longer defile themselves with all their crimes, but that they have become my people and I their God, says Lord Yahweh". It is not only the elders (by now almost forgotten), who by their perverse conduct demonstrate the necessity and possibility of a genuine relationship for the people. Yahweh's grace has a supply of negatives which is much richer than that. Since they exist, these pre-eminently unproductive realities can be used to set up the most fruitful of realities. A genuine relationship, proceeding from, and expressed in the people and situations of this world is so desirable, that it can be realized not only in spite of the colourless elders, but also in spite of idolatrous stranger, Israelite and even prophet. The contorted theology of the passage keeps the hearers on tenterhooks right to the end, for their own good, that they might finally receive the full weight of its possibilities. It shows that out of so much deceit a genuine, integral relationship can emerge expressed in the term "house of Israel", and in the statement of reciprocity "They will be my people, and I shall be their God".

8. THE EXILES GIVEN STRANGE CONSOLATION: 14:12-23

If the people are to react positively, they must accept responsibility for themselves. Ezekiel has continually insisted that the exiles can find no security in Jerusalem. Chapters 8,11,13 and 14 have also shown that not even in the leaders of the people can any confidence be placed. It would have been a good way of avoiding the issue, to seek hope amongst the leaders. These considerations form a good background to 14:12-23. The idea that some exemplary individuals might have enough merit to save the whole of Jerusalem is what may have precipitated them. But the point of 14:12-23 is that all the people are individually responsible for themselves.

This section begins in a general manner, making the final application to Jerusalem all the more effective:

Son of man, when a land sins against me by acting faithlessly and I stretch out my hand against it and break its staff of bread, sending famine against it and cutting off from it man and beast, then even if these three men were there - Noah,

70

> Daniel and Job - They would save only their own
> lives by their righteousness, says Lord Yahweh
> (14:13-14).

The word of Yahweh speaks first of any land, to show his
universal justice, and proceeds at once to mention judgement in
one of its traditional forms - famine. Other traditional forms
of judgement are used in the same connection in vv.15-16 (wild
beasts), vv.17-18 (sword) and in vv.19-20 (pestilence). In
each of these later cases, the point is made again that it is
impossible to transfer the righteousness of Noah, Daniel and
Job to others; nor is it the particular nature of judgement
which matters, but, whatever judgement comes and wherever,
there are no guarantees at all. If Noah, Daniel and Job are
not guarantees, three names known popularly in Ezekiel's time
as figures of great traditional piety, there could not possibly
be any others.

The power of their appeal is perhaps illustrated by the fact
that their associations would not necessarily be the same as
might arise in a modern reading of the Bible. For in Ezekiel's
time such figures belonged to an earlier, popular,
extra-biblical tradition. There is a well-established
tradition outside Israel of Daniel as an exemplary wise and
just man. Something similar seems likely in the case of Job
since the biblical book is set outside Israel; and it is
certainly not impossible that Ezekiel and his contemporaries
also knew an extra-biblical tradition of Noah(1). If all these
figures were recognized outside Israel, then this would fit in
with the application of Yahweh's universal justice to any
country, emphasising that the righteousness of Noah, Daniel and
Job would not be effective for anyone but themselves anywhere.
As subsequent traditions confirm, all three experience some
kind of deliverance, expressed here four times: "they would
deliver only their own lives by their righteousness" (14:14);
"they would deliver neither sons nor daughters but themselves
alone" (vv.16,18 and similarly, 20). But even so the whole
matter is expressed hypothetically.

The section beginning with v.12 is again expressed as the
word of Yahweh coming to Ezekiel. Yahweh's word is
transparently clear to anyone who can judge the condition of
people: that there is no way of saving Jerusalem, which is the
particular application of the general rule. If in any land
where Yahweh's justice is applied exemplary figures can save
only themselves, how much more reason is there for all the
inhabitants of Jerusalem to be responsible for themselves?
Such total judgement is expressed by the phrase "man and
beast":

> For thus says Lord Yahweh, How much more when I
> have sent upon Jerusalem my four sore acts of
> judgement, sword, famine, wild animals and
> pestilence, to cut off from it man and beast
> (14:21).

It is not that the Old Testament is unacquainted with the idea that the righteousness of some can be of benefit to others (see Genesis 18); but with Jerusalem so corrupted, people must be prepared to take responsibility for themselves - all the more so in a place where there has been a special relationship with Yahweh.

The strange consolation for the exiles is that,

> If there should be left in it (Jerusalem) any survivors who bring out sons and daughters, when they come out to you, you will see what they are like, their evil deeds, and you will be consoled with regard to the catastrophe which I have brought upon Jerusalem ... (14:22) (2).

Once again it is the exiles who are addressed; they are to see for themselves the nature of the Jerusalemites. It is indeed a strange consolation that the sole purpose of the survivors is to demonstrate that the destruction has not been without cause. Chapter 12 had returned to what was happening, the exile, and the understanding which the people must bring to it; chap.13 showed that even the prophets are not capable of understanding; and chap.14 establishes through the elders (and others) that from a negative relationship can come a positive one. The great responsibility necessary for this is invoked in the second part of chap.14. If, for the Jerusalemites, there was no hope even in righteous individuals such as Noah, Daniel and Job, for the exiles there is no hope even in the survivors from Jerusalem. At most, hope lies in what the exiles see in them, and in the responsibility which develops from that.

9. THE REALITY IS THE WOOD NOT THE FRUIT: 15

The exiles are slow to understand. They have recourse to all sorts of excuses before the difficult solution at the end of chap.14 is accepted. With no hope possible in the prophets and elders, there is all the more reason to seek it in kings or their own positive qualities. Judging from what is said in chap.15, it seems that the people liked to speak of themselves in attractive images such as "we are the vine". From chap.15 onwards a whole series of images(1) makes it likely that the collectors of the material knew that a presentation by image characterized at least a certain stage of Ezekiel's activity.

With his images of destruction of Jerusalem Ezekiel has already wounded the people both religiously and politically. These images in chap.15, unrestrained, wound the people emotionally, for the people are compared not with the fruit, but with the useless wood of the vine. The people are provoked

when the word of Yahweh comes in the form of a series of
derogatory questions, a provocation especially striking since
the vine had an honourable tradition in Israel. Its positive
place in the life of Israel could surely be taken for granted.
In Psalm 80, for example, the description of Israel as the vine
which Yahweh brought out of Egypt and which he himself planted
justifies a petition to God to have regard for his vine. But
here, Yahweh questions its special status:

> How does the wood of the vine surpass that of any
> creeper which is among the trees in the forest? Is
> wood taken from it to make anything? Does anyone
> get a peg from it to hang anything on? (15:2-3).

The answer to the latter two questions is obviously "no".
Surely the vine is mainly valued for its fruit? But it is
clear that the emphasis is on its wood: "How does the <u>wood</u> of
the vine surpass the wood of the creeper?" As wood the vine is
of no more consequence than the humblest creeper. Psalm 80 may
clarify this comparison, for though this psalm does not
explicitly use the term "wood", it does speak of the whole
plant taking root, and showing such significant growth that it
covers the mountains with its shade and sends out branches to
the sea. The image relates to the plant <u>as a whole</u>, so that
Ezekiel can be justified in turning his attention to the less
attractive parts which still, unquestionably, belong to the
whole. As wood, an essential part of its nature, the vine
would not even provide a peg. It has one undeniable use - as
fuel for the fire - but even for this it is inadequate:

> If it is given as fuel for the fire and the fire
> burns its two ends, leaving its middle part
> charred, will it then be of any use at all?
> (15:4).

Whether the fruit or the wood of the vine is spoken of, it is
an obvious image for Israel. Just as what happens can be
understood in terms of the people's conduct, here the image
emphasizes the people's nature. Images can attract the
imagination and give pleasure, lending an importance which is
not necessarily obvious in the thing itself. On the other hand
an image may obscure a reality which does not correspond
exactly to the image. One may need to change the emphasis if
the image is to be used as a faithful representation of
reality. This is what Ezekiel does in switching the attention
to the wood of the vine, and he leaves the people under no
illusion as to whom the wood of the vine represents:

> Therefore thus says Lord Yahweh, As it is the wood
> of the vine among all the wood of the forest which
> I have given to the fire for fuel, so I give the
> inhabitants of Jerusalem (15:6) (2).

The very deliberate wording states unequivocally the identification of the image and the fate of the vine. Those so clearly identified in the image will know Yahweh in the inevitable reality:

> I shall set my face against them; they have escaped from the fire, but the fire will still consume them - then they will know that I am Yahweh when I set my face against them (15:7).

This statement points to a time between the two Babylonian conquests of Jerusalem in 597 and 587 B.C., a time when the reality of further destruction was plain for those like Jeremiah and Ezekiel who had eyes to see. Yahweh will be known when the reality applicable to everyone (and already clear to some) is universally recognized. The image may be used not to conceal the reality, but to expose it.

10. REFLECTIVE SPEECHLESSNESS ON THE STATE OF JERUSALEM: 16

To be denounced in terms of their own nature was disturbing enough to the people in chap.15, but in chap.16 it is shattering. Here, Jerusalem is presented in a vividly drawn image as a faithless, brazen prostitute, a much more personal and comprehensive account of the conduct of the people than that of the abominations in chap.8. Although this must have had great emotional impact, it does not tear at the emotions with extravagant language. It is actually rather cool, written more as a factual report than as a list of sins calling forth moral indignation(1). The effect of using an apparently factual report of Jerusalem as a prostitute is to leave the hearers in a state of reflective speechlessness. It is achieved by means of a boldly, even crudely drawn picture; the crudeness lies in its brutal directness.

Ezekiel's usual opening with the word-event formula "The word of Yahweh came to me..." (16:1) shows it to be a direct address. The next verse makes the unadorned accusation: "Son of man, make known to Jerusalem her abominations." The abominations expose Jerusalem's very origins:

> You are to say, Thus says Lord Yahweh to Jerusalem, your parentage and origin go back to the land of Canaanites; your father was an Amorite and your mother was a Hittite (16:3).

This is one of the most astounding statements in the Bible. Nowadays the widespread impression is that the Old Testament places Israel in an elevated position, apart from other peoples. This one statement is enough to shatter such a view, for it appraises Israel's origins soberly, without posturing, without mythology, without heroism. Jerusalem has in no sense been set apart as something special, untouchable, from the beginning. To say that its parentage reaches back to the land of the Canaanites is to place Jerusalem in the most earthly and profane of spheres. There may be some awareness here of the fact that the origins of Israel as a whole lay outside Canaan, while those of Jerusalem did not(2) - but the point is that to all intents and purposes Jerusalem has become Israel. To say that the origins of Jerusalem reach back to the land of the Canaanites is offensive enough, but more offensive is the blunt declaration that "your father was an Amorite and your mother was a Hittite". More hurtful than just saying "you are a bastard", this rejects with particular brutality the notion of "pure race" which some people like to attribute to themselves. It is the ultimate in mixtures that Ezekiel is talking about. He may have been almost as vague as we are about the exact definition of "Amorite" and "Hittite"(3), but such vagueness serves his intention well: Jerusalem is the random product of an unknown union, the bastard child of nobodies.

Rather than becoming what she did become, Jerusalem could have been, should have been, of no account. For not only is she a bastard child, but one abandoned at birth:

> Your birth was like this: on the day you were born, your navel cord was not cut, you were not washed for cleansing, you were not rubbed with salt or swaddled (16:4).

We do not know the significance of rubbing with salt (it may have been apotropaic)(4), but in any case the ordinary parental care of the time is obviously not being given to this unwanted baby:

> No eye pitied you to do any of these things for you out of compassion for you. But you were cast out into the open field in complete neglect of your person on the day you were born (16:5).

Jerusalem was thus a foundling, exposed, and left to die. The very existence of this city, let alone its achievement, could in no way be taken for granted.

Ezekiel's reason for relating all this is to stress that she did not in fact die, and that indeed she did accomplish much. No natural reason or intrinsic ability accounted for this, only the fact that Jerusalem received an address giving life and growth:

> When I passed by you, I saw you floundering in your blood, and I said to you while you were still lying in your blood. Live [and I said to you in your blood, Live] (5) and grow up like the plants of the

75

field [I granted you]. So you grew up, came quickly to menstruation, your breasts were formed and your hair grew. But you were still naked and bare (16:6-7).

Jerusalem was thus not abandoned but "found". Far from being absorbed indistinguishably into the land of the Canaanites, she was enabled to develop individually. Nor did the care cease in the early period. She was naked, and when Yahweh saw that she was sexually mature, he spread the skirt of his garment over her to cover her nakedness, engaging himself to her so that she became his (16:8).

Such a bold sexual image of the relationship between Yahweh and his people, even more explicit than in Hosea, alters the tone from unsentimental realism to extreme tenderness. For the care continued: Yahweh washed and anointed Jerusalem, clothed her with fine clothes, and adorned her with jewellery so that she became very beautiful (16:9-14). From being rejected, unwanted, Jerusalem progressed to the opposite, the fullest degree of relationship.

The unwanted bastard was accepted as the beloved fiancee, which only serves to emphasize what Jerusalem has made of herself by contrast:

.But you trusted in your beauty, and were able to prostitute yourself because of your reputation; you lavished your licentious favours on anyone who passed by [may it be his](6) (16:15).

The bastard who became a fiancee has herself chosen to repudiate her given relationship, wantonly to prostitute it to an indifferent people. The verb for prostituting (zānâ), used about twenty times in this chapter and the related chap.23, expresses the licentious excess of wantonness(7) which seems inexplicable considering Jerusalem's favoured treatment by Yahweh. But this is because she "trusts in her beauty". Trust can be falsely placed in a superficial quality, which, though superficial, can be used to exercise power. This is what Jerusalem does: she is prepared to give up her unique relationship with Yahweh for the sake of passing popularity.

This is not a temporary lapse, but the rudest and most brazen provocation, since it is worsened by being prolonged. No doubt the original narrative intended to make this impression, but even modern readers who have got so far without being irritated, are likely to sense from about 16:15 an over-emphasis and reject it as distasteful. For example, Jerusalem is said to have decorated cultic places with coloured clothes for the purpose of prostitution (16:16) (8). After considerable digression, it is said in vv.24-25 that she built herself pedestals, high places in every square and at the head of every street. Here she prostituted her beauty and (using the coarsest phrase in the whole episode) spread her legs for anyone passing. Then, after another gap, much the same thing is repeated in vv.30-31, saying with what feverish lust she is acting, and characterizing her actions as that of a brazen prostitute. The personal disgrace of Jerusalem's conduct is made utterly clear.

Prostitution in public places is the main theme, but at least two others are also significant. In 16:17 Jerusalem prostitutes herself with male images made from the very jewellery which Yahweh had given her. In vv.18-19 she puts before them the cultic gifts which rightfully belong to Yahweh, materials like oil, incense and flour, and in vv.20-22 she sacrifices children to these male images. Another recurrring theme is that of giving herself to men of all different nations. In 16:26 she has intercourse with Egyptians who, it is said, are men with large penises - a remark betraying the sexual jealousy and fear sometimes directed towards other peoples (see 23:20). The composite nature of the narrative is revealed by a remark of a different character in v.27 to the effect that even the greedy daughters of the Philistines are ashamed of her lewd conduct. Again in vv.28-29 Jerusalem is not even satisfied by intercourse with the Assyrians and with the mercantile land of the Chaldaeans. "Trading" probably alludes to the fact that her desires are quite insatiable, while the theme as a whole is a probable addition interpreting Jerusalem's prostitution as foreign political alliances rather than as cultic malpractice.

The final theme is taken up in 16:31-34 directly after the last mention of the building of the pedestals. With savage irony it is argued that she is not like an ordinary prostitute because she scorns any payment. In v.32 an emotional outburst about the adulterous woman who receives strangers instead of her husband is followed by the conclusion in v.33-34 that instead of taking money from men she bribes them to come to her from all sides. She is the opposite of any ordinary, decent prostitute; she is insatiable. The inference is perhaps that where there is no meaningful basis for a relationship, it is not possible to be satisfied.

If Jerusalem is insatiable in her prostitution, it might be thought that the narrative is similarly insatiable in describing it! But the quantity of unnecessarily frank detail is due in large part to a series of additions to a comparatively short basic text(9). And while the additions certainly give a different character to the basic text by being too emotionally indignant, they do bear witness to the vigour of the intention. It was not so much the narrative itself as the image of Jerusalem which caught the imagination - so much so that embellishments were continually made to intensify the theme of insatiability.

The principal climax is the account of the brazenly exposed prostitute in 16:25, which leads to the matter-of-fact notice of the consequences of such conduct in v.35: "Therefore, you prostitute, hear the word of Yahweh..." Other verses within 35-43 are similar to the emotionally indignant additions, but statements in vv.35, and possibly 36a, 37a, and in 39-41a, take up once again the factual report without the emotional indignation. Appropriately, considering the superficiality of Jerusalem's relationship with her lovers, the punishment comes from the lovers themselves. Jerusalem is given into their hand; they break down her pedestals, strip her of her clothes, stone and slaughter her. They burn down her houses and she is judged in the sight of other women. The metaphorical presentation of Jerusalem as a prostitute leads to an acknowledgement that a judgement of public humiliation is appropriate.

After all this, it might well have been asked: who then can be saved? The narrative would leave the listeners speechless, emotionally affected by the depiction of their beloved Jerusalem as a prostitute, but reflective, not totally consumed with indignation. The added emotional dimension could be used to inspire people towards a new start. Who can be saved? Not Jerusalem, but those amongst the exiles who hear and see.

The matter does not conclude here. Just as there are additions within the fabric of the basic text on Jerusalem as a prostitute, so there are extensions outside it. Successive commentators never seemed to fathom this emotional image, could not feel they had exhausted it. The first of these commentaries, in 16:44-58, introduces an image of mother and daughter which is not immediately clear. Until recently, Jerusalem had been developing as a girl in her own right, the unwanted child of unknown parents. But now a particular proverb is applied to her: "Look, anyone who uses proverbs will speak this one about you: Like mother, like daughter" (16:44). The wording of the statement shows that it was a proverb in current usage, not necessarily connected with the stridently detailed picture just presented, which did not emphasize Jerusalem's place as a daughter. We know, however, that this proverb is not commonly used as a compliment. It makes an unfavourable characteristic more graphic and apparently more incontrovertible by saying it applies to more than one member of the family. The next verse, 45, elaborates on the astounding statement of 16:3, though drawing details from it which are not explicit there:

> You are the daughter of your mother who abhorred her husband and her children, and you are your sisters' sister who abhorred their husbands and their children: your [plural] mother was a Hittite and your [plural] father was an Amorite (16:45).

The quotation is plainly a commentary on 16:3, but whereas the original only stresses Jerusalem's foreign and mixed parentage, the present commentary says that Jerusalem is like her mother who abhorred her husband and her children. This may be an allusion to Hittite women as camp prostitutes, but in any case Jerusalem is branded here as having infamous relations, in particular the closest, her mother. And by such association, her own disreputable nature is underlined.

The commentary broadens and intensifies the seriousness of the matter by introducing sisters, who are not presented at all in the basic text. The reader soon discovers that the sisters are Sodom and Samaria. (In chap.23 the theme of the sisters will be independently elaborated.) The commentary in chap.16 has apparently taken the theme of the sisters from the material now in chap.23 (10), and adding Sodom to make the evil even plainer, has fused it with the theme of "like mother, like daughter". Jerusalem is thrown into contrast as the most evil figure of an evil brood, assisted by another subtle change in the quotation from 16:3: there the phrase "your mother" refers only to Jerusalem's; here the "your" is plural and the mother is also Samaria's and Sodom's.

This is made explicit in 16:46:

> Your elder sister is Samaria who lived with her daughters to the North of you, and your younger sister is Sodom who lived with her daughters to the South of you.

Jerusalem appears much the worse for having Sodom as a sister as well as Samaria. Moreover, she is said to have acted even more corruptly than they; indeed, Yahweh swears that Sodom and her daughters have not acted like Jerusalem and her daughters (16:47-48). There could not be a more unequivocal way of saying that Jerusalem is the most depraved of all. (To compare Sodom favourably means that the matter is beyond all doubt.) This theme will be developed, in various surprising ways.

It is difficult to conceive why any more commentary was felt to be necessary after the stark image of prostitution in the basic text of chap.16. Anything can lose its effect in the course of time though, and the very starkness of the image may have made it easier to disregard, so that a need was later felt to make more concrete comparisons with other peoples. Sodom's guilt and pride is in having more than enough food and prosperity; she did not help the poor, but was haughty and committed abominations (16:49-50). This is an unexpected definition of Sodom's guilt considering the tradition in Genesis 19, but it may be that her guilt was seen as no worse than this; she did not commit the prostitution associated with Jerusalem in the basic text(11). Something similar is said pointedly in the comparison between Jerusalem and Samaria:

> Samaria, moreover, has not even committed the half of your sins, for you have committed far more abominations than they have, and through all the abominations which you have committed you have justified your sisters (16:51).

Samaria is not of course sinless, but to put it this way is to show how bad Jerusalem is, so bad that she can only justify Samaria and Sodom by comparison(12).

Thus a surprising development of the theme is that reaction to Jerusalem in terms of her own nature begins to take on a universal regenerative aspect, a possibility already touched on in chap.14, but here much broader. In the first part of 14, the deceitful elder or any Israelite can be used to claim the devotion of other Israelite idolaters for Yahweh. The stranger in Israel or even the prophet can be used for the same purpose, so that the guilt of any group in Israel can be turned to the benefit of another group. In the particular application of the second part of chap.14, survivors from Jerusalem can comfort exiles concerning the destruction of Israel. But here in chap.16, the sin of Jerusalem as a whole, applied to other peoples, can have the effect of justifying them. So a negative can effect a positive. If other peoples recognize the extent of Jerusalem's sin, the conviction may grow that their own is not past redemption. It is a curious example of anything being possible as God's purpose. It is not the main theme, which remains Jerusalem's sin, but the author continues to use it to express the fact that Jerusalem must acknowledge her disgrace openly. In doing so, she bears favourable witness (the term is a legal one) for her sisters who are less guilty than she is.

Jerusalem herself must be convinced of and acknowledge her disgrace openly, but not in the abstract; it is achieved in justifying her sisters (16:52). These two things are closely linked: Jerusalem's disgrace can justify other peoples, and her disgrace can also be impressed on her in justifying them. The last part of 16:52 reads literally: "bear your disgrace in your justifying of your sisters", that is, there is real pain in justifying her sisters by the acknowledgement of her own greater sin. But it is the means by which such justification may be effected. Those who see another taking the suffering of their disgrace upon themselves may be moved by that to repent of their own.

Greater responsibility is required of the sinner, Jerusalem. Rather than have her guilt declared by someone else, she must do so herself in full knowledge that this exposure can redeem others. If it is the responsibility of the watchman in chaps.3 and 33 to draw attention to the guilt which he does not himself share, here Jerusalem is called on to draw attention to her own guilt, which exceeds that of others. This commentator is adding in a remarkable manner to the image of Jerusalem as a prostitute. It may weaken that particular image, but intensifies another - that of the humiliated mediator.

The significant effect which Jerusalem can have on other peoples is taken up by Yahweh in 16:53:

> I shall turn their fortunes, those of Sodom and her daughters, and of Somaria and her daughters, and I shall(13) turn your fortunes together with theirs...

Yahweh's restoration of all countries is implicit in Jerusalem's bearing of her disgrace for the justification of her sisters. The reference to restoring fortunes also makes it likely that this passage comes from after 587 B.C.(14), whereas the basic text in chap.16, which presents Jerusalem in disgrace, predates that time. So here the restoration from exile is linked with Jerusalem's responsibility to acknowledge her disgrace to other peoples. The restoration of Jerusalem can now be spoken of together with that of her sisters:

> ..in order that you bear the responsibility for your disgrace and are put to shame on account of all you have done whereby you become a comfort to them (16:54).

But restoration does not mean that Jerusalem is now excused from exercising her responsibility; on the contrary, it must be maintained so that the effect on the others may be continual. Once only the disproportion of guilt between Jerusalem and her sisters was stressed; now Yahweh's restoration of them all shames Jerusalem, providing a strange but well-founded comfort to the other peoples. If Jerusalem's restoration can come about in spite of her manifest guilt, how much more can the others be confident of their restoration! Yahweh's restoration, founded on Jerusalem's acknowledgement of her nature provides a realistic basis for a future not only for Jerusalem but for other peoples as well.

The unexpectedly positive course which the argument has taken from such seemingly unpromising ground may be the reason for its repetition in slightly different words in 16:55-58. In a somewhat heavy-handed way, the verses emphasize Jerusalem's disgrace without explicit mention of its positive benefits. Jerusalem supplants Sodom as the city of exemplary shame.

But the elaboration of the image of a prostitute continues also. The image is toned down, with a further contribution being made mainly in more theological terms. The basic text is strongly emotional, though seeking to be "recollected in tranquillity". But while 16:44-54 presents the unusual but extremely stimulating theology of the unrighteous mediator, 16:59-63 employs the more orthodox theology of covenant. Later commentators may have been surprised that the basic text did not make more of the term berît mentioned in 16:8 (the word usually translated, not very adequately, by "covenant"). However, if the term berît had been as important in the basic text as it is for those parts of the Old Testament which use it deliberately, then it would have been used significantly throughout. As it is, the sense in 16:8 is a specialized one of "engagement for marriage", used to make that particular point.

Otherwise the term tends to be applied in the Book of Ezekiel towards the end of originally diverse material, as it is here (16:59; 34:25; 37:26), and it is not used at all where it might be expected, in chap.36 for instance. This indicates that the basis of the book did not employ the word as a central theological term(15), whereas in 16:59-63 it is the most

suitable word to express the sure basis of lasting forgiveness.
Verse 59 apparently refers to judgement, but this is clearly
not the main purpose. The judgement is not specified and the
statement quickly goes on to an assurance of Yahweh's
constancy:

> For thus says Lord Yahweh, I shall act with you as
> you have acted in despising the oath and breaking
> the covenant, but I shall remember my covenant with
> you in the days of your youth and I shall establish
> for you a permanent covenant (16:59-60).

The emphasis of Yahweh's assurance is just as much on his
remembering what Jerusalem has despised and broken as on the
covenant itself, which in turn brings Jerusalem back to a
correct remembrance in v.61 (also in v.63):

> Then you will remember your ways and be ashamed
> when <I>(16) take your sisters from you, both the
> elder and the younger and give them to you as
> daughters, though not on account of your
> covenant(?).

Other countries, changed from sisters to daughters, are
evidently to be brought into closer relationship with
Jerusalem. It is not clear what is meant by the last phrase,
which seems to disassociate the new relationship from the
covenant(17). Possibly the intention is to say that what
Yahweh intends now is so comprehensive that it goes far beyond
the original covenant. In this remarkable new relationship,
where sisters become daughters, (and in the larger context it
applies even to Sodom), faithfulness is not forgotten but
reinforced on the basis of the covenant. "The everlasting
covenant" (v.60) as it is often translated, does not have a
transcendental meaning, but signifies rather something of
permanent validity. Exactly this is necessary if Jerusalem is
to remember her former nature and apprehend the difference
between that and her superabundance.
Yahweh's covenant, although broken once, becomes the basis
for permanence. It expresses the confidence that people, if
they gain insight into their former nature, may be transformed.
16:61 takes up the concerns of both the first and second parts
of the chapter and sees the prostitute (no longer called that)
as having an entirely different future with the very sisters
whom she surpassed in evil. With confidence it is said: "I
shall establish my covenant with you and you shall know that I
am Yahweh" (16:62). Berît is the appropriate word to establish
confidence in the possibility of forgiveness even for Jerusalem
as she was,

> ..in order that you might remember and be ashamed,
> but no longer open your mouth on account of your
> shame when I forgive you for all you have done,

says Lord Yahweh (16:63).

The recipients of restoration are forgiven and no longer burdened with guilt because they remember.

11. A NEW CHANCE REJECTED: 17

In chap. 15, Jerusalem is compared with the wood of the vine rather than its fruit, which might give the impression that this is a natural state which cannot be remedied. But the image of the bride and the prostitute in chap. 16 makes it clear that, when Jerusalem had been offered entirely different possibilities, she repudiated them in the coarsest manner. Chapter 17 corresponds to some extent formally with 15 since both use an image followed by a series of questions and then go on to a direct application of judgement(1). In this chapter, however, we hear of seed being planted by an eagle (that is the Jerusalem king Zedekiah by the Babylonian Nebuchadrezzar)(2). This means that Jerusalem, compared once again with a plant, is being given another chance even in a time of extremity. It communicates the extreme seriousness of the people's situation, while revealing the inadequate reaction, even of their greatest representatives such as the king. In this way, chap. 17 links with 15 and 16 as well as with the earlier chapters on the prophets(13) and the elders(14).

A special effort to show the people what has been made of their opportunities occurs when the word of Yahweh comes to Ezekiel as a commission to "... put a riddle and tell a parable to the house of Israel" (17:2). It is necessary to go to unusual human lengths to make the word of Yahweh understood. By the use of "riddle" (hîdâ), Ezekiel does not intend a puzzle, and that may be why the term "parable" (māšāl) is used immediately afterwards(3); rather he wants to catch the people's attention in a popular way and set them thinking for themselves. The form here differs from that of chap. 15 where the image adopted is one which the people already use.

The image is a composite one, that of an eagle of great proportions (described in some detail) coming to Lebanon, and taking from there the top branch of the cedar (17:3). It becomes clear later (v.12) that the eagle is the Babylonian king Nebuchadrezzar, who in 597 B.C. took into exile the Judaean king Jehoiachin, here represented by the top branch of the cedar, the noblest tree known to the Israelites. Jerusalem was not only deprived of her king, but also of the princes; she is in the parlous situation of being stripped of her leaders. This is represented in v.4 by the eagle picking the cedar's topmost twigs as well, and bringing them to the land of trade (Babylon). The land is not, however, abandoned to this state of deprivation. The eagle takes some of the seed of the land and plants it in fertile ground by a plentiful water supply (17:5). Thus even in the time of extremity after the first Babylonian conquest, Jerusalem is given a new chance to develop. This indeed happens: the plant grows and becomes a vine (Zedekiah), spreading out thick and low as a vine should, turning its branches towards the eagle and taking firm root (17:6). It is particularly significant that the new plant is a vine, and one full of promise.

What does the vine make of its promise? It abuses it. Not satisfied with its present relationship with Babylon (clearly regarded as the only realistic option), the vine takes advantage of another great eagle (17:7). The eagle (Egypt) is not more magnificent than the first, but the refusal of the Jerusalem king to accept the realistic opportunity and his passion for novelty are expressed in the image of the vine actually twisting its roots towards this new eagle, spreading out its branches towards him in order to be watered in a bed different from the original. The vine is then transplanted to other good ground near plenty of water, in the hope that it will once again grow and bear fruit and become a noble vine (17:8)(4). Such is the expression of Jerusalem's aspirations in rebelling against Babylon and turning to Egypt for help.

The episode necessarily prompts questions. Transplanting is risky, and Yahweh himself asks: will this succeed? Won't it be pulled up by its roots, stripped of its fruit so that all its fresh shoots shrivel up? Or, as a transplant, won't it dry up when the east wind strikes it? (17:9-10). This transplantation, this change of loyalty, will plainly be disastrous. The end of the parable, before the interpretation in 17:11ff, significantly does not speak of Yahweh intervening to punish, since it is quite clear that the matter will of itself turn out badly. It is also significant that it is the interpretation which is introduced by "Thus says Lord Yahweh"(5), which means that Ezekiel interprets what happens as a manifestation of Yahweh speaking. If people do not take the opportunities they are offered, there will be certain consequences which have to be accepted.

The interpretation adds another dimension. Some specific information (such as Zedekiah breaking a treaty with the Babylonians, v.18) shows that it was written at a later time than the parable itself, probably after 587 B.C. when Zedekiah was about to be taken into exile(6). But the interpretation says (v.20) that Yahweh himself takes Zedekiah into exile. This means that God is manifest in what is happening now as the inevitable and right consequence of what people had both done and failed to do in the past. The prefacing of this later interpretation with the word-event formula "Then the word of Yahweh came to me" emphasizes it. Usually the formula would introduce the whole unit. Its placing here means that the interpretation is a later addition informed by the developing situation, which is understood as the word of Yahweh. It is the clearest example yet that the people's understanding is the integrating factor between what happens and its acceptance as judgement for themselves. This is the word of God for the people. Ezekiel works towards this goal, urging people to respond to what is happening, putting a question which shows some impatience with the state of the people and their reactions. The impatience was naturally Ezekiel's, but it is also incorporated in the word of Yahweh: "Say to the rebellious house, Do you not know what these things mean? ..."(17:12). If in chap.16 the people have to understand their own nature, here in 17 they have to understand the significance of the events connected with the king.

The interpretation proper is then given in vv.12-15. It specifies Zedekiah's relations with the king of Babylon and with Egypt, with great emphasis (in v.13) on Nebuchadrezzar's making of a treaty with Zedekiah and placing him under oath(7), and concludes by asking whether a request to Egypt for an army will succeed. Will a man, who does such things as breaking a treaty, escape? Possibly the exiles viewed the breaking of the treaty very seriously because they were not merely prisoners, but hostages taken to ensure that the treaty was honoured(8). Verses 13-14, directly after we hear that Zedekiah is laid under oath, report that Nebuchadrezzar took away the dignitaries of the land, so that they would keep the treaty(9). Zedekiah rebelled (v.15), a clear proof that he did not appreciate the most realistic option open to him. The word of God is to say what must happen in the light of this: since the exiles are hostages their present status will now become permanent.

In 17:16-18, great emphasis is placed on the guilt of Zedekiah. A statement introduced solemnly by the divine oath formula ("As I live"), pronounces that Zedekiah will die in the country of his royal overlord whose oath he has despised in breaking his treaty. Egypt offers no military hope, and Zedekiah cannot hope to escape. Judaeans see their city of Jerusalem as deeply disgraced, even in their relations with Babylon. The fact that it is Babylon does not make it justifiable. For as vv.19-21 now emphasize, it is said to be Yahweh's oath which Zedekiah despised, Yahweh's treaty which Zedekiah broke; and this is charged to Zedekiah himself:

> I shall spread my net over him and he will be captured in my hunting net; I shall bring him to Babylon and enter into judgement with him there for the unfaithfulness with which he has treated me (17:20).

What Zedekiah has done to Nebuchadrezzar constitutes unfaithfulness to Yahweh, and Yahweh's judgement is in terms of Babylon. That is, the religious interpretation of this apparently political matter, far from providing an escape from inevitable consequences, confirms the necessity of their acceptance. It can also be said that Zedekiah has been unfaithful to Yahweh, because what is happening now shows up by contrast what could have been achieved earlier if the circumstances then had been fully exploited. That the unfaithfulness has been against Yahweh himself, and that it is Yahweh's judgement for Zedekiah to be brought to Babylon, means too that the reaction to be provoked from the people is an acknowledgement that there can be no possible hope for the exiles in Zedekiah or Jerusalem. Even a transplanted vine can twist itself away.

Some later editor(10),however, saw a different possibility in the treetop of the cedar; namely, that the Davidic monarchy could become something different from what it had been. Now it is said that Yahweh himself will take the same item as the eagle had taken at the beginning of the chapter:

> ..I myself will take from the treetop of the cedar
> [the high and will set] (11); from only its very
> topmost shoots I shall pick one and I myself will
> transplant it on a high and towering hill (17:22).

What Yahweh takes is even more choice than what the eagle took at the beginning, for it is probable that it signifies a new king who is directly related not so much to Zedekiah as to Jehoiachin. Zedekiah had failed, but even within the one family there are various alternatives. When one branch of a leading family fails, it does not necessarily follow that there are no new possibilities within that same royal family, possibilities which are extended to the generations of all people in chap.18. That no new generation, if it responds creatively, need have its life cut off by a previous generation's legacy, is one of the most insistent messages of the Book of Ezekiel.

The eagles thus play no more part, and Yahweh now plants the shoot on a high and towering hill. Zedekiah had been humiliated but now there is exaltation (12). The re-establishment of the "mountain of the house of Yahweh" is imagined as the rule of a new king, truly worthy of it. Certainly his scope goes far beyond Zedekiah's:

> I shall plant it on the mountain height of Israel
> and it will put forth branches and bear fruit and
> become a magnificent cedar. All the <animals>(13)
> will dwell beneath it, and all the birds will nest
> in the shade of its branches (17:23).

This plant becomes a protective cedar. That Yahweh plants it means that harmony will displace disharmony, not in the abstract but through an institution known to Israel. This re-established Davidic monarchy begins to have a universal significance. Its exact nature is not clearly stated, but other peoples are envisaged as being able to take up their place in relation to it. That its potentialities are seen, potentialities which would involve the renewal of life for all, whatever had gone before, is more important than the fact that the Davidic monarchy was not renewed, and never had the significance envisaged for it here(14). For the Jerusalem community was renewed along with its own leadership, and though this was not so grand or so exclusive as pictured here, some of the aspirations were realized through something more humble. Exaltation arose from humiliation as other peoples observed. The community could repeat it in their own lives.

> All the trees of the field will know that I Yahweh have humiliated the lofty tree, I have exalted the lowly tree; I have dried up the moist tree and made the dry tree bloom - I Yahweh have spoken and acted (17:24).

12. LIFE POSSIBLE FOR EVERYONE NOW: 18

Since chap.19, using the image of lions, is like chap.17 concerned with the king, it may be wondered why chap.18 breaks sequence, especially since unlike all the other chapters between 15 and 19 it is not based on an image. In chap.17, an attempt is made to force an answer from the people (17:12), which leads them away from confidence in kingship. The reason for the present position of chap.18 may then perhaps lie in the question: if even kings fail to take their opportunities and come to disaster, what hope for the people now? The editors thus take the conviction that the people could be activated, and contrast it with the the two surrounding chapters on the king(1). Past king and present people are quite different propositions. If it is true that the exiles were at first hostages to guarantee the loyalty of Zedekiah and felt themselves to have been betrayed by him, then this arrangement may express the need to see the greatest possible difference between the king's previous opportunity, which was not taken, and the people's present one, which can be. It represents the bold realization, also expressed elsewhere in the book, that the people's potentialities do not stand or fall with those of their leaders, not even those of kings. Responsibility is democratized: the realization of the freedom to choose what is most significant in life for oneself.

All this is only possible for the people if they react to their present nature, just as they have to react to the present nature of the prophets, the elders and kings. Thus it is appropriate that the unit as a whole begins with a word of disputation(2), quoting the people's own words:

> Now the word of Yahweh came to me saying, what do you mean by repeating this saying concerning the land of Israel: The fathers have eaten unripe

grapes and the teeth of the children have become
numb? (18:1-2).

What happens is now seen in the people's expression of an
attitude. Yahweh does not just quote the people, he demands:
what do you mean by repeating the saying? It implies that the
people should react by rejecting their present attitude to the
disaster. The saying may refer to the thin coating on the
teeth caused by eating unripe grapes, which makes the teeth
feel numb(3). Here it presupposes a view of retribution where
Yahweh himself punishes not only the present but also the
future generation for sin; but the saying is also cynically
used to avoid exercising any responsibility in the present
situation of acute depression(4). Just how serious such an
attitude is for the people's future, and just how necessary it
is to dispel it, is shown by there being not only an
introductory edge to the quotation, but also a sharp
prohibition against any repetition : "As I live, says Lord
Yahweh, You shall no longer repeat this saying in Israel"
(18:3). All lives belong to Yahweh - the life of the son as
well as the life of the father (18:4). The possibility of life
for all is not compromised either by leaders or by the people
themselves, so long as those in the present are prepared to be
responsible for their own particular circumstances and respond
appropriately. If the chapters as composed inhibit the people
from using what has happened to the kings as an excuse for
their inaction, the direct challenge of the present context is
to stop using the excuse of what has happened to the fathers.
It is a theology calling on people to take responsibility upon
themselves, in other words, to grow up.
   The possibilities when responsibility is freely grasped are
illustrated by examples from three generations. Verse 5-9
start with the righteous. Doing right is not something which
exists in itself but proceeds from being "righteous" (ṣaddiq):
"if a person is righteous and does what is lawful and right"
(18:5). "Being righteous" means having a proper relationship
with God from which in turn proper conduct stems. Relationship
integrated with conduct prompts what may seem to be the
particularly uninspiring moralistic list which follows. The
exemplary righteous person doing what is lawful and right does
not eat on the mountains or lift up his eyes to idols; he does
not defile the wife of his neighbour nor approach a woman
during her menstruation (v.6); the righteous man does not
oppress, restores the pledge to his debtor, does not steal,
gives food to the hungry and clothes the naked (v.7); he does
not lend at interest, refrains fron iniquity, and executes true
justice between people (v.8).
   This list, which might be called a "guide for
self-examination"(5), originated when people seeking entry to
the sanctuary were given such a paradigm by the priest(6) (see
Psalms 15 and 24). Since it is based on a relation with God,
it is appropriate that the "guide" ends in v.9 by saying that
the righteous person doing what is lawful and right "walks in

my (Yahweh's) statutes and keeps my ordinances in order to deal truly", summing up life as an integral whole. The matters listed would all have been relevant to life in a foreign country, but it is not necessary that there be proof that every detail of the "guide" has been adhered to. It is sometimes quoted in much shorter form (33:15), and it ends with a declaratory formula(7) proclaiming through the priest over the righteous person the judgement of God himself: " - that person is righteous, he will indeed live, says Lord Yahweh" (18:9).

Even with such a guide at his disposal, no one can judge himself to be righteous. It opposes the common modern view that to become a virtuous person, one has only to conduct oneself rightly. But the significant factor here is that life is still possible outside the sanctuary and even in exile. Such an integrated life is transferable; it can be realized here and now; it is not to be compromised by people of other times. This life is the realization of Yahweh's gift and the response in everyday life, and it is only on such conditions that it is now being offered to the exiles, whatever their fathers have done. It is the awe-inspiring but wonderful challenge to be themselves.

The challenge is sharpened by saying that the right decision of the fathers will not necessarily benefit their children if they decide otherwise. Ezekiel 18:10-13 tells of the son of the righteous man who has become a robber, using a word (pārîs) which draws together all violent actions(8). This person of the second generation bears his own responsibility, not his father's. He is a shedder of blood, acting in the very manner which his father, a righteous man, did not (18:10-13).

Such a person cannot live, is not sharing that life with God and the community stipulated in the details of the "guide". As the Hebrew puts it, "his blood will be upon himself" (v.13), which means there is no escape from his own guilt, he is entirely responsible for himself. No wonder that Yahweh asks somewhat testily, "What do you mean by repeating this saying ...?" The guilt which makes their teeth numb is their own.

But, once again, there is no chain of guilt which cannot be broken. Things can change again with this guilty man's son, for now it is the turn of the third generation (18:14-18). Capable of learning from the sins of his father and of avoiding them (v.14), this man, like his grandfather, does not do the things his father had done (vv.14-17). He will thus not die for his father's guilt, but will certainly live, as the contrast between his life and his father's fate makes clear (v.18). The contrast between what happens to the different generations brings out the potentialities of their own responsibility. (This conviction that families should not be stereotyped implicitly contradicts the proverb quoted earlier: "like mother, like daughter" (16:44).) Examples from three generations show that life is possible for everyone, in any place and at any time, and whatever the family history.

However cynically the people may have uttered the saying quoted at the beginning of the chapter (18:2), they still prefer to cling to tradition. The people are quoted again: "Why should not the son suffer for the guilt of the father?" (18:19). This seems strange, since this was the very complaint the people were making at the outset. But it is not totally strange when one considers how much responsibility the answer which has been given lays on the people themselves. The people's reaction now shows them to have comprehended some of the implications, for, far from wanting to realize the possibilities of responsibility, they seek an excuse not to. It is easier after all that the son should suffer for the guilt of his father, for he is then absolved of any blame himself.

Only one sensible rejoinder can be given. If the son has done what is lawful and right, he will live (18:19).

> It is the life that sins that will die. The son will not bear the guilt of the father nor the father the guilt of the son. The righteousness of the righteous is up to him, and the guilt of the guilty is up to the guilty (18:20).

Thus Ezekiel calls for responsibility to accept life within the present generation.

Having shown that the people's past is no hindrance to life, he shows that even an individual past is no hindrance either:

> If the guilty man turns from all the sin which he has done, keeps all my statutes, and does what is lawful and right, he will certainly live and not die. All the crimes which he has done will be remembered against him - he will live in the righteousness he has done (18:21-22).

He emphasizes the positive effects on a person's life when it is not burdened by the past, an idea underlined by the sudden introduction of Yahweh's emotions:

> Should I have any pleasure at all in the death of the guilty, says Lord Yahweh, and not rather that he turn from his way and live? (18:23).

Such a question introduced into the matter-of-fact argument is one which compels an answer.

Even this appeal has to be made within a realistic context. That there is no hindrance whatsoever to the acceptance of life cannot remove the urgent need for the people to make a positive response, a need best emphasized by the person who was once righteous and has now failed. When a righteous person turns from his righteousness and acts like a guilty one, then his righteousness will not be remembered; he will die on account of his treachery and sin (18:24). Responsibility is total; it cannot be turned on and off, nor calculated. Responsibility is the opposite of the legalism which balances bad deeds with good. If the present time is excepted, then the response has no meaning.

Out of their fear of the need for present responsibility the people complain: "The way of <Yahweh>(9) is not just" (18:25). The conversation with the people exposes them at their most debased. Here the people's desire to avoid present responsibility by playing off the present against the past is revealed without any pious protestations. The people extend their dissatisfaction with God beyond the issue of what happens between the generations - to claiming it is unfair that the righteousness of a person who has become wicked should be forgotten.

The arguments in this passage are often interpreted as individualistic, but it is the people who show themselves to be individualistic. They want to be judged in terms of both their strengths and weaknesses, whereas the emphasis on present responsibility is to insist that people are hampered neither by their past family history nor their own, and may respond to an offer transcending their present state since it comes from God through another person. The offer involves a response to others, expressed in a life of fellowship with others. Within such communication there can be no individual calculation.

One must therefore oppose the people's objections with facts: they, as the communal house of Israel, are asked to answer the question as to whether their own ways are unjust compared with Yahweh's. A righteous person who has turned away from his righteousness can only die in his iniquity (18:25-26). The positive counterpart is then put forward:

> When the guilty person repents of the wickedness he has done, and does what is lawful and right, he will save his life. [for he saw] (10) He has repented of all the crimes which he had done and therefore he will certainly live and not die (18:27-28).

But the people are frightened of such a life, not of the fact that their righteousness will be forgotten. If this were not so they would not react in the way they do. Therefore they have to see that it is not Yahweh's ways which are unjust, but their own (18:29). "Therefore I shall judge each man according to his ways, house of Israel, says Lord Yahweh" (18:30). Once again judgement accords with their way of life. Just as the people reacted to the nature of the kings and other Israelite officials so they must to themselves. The people's own conduct, even their own nature, takes on an ever more personal aspect from chap.15 onwards - even in chap.18, which contains no image.

Finally must come the offer of repentance. The people must recognize their true nature, but once this is acknowledged, it need not hinder them from the acceptance of life any more than the failure of the kings:

> Repent and turn from all your crimes to avoid guilt
> becoming a stumbling-block to you. Cast away your
> evil deeds and all the crimes you have committed,
> and get yourselves a new heart and a new spirit;
> for why will you die, house of Israel? (18:30-31).

They are told to avoid being inhibited by their guilt. The
strong exhortation itself sets the possibility in motion, and
then there follows a remarkable exhortation to "get
(themselves) a new heart and a new spirit". The imperative
here, in contrast with the indicative in 11:19, emphasizes
strongly the necessity and potentiality of the people's own
response(11), prompted by the plaintive question, "Why will you
die?" To apprehend the possibility of response is to realize,
with other people, that indeed one need not die. The people
must react and answer the question, acknowledge the reality of
the offer of life. They have the greatest possible assurance:
"For I have no pleasure in the death of the person threatened
by death, says Lord Yahweh" (18:32). His commitment to life
overcomes the people's present cantankerousness.

13. THE END OF THE WHOLE ROYAL HOUSE: 19

Before making the offer which is now to be found in chap.18, it
was necessary to turn against the king more than had been done
in chap.17. Chapter 19 indicates that the people should make a
final reaction to the kings of Israel. The kings are first
presented in a positive light as young lions, their mother a
paragon: "What a lioness was your mother among lions, she
couched among young lions rearing her whelps" (19:2). Some
scholars think that the lioness refers to Hamutal, wife of
Josiah and mother of Jehoahaz and Zedekiah, and assume that as
Queen Mother she would have exercised great influence in
court(1). Whatever influence she had was clearly not lasting,
for the image of the lions has already been introduced not as a
word of Yahweh but as a lament: "But you, take up a
lamentation over the princes of Israel ..." (19:1).
  The dirge over the princes of Israel is in fact a potent
threat of death(2). Whatever pictures one can give of the
past, and however much influence this may still have on the
present, the future is already compromised. For though the
lioness brought up one of her whelps so that he learned to
catch prey and devour men, nations summoned troops against him,
he was taken in their pit, and they brought him with hooks to
the land of Egypt (19:3-4). Thus what seems to be most secure
in the young lion's upbringing is soon changed; whatever the
appearances they can be reversed. This almost certainly refers
to Jehoahaz whom the people of the land made king after Pharaoh

Neco killed his father Josiah. But Neco made his half-brother
Jehoiakim king in his place, taking Jehoahaz prisoner to Egypt
(2 Kings 23:30-34).

Another possibility exists. Indeed, that was the problem in
Judah: after one failure they could always turn elsewhere for
deliverance, and then were disabused of that also. When the
lioness sees her first hope disappointed, she takes another of
her whelps and makes him into a young lion (19:5). This one is
more successful than the first (compare vv.6-7 with v.3). He
prowls among the lions, learns how to catch prey, devours men,
but also <ravaged> their <strongholds>(3), laid waste their
cities so that the land and all in it were appalled at the
sound of his roaring. This last description, which goes far
beyond anything which the first young lion did, does not
exactly fit any of the kings who might be represented by this
second lion (Jehoiakim, Jehoiachin or Zedekiah), especially if
it stands for activity directed against other nations. Perhaps
it refers to threats to peace and persecutions made during the
reign of Zedekiah, in the period between the two Babylonian
conquests of Jerusalem in 597 and 587 B.C. This seems the most
likely interpretation if a choice has to be made between the
three kings. "Ravaging strongholds" and "laying cities waste"
is inappropriate though - at least in literal terms - for the
rather weak Zedekiah, manipulated by a war party in Jerusalem;
and one wonders whether the emphasis is not rather on the last
desperate stages of the Judaean kingship as such(4).

In any case, even this lion who appals by his roaring, is
taken, and just as there was more detail given of the second
lion's violence than the first's, so now the desperate
description of his capture is more detailed (compare v.4 with
vv.8-9):

> They set nations against him from the province
> round about, they spread their nets over him and he
> was taken in their pit. They put him in a
> neck-stock(5) [with hooks] and brought him to the
> king of Babylon [they brought him in hunting nets]
> (6) in order that his voice no longer be heard on
> the mountains of Israel.

This lion is not only caught in a pit, but has nets spread over
him; being put in neck-stocks corresponds to being taken with
hooks in v.4, although otherwise nothing more is said about the
first lion's transportation to Egypt. The second lion is
humiliated and silenced: he is brought to the king of Babylon
"...in order that his voice no longer be heard on the mountains
of Israel". Here is the end of the royal house. The fate of
the two young lions confirms the final silencing of the
kingship in Israel; one is taken with hooks to Egypt, the
other in neck-stocks to the king of Babylon. The Israelite
kingship has been totally annihilated and crushed. It is
superior to no nation. The exiles must see that there is no
more hope even in this great institution, as the image makes

clear. Even a lion, indeed two young lions, can be silenced. The proverbially strong are of no avail.

Since no details are included about Zedekiah being taken blind to Babylon, this passage was probably a prediction written before the final fall of Jerusalem in 587. The dirge, with its almost regular rhythm of three strong stresses followed by two, is all the more effective since it is sung over a kingship still not dead. Verses 10-14 change the image to that of a vine, ending with the words, "This is a lament and has become a lament". It makes it sound as though what is described here has actually happened already: the execution of the predicted judgement. So the prediction is linked with what happens, probably in terms thought more suitable at a later time(7). The lioness thus becomes a well-placed vine(8): "Your mother was like a vine full of shoots because planted by water, she was fruitful with many branches by abundant waters" (19:10). It develops in a special way:

> There grew up on it strong branches which became rulers' sceptres [its growth reached high among its branches, and it became visible on account of its height in the abundance of its foliage](9) (19:11).

Even this plant however is uprooted and thrown to the ground. An east wind dries it up, its fruit is stripped off, and fire consumes it (19:12). This description may well betray a more detailed knowledge of the fate of Zedekiah (though Jehoiachin's has also been suggested); but in any case, what had seemed well-planted and strong has been rooted out, and destroyed. After this it seems strange to hear of transplantation, so that vv.13-14 may be a further addition:

> And now it is transplanted in the wilderness in a dry and thirsty land [and fire went forth from the branch, consumed its shoots, its fruit] (10), so that no strong branch remained on it, any sceptre for ruling - this is a lament and has become a lament.

These verses may refer to Jehoiachin (the king taken into exile in 597 B.C.), but are particularly poignant here. If even this plant is dried, stripped and burnt, what hope then for the plant when, far from being planted by abundant waters, it is planted in dry ground? Even in the exile, it implies, there is no hope for the king. The reality is the lamentation, and not only in Jerusalem. The withered vine image of chap.17 has come true. One need not talk about the wood of the vine as in chap.15 - failure comes from its most luxuriant growth.

If there is no hope then in the position as such, where is hope to be found? The answer could only be in the judgement itself, the exiles' acceptance as legitimate of the judgement which they have seen happening. Even what is saved and brought to them cannot be a carrier of hope. If anyone is to receive restoration, it is those who accept the judgement.

14. RECOGNITION OF PAST EVIL FOR THE PURPOSE OF
TRANSFORMATION: 20:1-44

It is noteworthy that like the call vision and the vision of
the abomination in Jerusalem (chaps.1 and 8) chap.20 starts
with a full date: "Now it happened in the seventh year, in the
fifth month on the tenth day of the month ..." Since the two
preceding dated passages are clearly of vital importance, we
can guess that this will be too. The reader soon discovers
that in chap.20 not just one event is depicted but the total
history of Israel as a history of sin. It states conclusively
the need for judgement on all that has happened previously.
This is a suitable place to summarize the preceding sections,
the necessary background to chap.20, which then surpasses the
others.
The way Ezekiel is presented during the siege in chap.4 shows
that those who face up to appalling events gain some relief
since they are coming to terms with reality. Those people who
respond to these appalling events are potential recipients of
restoration, since they are people who persevere. In 5:3-4 an
addition, contradicting what has gone before, speaks of some
survivors. Thus nothing is fixed for all time; theology is
not comprehended by only one period. Judgement is recognized
by those who have once known God and who are prepared to make
distinctions with regard to what happens to them at different
times. Despite what Ezekiel sometimes said about the
destruction of everyone, his disciples were prepared to add
that some did escape after all. The disciples are able to see
both the destruction of Jerusalem and the exile experience as a
judgement. They understand better what they were, and so what
they can still become.
Restoration for those exiles who view and accept the
judgement of Jerusalem is an idea most explicitly formulated in
chaps.8-11. Though they contain a vision of judgement on
Jerusalem, they begin and end with the exiles who are with
Ezekiel when his vision commences, and to whom it is explained
at the end. Embedded within this as a later addition are the
first two parts of chap.11; the first tells of judgement on
the most important officials in Jerusalem, while the second, in
contrast, announces restoration to the exiles. This is all the
more striking since the announcement of restoration explicitly
contrasts with the Jerusalemites' claim to the land and their
depreciation of the exiles whom they see as being remote from
Yahweh (11:15-16). Within these chapters too the seeds of
restoration are seen in the one person who cares. Ezekiel's
concern is expressed in his question as to whether Yahweh is

going to destroy everything which remains in Israel (9:8; 11:13). For such a person the source of restoration is certainly removed (the glory of Yahweh, 10:18-19), but does not disappear. Hope remains with the exiles who are told of the vision at its conclusion. For these exiles, Yahweh becomes a sanctuary even in exile (11:16). While this manner of expression does retain a continuity with Jerusalem, it also makes clear that the future lies only with the exiles. But this by itself is not enough, for the renewal of the nature of the people must be added (11:19). Thus the destruction of Jerusalem is not the end in any significant sense.

Total commitment to exile however is the necessary condition. In chap.12, the exiles are told that even those still left in Jerusalem have to go into exile, and Ezekiel himself becomes a sign to them as an exile. The following chapters make it clear that there is no escape - not even the people's most pre-eminent representatives, prophets, elders or kings can change the situation. After the offensive narrative of Jerusalem as a prostitute in chap.16, the people are left to reflect in silence about themselves. Chapter 14 had already made it clear that the recognition of others' guilt can be beneficial for those prepared to see, and the additions to chap.16 go so far as to consider such recognition as redemptive of other peoples. Jerusalem bearing her disgrace can thus have totally unexpected consequences reaching out, as Yahweh's restoration, beyond herself. Restoration, it is clear, comes from recognition of the worst. Those making the additions to chap.16 use the term "covenant" to express Yahweh's constancy as a sure basis for lasting forgiveness. Even something which the people have broken can become the basis for a new permanence. Chapter 18 states further that the recipients of restoration are no longer burdened either by their collective or individual pasts.

But before people can properly appreciate that they need not be burdened by their past, they have to accept a total cancellation of the past as refuge. Chapters 16, 20 and 23 intend in their different ways to bring the exiles to a complete alienation from their own people in the past, so that the way may be opened to create a new people for the future, open to restoration. In his account of the history and nature of Judah, Ezekiel wants the exiles to see that there is nothing in which they can put their hope, for it is only when alienated that they can begin the process of restoration. Emotion to be recollected in tranquillity characterizes the listeners' reflective speechlessness about Judah in chap.16. In 23, as will be seen, the hearers are alienated even more by the comparison between the sisters Samaria and Judah, for Judah is seen to be the worst; in 16 and 23, sexual imagery compounds their alienation. On the other hand, these powerful pictures are almost too effective in that people could easily deny that such a thing applied to them. Or, they could be applied too literally to other people, as in 23:48.

Alienation results not only from sexual imagery, but from a narrative of the utmost directness. Chap.20 is a savage, uncompromising address which speaks plainly of the exiles' own people. By alienating them from the present reality it provides the presupposition for restoration. Grave as the people's sin is, the very fact that they are continually told, "Do not walk in the statutes of your fathers" (20:18), implies that they do not have to take such behaviour for granted.

It is significant too that, like chaps 8-11, the basic text(1) of chap.20 begins (vv.1-4) and ends (vv.30-31) with the exiles. At the beginning the elders of Israel are said to come at a particular date (about 591 B.C.) to sit before Ezekiel and inquire of Yahweh, possibly expecting to hear something hopeful about their return home(2). Their inquiry is, however, even more abruptly rejected than it had been in chap.14: "Have you come to inquire of me? As I live, I will not be inquired of by you, says Lord Yahweh" (20:3), a rejection emphasized by the apparently irrelevant judgement on the exiled elders through the abomination of their fathers: "Will you judge them, yes judge them, son of man, by making known to them the abominations of their fathers" (20:4). To tell of the abominations of the fathers is indeed to judge the exiles, for they are not yet aware how little reliance can be placed in the past tradition of their people. It also gives a much better reason to reject their inquiry than had been given in chap.14.

In letting the exiles know of the abominations of their fathers, Ezekiel unexpectedly inserts a section in 20:5-7 on what Yahweh had originally tried to do for them. This is a pattern repeated three times throughout the narration(3), which emphasizes that the abominations of the fathers must be seen in contrast with the totally different life available to them which they rejected. The contrast is underlined by one of the very few references found on the prophets to Yahweh choosing Israel ("election"):

> On the day I chose Israel, I solemnly made myself known to the descendants of the house of Jacob in the land of Egypt, and I swore to them saying, I am Yahweh your God (20:5).

Yahweh has established a special relationship even with prisoners and made himself known in an alien environment. Yahweh promises more in v.6: he will lead them out to a land which he himself has searched out for them, "the fairest of all lands". That Yahweh made himself known to them in Egypt, a land of bondage and idols, indicated to the fathers that they did not have to stay there. The people had to make a deliberate choice, and they were given the opportunity to throw away the idols they were so attached to (v.7). The second instance of the fathers' abominations reports on their rebellion against Yahweh, when they would not listen, and refused to cast away their detestable idols (20:8). Since this is the only place in the whole of the Old Testament where it is said that the Israelites worshipped idols as far back as in Egypt, it is extremely doubtful that the information was historically founded. It is an extreme means to express the conviction that Israel's rejection of the life which Yahweh stands for has deep roots, and is not easily redeemed. The exiles must be totally alienated from the root of Israel's being.

Israel's rejection of the life offered by Yahweh leads to the third section in the pattern of Ezekiel's narration. Faced with Israel's perverse responses, Yahweh's naturally expected reaction would be to destroy his worthless people: "Then I intended to pour out my wrath upon them in the land of Egypt" (20:8). This however serves as a contrast to highlight what actually does happen. Now and twice more in the pattern it is said:

> But I acted for the sake of my name that it be not profaned in the sight of the nations among whom they were living and before whom I made myself known to them to bring them out from the land of Egypt (20:9).

This is one of the most striking theological statements in the whole book. It is a realistic (some might say, over-realistic) way of expressing the mercy extended by Yahweh to an undeserving Israel: Yahweh acts for the sake of his name, for his own sake. It seems therefore to be only a question of his name and his reputation among the nations where Israel was dwelling. Such a thought is certainly present(4), but it is also true that the possibilities of life inherent in Yahweh would be present no longer if Israel were no more. Thus to refrain from destroying Israel implies that it is only through Israel that Yahweh can be known. Without her, there would only remain profanation among other peoples. Thus Yahweh's life with Israel is to continue, however total Israel's corruption may be. The pattern, with its four components, which repeats itself twice more, shows a determination to make this life known, while bringing out the increasing opposition which is directed against it.

Yahweh manifests himself by bringing the people out of Egypt and leading them into the wilderness (20:9-10). Yahweh is known by what happens to the Israelites. In deliverance and in the provisions made for the life of deliverance, it is still possible to controvert the idols of Egypt. In 20:10-12 appears the second statement of what Yahweh attempts to do for the people in spite of their rebellion. He makes known to them the statutes and ordinances by the observance of which people can live; he also gives them his sabbaths to be a sign between him and them so that they might know that Yahweh sanctifies them. Here the wilderness is a place quite different, for example, from the great and terrible wilderness of Deuteronomy 8:15; it is a place where people can begin to know God in the detailed concerns of everyday communal life. The statement acknowledges not only the mere fact of being delivered, but of having life filled with direction. Deliverance is not sufficient in itself, for life has to be lived after it. But even this general direction can be enhanced by something special within it, by the sabbaths as a punctuating period in which to know the relationship established with Yahweh. People have to know for themselves, have to be given an opportunity of knowing, and this is what the sabbaths provide: a particular expansion of the statutes by which people can live.

But once delivered from Egypt they reject the statutes which promote communal life, and deliberately profane the sabbaths which could make them holy. In 20:8, the fathers had merely persisted with their previous behaviour, but now in v.13 it is worse: they rebel for a second time in actually refusing the opportunity offered them. It is an interesting indication of the importance of the opportunities offered, that rebellion itself is not an action, but a refraining from action, a failure to accept the opportunities of life. This, though the formal pattern is the same, makes the matter worse. After the second mention of Yahweh's anger being withheld for the sake of his name (20:13-14), a threat is now added in vv.15-16. The promise of bringing them into the fairest of all lands may not be fulfilled because of their rejection. This threat is immediately withdrawn (v.17), showing the supreme importance of the life which Yahweh is trying to offer. But clearly God's promises cannot be taken for granted, and the people's responsibility is all the more urgent.

The third phase of the pattern begins in vv.18-20, and gives an odd twist to vv.10-12. The list of Yahweh's statutes, ordinances and sabbaths in vv.11-12 is sharpened by making them direct commands:

> I am Yahweh your God; walk in my statutes, keep my
> ordinances and do them; hallow my sabbaths so that
> they may be a sign between me and you for knowing
> that I am Yahweh your God (20:19-20).

This, however, has been preceded in v.18 by a command not to follow "... the statutes of your fathers; do not keep their ordinances and do not defile yourself with their idols". This means that the benefit which Yahweh is now finally trying to confer on the people is to warn them not to do what their fathers have done. The life of relationship with Yahweh can be achieved only by protecting the people from their own kind. The attempt is made, and even in the most pessimistic evaluation of Israel, past failures do not necessarily entail future ones. It is still possible to hallow the sabbaths; indeed since the sabbaths were given previously (v.12) as a sign that Yahweh hallowed the people, they now have the opportunity to hallow themselves and so make them into a sign of knowing Yahweh as their God. This expresses tangibly the difference between what the fathers have done and what is still possible.

The people still fail to respond, rebelling by doing the opposite. Yahweh again expresses his wrath, though he still restrains himself (20:21-22). This time, however, his threats become much more pointed than they had been before. The listeners know that the threat of v.15 not to bring them into the new land(5) had not been carried out - in contrast with that of v.23, which they themselves were at that moment bearing the full force of.

> Moreover I swore solemnly to them in the wilderness that I would scatter them among the nations and disperse them through the lands ...(6)

They would also know the reason:

> .. because they did not keep my ordinances but rejected my statutes and profaned my sabbaths and directed their whole desire after the idols of their fathers (20:24).

The same pattern is thus repeated three times, not entirely identically, but gradually working right into the present situation of exile. The exiles hear that far from there being any hope in their own people, the latter have brought them into this plight.

The climax of Yahweh's speech goes even further than the accusation of worshipping idols in Egypt (20:8):

> Moreover I gave them statutes which were not good and ordinances by which they could not live, and I defiled them with their gifts in making them offer all their first-born by fire that I might appal them so that they might know that I am Yahweh (20:25-26).

Since at no other place in the Old Testament is it said that Yahweh deliberately gave Israel bad commandments, this is perhaps the boldest of many bold theological statements. To say that Yahweh gave them commandments by which they could not live is meant deliberately and provocatively to contradict the very purpose of life in the commandments already mentioned in v.11. This contrariness is most provocatively expressed in the example of child sacrifice: they must surely react in revulsion to the practice of such degrading evil. It is the most extreme way of saying that they have gone so far that no positive offers of any kind can affect them; the only hope is that they will be appalled by the extent of their own evil-doing. The reference to child sacrifice may be to a fragment in the law (Exodus 22:29), or to child sacrifice in the time of Ahaz and Manasseh, or both; to say Yahweh himself prompted it is to declare that even the most extreme evil might, as a last desperate appeal, be the means of bringing them back to life. Utterly realistic about the people's state, the appeal suggests that things need not remain as they are.

That Yahweh himself appals the people is significant. In the account of the siege in chap.4, Yahweh himself commands the eating of food in an unclean way, which elicits an indignant reaction from Ezekiel. In chap.6 the people react to themselves with revulsion. Here in chap.20, however, things have gone so far that Yahweh himself must shock the necessary reaction from them. What is said is a significant variation of chaps.14 and 16. In the former, the people's devotion to Yahweh can be renewed by rejecting the idolatry of the elders. In the latter, Jerusalem bearing her disgrace can even be a means of justifying other peoples. In both these instances, the evil of some can be used for the benefit of others. Here in chap.20, one's own evil can be used as the means for recognizing its opposite. The ultimate importance of this apparently curious theme is thus given clear expression by its many variations.

Ezekiel now receives a new commission to speak: "Therefore speak to the house of Israel, son of man, and say to them. Thus says Lord Yahweh ..." (v.27); and, "Therefore say to the house of Israel, Thus says Lord Yahweh ..." (v.30). To draw a consequence twice tends to blunt the point of both occasions. Verses 27-29 are doubtless an accusation using different details and concepts from what has gone before(7), while vv.30-31 relate thematically to v.26 and are therefore to be regarded as the original consequence. The theme is related in a direct question to the house of Israel: "Will you defile yourselves after the manner of your fathers and prostitute yourselves in pursuance of their destestable things?" (20:30). We are thus brought back to the exiles with whose inquiry we began (v.1).

> When you offer your gifts and sacrifice your children by fire, you are defiling yourselves with your idols until the present, and I am to be inquired of you, house of Israel? As I live says Lord Yahweh - I will not be inquired of by you! (20:31).

The exiles were almost certainly not making child sacrifices but are addressed as though they are. This indicates that they do have to identify themselves with their fathers. The purpose of narrating the whole history of Israel's sin, and of provoking a reaction of revulsion is to make them acknowledge that they are not the kind of people who can justifiably inquire of Yahweh. There will be no realistic basis for an inquiry unless this acknowledgement is made.

The alienation of the readers from the fathers of Israel has been focused on to such an extent that they may have forgotten their primary concern with the exiles. These present exiles must see the nature of their people and, as they still identify with them and can be identified with them, their own nature. The additions following in 20:32ff show that the outcome was to see such judgement as restoration. Above all other chapters the two parts of chap.20 show how far back in time the recipients of restoration have to be taken, in order to become aware that there is no hope in Jerusalem (Judah) nor in the whole past history of Israel. Only restoration can provide a totally new start.

It is this totally new start which the later material(8) in 20:32-44 (vv.45-49 belong to the material in chap.21) is concerned to present, setting the necessity of transformation against the total corruption presented in the first part of the chapter. In the first part, in 20:4, Ezekiel had been commissioned only to judge the exiles in terms of the abominations of their fathers, and v.31 shows how determined he was to do this, and to hold them at that point. It would have been impossible to execute this commission, and it would have been irresponsible to do so, if he had gone on directly to speak of restoration. His determination to confront and go on confronting the exiles with the necessary judgement is seen in the oath formula as conclusion; "As I live, says Lord Yahweh, I will not be inquired of by you" (20:31). This makes a very deliberate end for it is quickly followed by another oath formula in vv.33(9) This suggests that the oath formula is now being used as a linking device, and that v.32 has been inserted to introduce the second part, linking it with what the exiles were saying:

> That which you are thinking will never come to pass, namely what you are saying: We shall become like the nations, like foreign tribes worshipping wood and stone (20:32).

This could well be a word taken from some situation in Ezekiel's and the exiles' life, not further elaborated here, where the people express the fear that they will be absorbed by other nations. It remains to this day a matter of wonder that they survived as a separate entity, and one reason that they did is due to the fact that there were individuals like Ezekiel amongst them, who were prepared to resist absorption. His resistance to the people's claim now provides the basis for a discussion where the possibility of idolatry for some is no longer entirely denied (v.39), but combined with an even stronger conviction that there will be true worship of Yahweh in Israel's own land. What the people said at the beginning of this section roots the hope for the future in their own nature, and draws them into that future. The idols will not dominate Israel; on the contrary,

> As I live, says Lord Yahweh, it is with a strong hand, an outstretched arm, and with wrath outpoured that I will be king over you (20:33).

The people themselves are drawn here into hope for the future by salvation and judgement.

The images of the "strong hand" and "outstretched arm" are commonly used in the salvation act of the exodus (e.g. Deuteronomy 26:8) (10), but here they are connected with wrath and Yahweh's being king over them. This is the only place in the Book of Ezekiel where Yahweh is spoken of as being king, and so the expression is likely to be emphatic(11). It probably implies that Yahweh has sole, overriding rule over the nations and their gods. The exclusive role of Yahweh is asserted, not as something forced on the Israelites, but manifested in their lives by both salvation and judgement. The thought of the people in 20:32 is not now bluntly contradicted, but discussed reasonably. Yahweh's words express a lordship over the people which is not yet exhausted despite the dangers of worshipping wood and stone. Such a manifestation in Israelite lives is clearly of importance, for the new language of exodus and wrath recurs in v.34.

The new start is to be thought of in terms of a face to face judgement of what they are:

> I shall bring you into the wilderness of the peoples and will enter into judgement with you there face to face; as I entered into judgement with your fathers in the wilderness of the land of Egypt so I shall enter into judgement with you, says Lord Yahweh (20:35-36).

The phrase "wilderness of Egypt" probably explains the earlier phrase "wilderness of the peoples" as a place of judgement like Egypt, signifying that Israel can still regard herself as captive until she has gone through judgement(12). The face to face judgement is presented in 20:37-38 as an exclusion of those not prepared to give their sole allegiance to Yahweh:

> I shall make you pass under the rod and I will <count you off>(13) and purge out from you the rebels and transgressors against me; I shall bring them out of the places where they are staying, but they will not enter the land of Israel; then they will know that I am Yahweh.

"Passing under the rod" and "counting" constitute an image of shepherding. The rebels will be brought out from one fold into the other. The judgement of separation means that a totally new start can be made only with a certain kind of people, who are to be freed both from slavery and from those amongst them who are unworthy(14). The wilderness in this passage has a very particular function, comparable to Deutero-Isaiah's presentation of it as the place of Yahweh's revealed glory (Isaiah 40:3-5). Here, however, we see that the emphasis is on people totally devoted to the life represented by Israel. The efficacy of the judgement consists in their recognizing the end - "then they will know that I am Yahweh".

⁻n the first part of chap.20, references to the wilderness
are mainly negative. Although Yahweh delivers his statutes and
ordinances there, it is the place where the Israelites rebel
against him, the place where he plans to pour out his wrath
against them (vv.10-13). Later (v.23) it is the place where
Yahweh swears to scatter them. In the second part of the
chapter, however, the wilderness is ultimately positive because
it is the place where the people are purified. The importance
of the re-establishment of the people is shown by the exodus
ceasing to be an independent event, and being used instead to
lead up to that judgement in the wilderness which
re-establishes the people. The exodus theme connects from the
beginning (v.33) with the notion of Yahweh as king and judge.
Even the shepherd is a judge in this passage. Yahweh's goal is
revealed when the exodus and wilderness themes are replaced by
the holy mountain (v.40) as the foundation for a new people,
those who serve Yahweh(15).
In 20:39 a choice is given between the idols and Yahweh:

> So you, house of Israel, thus says Lord Yahweh, Go
> each one of you and serve his idols, but after
> that, if you are not going to listen to me, you
> will no longer be able to profane my holy name with
> your gifts and your idols.

The choice may be given, but one may not combine the workings
of idols with the worship of Yahweh. Allegiance to idols is
quite contrary to the correct worship of Yahweh, a prohibition
anticipating the programme of chaps.40-48(16). A particular
place and particular practices are needed to nourish the new
people, a clearly established centre for the people's life.
The exodus theme loses its independent weight, becoming
absorbed into expectation of the Jerusalem temple, which was
after all a specific institution which could be envisaged as a
centre of life and unity for all of them:

> For on my holy mountain, on the mountain of the
> height of Israel, says Lord Yahweh, all the house
> of Israel, yes all of it, will worship me there [in
> the land] (17); there too I shall accept them and
> shall require your contributions, the choice of
> your dues and all your dedicated offerings (20:40).

Everyone (stressed strongly) must serve and be accepted. The
expression "accept them" is sacrificial terminology (sacrifices
can be accepted by Yahweh), but applied in this case to people!
This is stated explicitly at the beginning of v.41, "As a
pleasing odour I shall accept you ..." The people accepted are
the ones now addressed, the exiles who have been brought back
from the places where they are still scattered (v.41). The
promise is that these can become a new people unified in their
response, and their unity and acceptance manifests the holiness
which is then visible beyond Israel (v.41). It might be said

that the alienation in the first part of the chapter has itself
become alienated, transformed into unity and acceptance.

It is this which puts into focus Yahweh's work of salvation
in finding its end "only" in the temple. Against the
background of unity and acceptance it is said that people will
know Yahweh when he brings them into the land of Israel (v.42).
In 11:16 the sanctuary expresses hope for the exiles' future.
Now that hope is fulfilled even when the people remember their
past evil ways and deeds by which they defiled themselves.
They now realize the significance of Yahweh's action in not
punishing them as they deserve for the sake of his name
(vv.43-44). It recognizes that the reaction of remembering
past evil rather then forgetting it, can itself be used for the
transformation of that evil. The two parts of chap.20 signify
that the total corruption of Israel can actually lead to the
recognition that even the greatest human evil does not preclude
restoration.

15. FINAL PUNISHMENT AND TOTAL REVOLUTION: 20:45 - 21:32

The material in previous chapters has shown that all the
leaders of the people, prophets, elders, kings, are corrupt,
with no saviours among them. But the reaction to evil which
leads to restoration was only possible after the realization
had come that the catastrophe was going to include everyone.
Now when the word of Yahweh comes to Ezekiel again, he is to
set his face towards the south and prophesy against the forest
land of the Negeb (20:45-46). The Negeb is generally used as a
geographical term for southern Judah, but two other words are
used for "south" in v.46. This taken together with Ezekiel
saying in v.49 that the people have understood him to be
talking in riddles, suggests that the people are being
deliberately provoked into wondering which territory will be
destroyed. The Negeb, we realize, is not a distant territory
in the south, because the interpretation in 21:2 speaks of
Ezekiel setting his face against Jerusalem. It thus seems most
likely that the Negeb stands here for Judah as such, being
thought of as south of Babylon(1). It is a question too of the
purpose of making an identification, as the forest of the Negeb
is a clear-cut image for something which must be burnt:

> I am kindling a fire which will consume every fresh
> and every dry tree among you; the blazing flame
> will not be quenched, and every face from the south
> to the north will be scorched by it (20:47).

All possible means are used to get a hearing, showing the
importance of the reaction of the people for any further

development. The riddle's purpose, getting people thoughtfully involved, is effected with vivid imagery. At the same time Ezekiel's own reaction in v.49 shows that the people need to appreciate what he is talking about: "But I said, Ah Lord Yahweh, they are saying to me, Is he not talking in riddles?" The riddle forces their involvement, but they must also be told directly.

Destruction by military catastrophe includes everyone, for "righteous and wicked" (21:3) is an expression of totality. This chapter shows that not only the leaders are concerned, but that the first emphasis must be placed on the people. They must recognize what is directed against them, indeed that their own God is actually determined on their total destruction (21:3).

The imagery of the sword applied to Yahweh himself now communicates this destruction in yet another way:

> Look I am against you, and I shall draw my sword
> from its sheath and shall cut off from you both
> righteous and wicked (21:3).

The drawn sword is a clear image of destructive intention. The destruction of the population of Jerusalem itself is so appropriate that it is expressed as Yahweh with drawn sword against his own people. To see Yahweh as a battle hero against the nations may have been natural enough for ancient Israelites, but as a soldier personally brandishing his sword against his own people could only have horrified them. The image of the sword effects face to face hostility, far more personal, for example, than Yahweh throwing the Egyptian horse and rider into the sea (Exodus 15:21).

Thus everything possible is being done, without equivocation, to convey the immediacy of what Ezekiel sees. At the point that the image of fire changed to that of sword, thus becoming more particular, a universal implication is drawn: "All flesh will know that I, Yahweh, have drawn my sword from its sheath; it shall not be returned again" (21:5). Not only is destruction coming, but no argument whatsoever can be made about its justice.

If it is an intense experience, it is also a broad experience. The face-to-face hostility which the use of the sword produces leads to an emotional reaction from Ezekiel, with his emotions themselves becoming part of the communication:

> Now you, son of man, sigh with breaking thighs and
> with bitterness; sigh where they can see you; and
> when they say to you, Why are you sighing? you
> shall answer, Because of the news. When it comes
> every heart will melt, all hands will droop, all
> spirits will become faint, and all knees will run
> with water. It is coming and will certainly
> happen, says Lord Yahweh (21:6-7).

Ezekiel's part in the news of the destruction of the people is to sigh, and this becomes a focus of attention for the people who are themselves drawn in by his personal participation. The breakdown of the whole physical and mental constitution of a people is represented in Ezekiel himself: the thighs (loins) were the place of male strength and this too is diminishing(2). So long after the defeat of Jerusalem and the exile of its inhabitants, it is hard to imagine what it meant for them, but the reader must realize that this is a complete crisis in confidence, the breaking of a whole people militarily, socially, politically - and religiously. How much more so when one's own God has caused it, when the foundation of religion as the meaningful integration of life is removed without compromise. It is a state of incontinence where people no longer have any control over themselves: a state comparable perhaps to that suffered by certain indigenous populations and brought about by white people.

Peoples who have not for a long time gone through total defeat and degradation have a great deal to make up in understanding. "It is coming and will certainly happen, says Lord Yahweh." It is even harder to accept that no complaint about the justice of such defeat and degradation can be made. Ezekiel's emotions are not those of a queasy weakling, with a supersensitive conscience unworthy of the people as a whole. In reacting as he does, he is a proper Israelite whose reactions will, of necessity, be those of all Israelites.

All this seemed so implausible that it was never really possible to present it in enough ways. It had to be elaborated in song, poetry, perhaps even dance(3). The sword is given both a poetic and a practical edge - for whirlwind slaughter:

> A sword, a sword is sharpened and also polished, it
> is sharpened for slaughter, polished to flash like
> lightning ... (21:9-10).

This "Song of the Sword" demands that the sword be taken seriously. It can be seen and addressed as glittering for action. Verse 11 emphasizes that the sword is polished for the very purpose of being handled; it is both sharpened and polished to be given into the hand of the slayer. This provokes a wailing reaction in v.12:

> Cry out and wail, son of man, because it has come
> against my people, against all the princes of
> Israel; they also have been <delivered>(4) to the
> sword together with my people - therefore slap your
> thigh.

The wailing occurs because the sword is being used against all classes of people, even all the princes. Slapping of the thigh is a sign of grief(5).

By wailing and slapping his thigh Ezekiel shows a personal reaction which is both inward and outward. Another outward reaction, handclapping(6), is to set in motion the multiple actions of the sword:

> Now then, son of man, prophesy and clap your hands;
> let the sword work doubly, triply; it is a sword
> to make slaughtered men, a sword of slaughter, the
> great sword penetrating them deeply (?)(7) (21:14).

The sword seems to have a certain independence (though commanded by Yahweh's word, v.17), which emphasizes its inevitable power. Its reality must be faced. The realistic background is further filled out in v.16 which possibly contains commands from military drill(8): "<Cut sharply>(9) to the right and thrust to the left where your edge is directed". Thus the sword itself is addressed directly, leading up to Yahweh's own words and confirming the prophet's gestures: "I also clap my hand and satisfy my fury - I Yahweh have spoken " (21:17). Yahweh himself lets loose the sword against his own people. The exiled hearers find this is so difficult to grasp that it has had to be presented to them in song.

The sword is no ornament, but for slaughter, and 21:18-24 demonstrates this by returning to the present and the imminent departure of the king of Babylon for Jerusalem. The date is probably 589 B.C. when Nebùchadrezzar set out for the west because of a rebellion against him(10). What happens is judged to be justly directed against Jerusalem, so that even the Babylonians' doings can be presented as a symbolic action. Ezekiel presents a literal picture full of dramatic tension. He is to sketch out two roads which the the sword of the king of Babylon cdould take, and also to show signposts on the roads, one leading to Rabbah in Ammon and the other to Jerusalem (21:19-20). The tension is heightened by making the listeners wait and see what the king of Babylon will do at the crossroads: will he perhaps after all choose to go to Ammon and not to Jerusalem?

The action continues, showing him using oracular means to decide:

> For the king of Babylon stands at the crossroads,
> at the parting of two ways. In order to receive an
> oracle, he shakes the arrows, he inquires of the
> teraphim, he inspects the liver (21:21).

The arrow oracle was not known in Babylon(11); it was possibly performed by shaking arrows in a quiver until one sprang out, or one was taken at random, like drawing lots. Zechariah 10:2, for example, suggests the teraphim may have been masks behind which a functionary uttered oracles. In fact the only procedure typical of Babylon mentioned here is the liver inspection: clay models have been found formed with divisions as marks for interpretation. Listing these various methods indicates that Nebuchadrezzar uses every available means to find out the will of his gods. So certain is the outcome that Israelites are obliged to accept the revelation even of Babylonian gods (12)!

> Into his right hand comes the lot for Jerusalem -
> [to set battering-rams](13) to open his mouth with
> a shout, to raise his voice with a war-cry, to set
> battering-rams against the gates, to throw up siege
> works and to build a siege mound (21:22).

The choice has now been made, leading directly to the violent siege of Jerusalem. Even now the Jerusalemites will not accept the obvious: "To them it seems like a false divination". "They swore great oaths", probably refers to Zedekiah's oaths of allegiance to the Babylonians after the first defeat of Jerusalem. They ought to have been prepared to recognize their guilt and the justice of what is happening. Even the Babylonian Nebuchadrezzar is a kind of public prosecutor before Yahweh, reminding them of their guilt (v.23) (14). Yahweh does not need to be reminded since they themselves, in making their crime plain, have been their own prosecutors (v.24). To say that both Nebuchadrezzar and they themselves prosecute means that their guilt has been demonstrated correctly in a legal way. Such is the nature of all Jerusalemites - plain in their own guilt - which Ezekiel wished to reveal to the exiles.

In 21:12 the sword is turned against Yahweh's people, including all the princes of Israel. Appropriately there follows 21:25-27 with the king himself (Zedekiah) being addressed thus: "But you, unhallowed godless man, prince of Israel whose day has come to the final judgement". What a brutally direct way of expressing the end of the hallowed Davidic monarchy and all it meant religiously, politically and socially for Israel! No hope is left now, even in the king. He is stripped of the insignia of rank:

> Thus says Lord Yahweh, Remove the turban and take
> off the diadem. Put a stop to everything as it is:
> exalt the low and abase the lofty (21:26).

The end of the kingship means that everything has to be subverted. A decisive end is reached for everyone, a totally new start must be made. The day of the king's final punishment entails the coming universal revolution. This being clear, it is not likely that v.27 is to be understood postively, far less messianically as has often been done(15). The meaning is rather obscure, but it may be something like this:

> A ruin, ruin I have made it, but this too will not
> have been until he comes to whom belongs the
> execution of judgement and I have given it to him.

On this understanding, it means that there will be a time when the ruin of Jerusalem is seen to be complete. But the exiles must realize that they still have the experience of this catastrophe before them. It is even harder to acknowledge that the execution of this judgement on Jerusalem has been legitimately given into the hand of none other than their own Babylonian captor, Nebuchadrezzar! Possibly a connection is intended with v.23 if Nebuchadrezzar is represented there as the official prosecutor; now he is the executor of judgement and it is given to someone both justified in having the office and capable of performing it. Such is the necessary inference from the linking of Yahweh brandishing the sword with the conquest by the Babylonians. The exiles can no longer be in doubt.

The last section on the Ammonites, in chap.21:28-32, is a later addition, but is appropriate in that it expresses the judgement on all people. The question arose: what happened to the Ammonites, allies of the Judaeans, the road to whose city Nebuchadrezzar did not take at that time? They do not escape the sword and the fire either(16). There is no respect for human life anywhere.

16. THE EXILES TO ACCEPT JUDGEMENT ON JERUSALEM: 22

Chapter 20 showed that no reliance could be placed in the history of Israel. Chapter 21 describes graphically the only thing on which people could rely: Yahweh's sword. Now chapter 22 demonstrates that the guilt bringing about the judgement of Jerusalem accurately reflects her nature. Jerusalem is the bloody city(1) (v.2), a very different name from the faithful city which Isaiah (1:26) envisaged, and more to be equated with the bloody city of Nahum (3:1). That city was Nineveh, a model of wickedness. No less a comparison than this is seen to be necessary. Perhaps something of the anguish this meant is found in the interrogative expression: "... will you judge the bloody city and make known to her all her abominations?"(22:2). "Bloody" is an expression for violent crime and for continuing guilt in all spheres of life. There can only be a direct accusation of her guilt, introduced by a description of her state: "... a city shedding blood in her midst so that her time (of judgement) comes, and making her idols so that she becomes unclean" (22:3). This is the first of a number of references to "in her midst" or "within her", which suggest that the city's own guilt is becoming endemic and is bringing its own consequences(2).

The accusation in terms of law lends another dimension to chap.20, which had been expressed in terms of history.

You are guilty through the blood you have shed, and

110

through the idols you have made you are unclean,
and hereby you have made the days (of your
judgement) come near, and you have come to the time
(of your end) (22:4).

The moral and cultic transgressions for which she is
responsible are here summarized. The catastrophe is about to
happen now, is obvious to everyone else, if not to Jerusalem
herself:

Therefore I have made you an object of scorn to the
peoples and a laughing-stock to all lands. Both
those near and far from you will mock you, O you
who have a reputation for uncleanness and who are
great in tumult (22:4b-5).

Jerusalem has become so infamous that she has removed herself
beyond the pale for everyone. If Jerusalem is an object of
scorn to peoples, she is in a state as bad as or even worse
than the exiles themselves. Nothing could throw the exiles
more on to their own resources than this.

The many instances of the expression "within you" show
clearly the fixed nature of Jerusalem. The princes within you
rely defiantly on their own power to shed blood (22:6);
in you, father and mother are treated with contempt;
sojourner, orphan and widow are oppressed (v.7); sabbaths are
profaned (v.8); there are slanderers within you and those who
commit lewdness (v.9); sexual transgressions in you
(vv.10-11); and in you there are those who take bribes and
demand interest (v.12). They do these things to "shed blood",
and since it is used of misdemeanours such as slander, not
necessarily connected with physical violence, the phrase
indicates the breakdown of relationships in all spheres of
life. That they do these things in such different situations
indicates that they have forgotten him, says Lord Yahweh
(v.12b). There is no future for the exiles in the city of
Jerusalem.

The verses in 22:13 -16 express a lack of permanence. Yahweh
claps his hands against their profiteering and violence,
probably meaning to make these disappear(3.) They are scattered
among the nations as a result. This is meant so seriously that
Yahweh will even allow himself to be profaned on their account
in the eyes of the nations.

Verses 17-22 show that all the people are involved. Here
there is an image of Jerusalem as a furnace to which the house
of Israel is brought. All of them, whether they be thought of
as silver, bronze, tin iron or lead have become dross as far as
Yahweh is concerned (22:18), and are brought into Jerusalem as
metals are brought to a furnace to be melted (22:19-22). The
Exodus has been described in a different way (Deuteronomy 4:20)
as Yahweh bringing the people out of the iron furnace to be his
own inheritance. But to say that Yahweh brings Israel to
Jerusalem to be melted in his wrath suggests utter rejection

rather than intimate acceptance. It may seem strange to be brutally insistent, but it shows how debased the population of Jerusalem had become. It is the opposite of the modern propensity to look desperately for extenuating circumstances in the case of one's own country while being all too quick to condemn another.

The final two units of chap.22 were probably originally independent of vv.1-16 (4), but they each have their own emphasis to add. The last (vv.23-31) describes a land without rain, intended to present the day of wrath as one of arid drought (v.24) (5): a suitable image for any place which has so exhausted itself with evil that it is quite incapable of bringing forth any new growth. All professions are involved: even the princes and officials of the land are likened to lions or wolves tearing their prey, consuming people, seizing valuables, making many widows, all for dishonest gain (vv.25, 27). It pictures corrupt administration, a noble class in power who deny themselves no violence in the execution of their power. But it is not only the princes: The priests (v.26), the prophets (v.28) and the people of the land (v.29) are also implicated, summing up much that has been said in previous chapters about the leading classes. The priests, rather than teaching Yahweh's torah, do violence to it. None of the traditions of Yahweh are used as a healing influence.

The prophets are introduced after the description of the officials who act for dishonest gain. But rather than carry out their proper function of exposing such conduct, they condone it. They fabricate false visions and make fraudulent divinations claiming, "Thus says Lord Yahweh", when Yahweh has made no communication at all. So not only the princes are at fault. What the princes do, even though it entails the suffering of the people, is intensified by the very people who should counter it. The destruction of Jerusalem is expressed brutally because there is no other alternative, when even its most creative representatives have been sucked into the prevailing destructiveness.

> The people of the land have practised extortion and committed robbery; the weak and poor they have oppressed, and they have <acted>(6) towards the stranger without redress (22:29).

Thus all those with power abuse it in a similar way. One cannot make the commonest human excuse, which is to place the blame on one particular class or section of society. The intense emphasis on the nature of the city leads to the acknowledgement that there is not one person anywhere who resists what is happening;

> I looked among them for a man who would build a wall and stand in the breach before me on behalf of the land so that it not be ruined, but I found no one (22:30).

Ezekiel probably elaborates a word of Zephaniah's (3:3-4) which, like other prophetic accusations (Micah 3:11; Jeremiah 5:31), makes a summary indictment; but Ezekiel goes beyond Zephaniah in not omitting even princes(7). There is no exception, it seems, even among them, the reason for the total judgement expressed at the end in 22:31. It demonstrates to those already judged, the exiles, the legitimacy of the judgement on all still in the land. Only thus is there hope for the future. The acceptance of the worst is not the worst, as is commonly thought, for it is the only way to a new beginning.

17. DO THE EXILES STILL WISH TO PUT THEIR TRUST IN JERUSALEM?: 23

The modern reader might think it excessive to find that, after depicting Jerusalem as a prostitute in chap.16, the Book of Ezekiel goes on in chap.23 to an account of the licentious conduct of the two sisters, Samaria and Jerusalem, the infamous Oholah and Oholibah passage. However, while chap.16 is concerned with Jerusalem's unfaithful conduct in the cult, 23 looks mainly at unfaithful conduct in political alliances. Thus we must realize that the Book of Ezekiel is not like a modern book; it speaks to different situations at different times, reinforcing convictions which had probably not made any lasting impression. Even so, there are more differences between chaps.16 and 23 than are at first apparent. This can be seen immediately after the word-event formula in 23:1:

> Son of man, there were two women who were daughters
> of one mother. They prostituted themselves in
> Egypt in their youth; they had their breasts
> pressed there, their virgin breasts handled
> (23:2-3).

The image of sisters, relations, was not present in the basic text of 16, which was primarily concerned with one girl. And whereas in 16 Yahweh directly addresses Jerusalem - an address which despite its savagery has a positive effect on their relationship - here in 23 the prophet receives a narrative from Yahweh, with the sisters being referred to in the third person. Thus when an address to Jerusalem does finally come in vv.22ff it is all the more abrupt(1). Even in 16 the effect on the audiences is to observe the degradation of Jerusalem at some distance, so that the long third person address in 23 has the effect of removing the participants even further from the hearer. Things are so bad with the participants, it seems, that they themselves are excluded until the final application is made.

Chapter 16 pictures a loving relationship between Yahweh and Jerusalem, existing from the time she is a foundling to the time when she is a young woman; 23, however, does not mention this, opening rather with the statement that the sisters prostitute themselves in Egypt in their youth (23:3). The substance of 23 must have originated at a time when the nature of Jerusalem was viewed even more seriously than at the time of 16. Israel's sin derives from the very beginnings and is a family characteristic, the second sister being more depraved than the first. The comprehensive charge is compounded not only with the whole history of the people as a family, but also with place. Instead of Egypt being the sphere of Yahweh's deliverance of Israel, it is now the place of her first, one might almost say, primeval, sin against him. The reference to sin in Egypt may mean that the passage can be dated in the last few years before the destruction of Jerusalem, when there has been a further rebellion against Babylon in the hope of obtaining help from an Egyptian alliance(2).

The passage belongs to a time of great urgency, which another difference between 16 and the very first verses of 23 confirms: while 16 has a description of illicit sex in its climax in v.25, chap.23 starts with one, and repeats it: "they had their breasts pressed there, their virgin breasts handled". Such poetry of abhorrence does not wish to procrastinate. There are now no extenuating circumstances whatsoever.

The names used may be intended to emphasize the abhorrence:

> Their names were Oholah for the elder and Oholibah
> for her sister; they became mine and bore sons and
> daughters [and their names: Oholah is Samaria and
> Ohlibah Jerusalem] (3). But Oholah had sexual
> relations elsewhere instead of with me ...
> (23:4-5).

Exactly what the names are meant to convey is not entirely clear(4). That a Hebrew word 'ōhel means "tent", suggests an association with the Bedouin, that is, the sisters were not natives to Egypt, but came from the desert, and belonged to those nomadic people who live in tents and herd animals. However, it is not really clear why Ezekiel would want to make such a point; he could possibly argue that these were people just like the Israelites, or at least like their ancestors. Even so, one wonders whether the term is sufficiently derogatory. It is possible that there is some allusion to "tent girls", that is, to prostitutes who attach themselves to the Bedouin.

In any case, the theology of v.4 means that they become Yahweh's. Yahweh is prepared to accept them after their promiscuity in Egypt. It is thus a clear case of Oholah's crass infidelity that she has sexual relations elsewhere. This is a bold theological statement; but the metaphor does imply that Oholah ought to have her sexual relations with Yahweh(5).

114

Oholah has callously perverted the most intimate relations.
The crudely effective image of the unnaturalness, lustfulness
and debasement of Samaria's relationships with the Assyrians,
is now described:

> But Oholah had sexual relations elsewhere instead
> of with me: she lusted after her lovers, towards
> Assyria, warriors clothed in purple, lords and
> governors, all of them choice young men, horsemen
> riding on horses. It was to them that she directed
> her sexual advances, all of them the pick of the
> Assyrians ... (23:5-7).

This description of her infidelity reveals Oholah's (Samaria's)
hankering after the flamboyance of foreign military
masculinity. Her punishment, appropriately, is at the hand of
her own "lovers":

> Therefore I delivered her into the hand of her
> lovers, to the Assyrians after whom she lusted;
> they uncovered her nakedness, seized her sons and
> her daughters, and slew her with the sword ...
> (23:9-10).

To be delivered by Yahweh back into the hands of the same
lovers brings out the ironic justice of being punished by her
own "lovers". It demonstrates the emptiness of what had gone
before; nothing genuine existed. The only role of the
Assyrians is to carry out the inevitable and disastrous
consequences.

If this happened to Samaria, it could not be ignored by
Judah, because they were sisters (23:2). But even though Judah
saw what happened to her sister, she behaved worse - as the
contrast shows: "Her sister Oholibah saw this, but her lust
was even stronger than hers and her prostitution even worse
than her sister's"(23:11). The shorter passage on Oholah at
the beginning functions principally to contrast with Oholibah,
on whom the main focus rests. In the time of exile, it is the
condition of Judah which must be faced without flinching.
Lusting after foreign men, Oholibah does something Oholah had
not done, sending messengers after the Babylonians (23:16),
brazenly attracted by mere appearances. She is worse than her
sister, for she does not see men in person at first, but only
portrayals of them on the wall (23:14). (This may refer to
reliefs outside Jerusalem, using minium to sketch outlines in
red(6).) Like someone who sees a colour photograph in a foreign
magazine, and sends for that person on the basis of the
superficial image,

> When she saw men portrayed on the wall, images of
> Chaldeans sketched in vermilion with sashes around
> their waists and flowing turbans on their heads,
> all of them looking like officers, a likeness of

Babylonians whose home is in Chaldea, then she lusted after them from what her eyes saw and she sent messengers to them to Chaldea (23:14-16).

"All of them looking like officers" sounds like a typical impression of the uniform of a foreign army. Her hankering after such attractive but superficial appearances leads to a degrading lack of satisfaction, because though "The Babylonians came to her bed of love and defiled her with their sexual acts, after she was defiled by them her desire suddenly turned away from them" (23:17).

Thus Oholibah rapidly tires of what she had hankered after, and what hope could be placed in such a person? The exiles must recognize this about Judah. They can only turn away in disgust; 23:18 puts it conclusively in terms of Yahweh's turning away. The blunt thrust of the argument, however, is continued in vv. 19-20:

> Yet she increased her prostitution remembering the days of her girlhood when she had sex in the land of Egypt. She lusted after the gigolos there who had penises like asses and who ejaculated like stallions.

The need to be brutally frank in painting the picture of Judah just before the final castastrophe is shown by the way in which even the statement of 16:26 is added to. Such coarse language shows that, although Judah has turned unsatisfied from the Babylonians, she greedily craves still more: Oholibah is insatiable. Is this where the exiles want to put their trust? The question must be posed by every possible means.

The first direct address to Judah, exposing the consequences of her conduct, occurs appropriately here: "Therefore, Oholibah, thus says Lord Yahweh, I am rousing your lovers against you, those from whom your desire turned away ..." (23:22). Oholibah is not to imagine that in turning away from them, she is rid of them. Once relationships, however unsatisfactory, have been established, they keep making their claims. Indeed the more unsatisfactory relationships have been, the more likely the lovers are to react in anger. Thus it is fitting that Judah is punished by her own "lovers", listed in 23:23 as the Babylonians and the Chaldeans, Pekod, Shoa and Koa (the Assyrians probably having been added from the account of Oholah). Pekod, Shoa and Koa might have been mentioned because of the foreboding o sound in their names, the first being an Aramaic tribe in East Babylonia, and the other two possibly nomadic groups from the Syrian-Arabic desert(7). A great array of troops is mustered against Judah with chariots, wagons and a host of people with large shields, small shields and helmets (23:24). "I shall give them authority and they will pass sentence on you using that authority". That Yahweh gives them the authority emphasizes more explicitly than 23:9 that Judah is justly punished by her own "lovers".

Judah's attempt to use other peoples has met with the most serious consequences, and appropriately it is the loathsome Babylonians themselves, and numerous other obscure peoples, bringing punishment upon Judah. Yahweh himself confirms the conquest by the Babylonians: "I shall direct my zeal against you and they will deal with you in anger" (23:25) - the reciprocity of this statement with Yahweh directing and the Babylonians dealing makes it quite plain that Yahweh's zeal for his people is seen in what the Babylonians do. The nature of Jerusalem has led to the most vigorous reaction against what the Judaeans are and do. The harshness of this reaction is indicated by the cutting off of nose and ears (23:25). Punishments by mutilation are rare in Israel's law(8); here they are not ends in themselves, but occur so that "I shall put an end to your lewdness and your prostitution from the land of Egypt that you will not pay regard to Egypt or remember it any more" (23:27). Not remembering Egypt means not that it is literally to be put out of mind, but that the ways associated with it will no longer be of any effective influence.

Thus this long and degrading narration ends offering no hope for Judah in alliance with the Egyptians: Judah herself has changed the association of Egypt with deliverance to degradation, which goes further even than chap.16. Moreover, the idea that Judah, out of her degradation, will pay no more heed to "Egypt" means that the purpose of this objectionable harangue is to afford just a hint of hope even in the midst of destruction by the Babylonians. If all confidence is lost in that which provides no true basis for confidence, then something will have been achieved.

23:27 brings the narrative to an unexpected but clear conclusion. A strong statement of the destruction of Judah for which she is herself responsible follows in vv.29-31. This adds nothing except that in v.31 there is a strange new image of Judah's sister's cup now given into Judah's hand. This image has no doubt been taken from the poem quoted in vv.32-34, and v.31 is a transitional verse introducing it. The use of the poem in a composite secondary passage gives poetic expression to the fact that Judah had to suffer the same consequences as Samaria - an insult which few Judaeans would have accepted easily. Verse 35 states once again, in prose, that the consequences must be borne.

These additions are so close to the basic narrative that they are somewhat repetitious. This is not true of what still remains in 23:36-49 (9) which uses language with cultic details not mentioned before. Even more repelled by the illicit conduct of Samaria and Judah(10), the verses show that later there were groups who could conceive of it only in cultic terms. In vv.40-42 there is a further reference to sexual relations, with (in addition) sending for men and making up for them. Based as much on chap.16 as on 23, they show that in later times the narrative broadened with continual elaboration of the shocking conduct in a tone of moral indignation.

117

Finally, after the two obscure verses 43-44 (11), vv.45-49 further describe the punishment. Verse 48 makes a particular application quite different from anything before, because now the aim of putting an end to the lewdness is that "... all women may listen to reason and not act lewdly as you have done". Thus the narration proceeds to a general warning to all women in the sexual sphere. Men are left out, which means the whole point of the image is missed. Judah's extreme political and theological unfaithfulness has now become a question of female sexual morals. Some relevance to a later situation where the narrative's characterization of Judah was not so pressing must have been desired. But it effectively singles out women for attention and makes it easier to avoid a comprehensive responsibility(12). This was the intention of the original bold image. It was not a question of women alone taking warning, but of the exiles seeing the people as a whole turning promiscuously from Yahweh, which means giving up all hope for Judah in her present state. Restoration did not lie in the preservation of the status quo, but in its elimination.

18. THE PEOPLE MUST RESPOND: 24:1-14

The hope for restoration could be realized only after the siege. It is thus appropriate that chap.24 at the end of this section (like chap.4 at the beginning) returns to the siege. The ardently expected climax is now expressed: "Son of man, write down the date of this day, this very day, the king of Babylon has laid siege to Jerusalem this very day" (24:2). Finally, after all that Ezekiel has said, the time has come. The giving of a date in v.1 makes it definite: this word of Yahweh comes to Ezekiel on the tenth day of the tenth month of the ninth year of the exile, the date of the beginning of Nebuchadrezzar's siege of Jerusalem towards the end of 589 B.C. That the exiles would not necessarily believe Ezekiel's claim that the siege had actually begun, is the reason for his insistence that the exact date of the day be written down. He is deeply concerned that the exiles are again aware of what is happening to Jerusalem.

Confirmation is offered in another way when Ezekiel tells the rebellious house a parable (māšāl) in the form of poetry, a song, probably a work song (24:3) (1). Introduced by "Thus says Lord Yahweh" its effect is to present Yahweh as foreman who makes the command to do the work extremely authoritative; moreover the song has the rhythmic swing of the work in progress:

Put on the pot, put it on,   and pour water in it too.
Put pieces of meat in it,   every good piece,

Thigh and shoulder,   fill it with the best bones
                    Take the best of the flock,
And pile the <logs> under-
                    neath it: boil its <pieces of meat>(2),
Then its bones will also have been boiled inside it (24:3 -5)

The poem by itself speaks only of a preparation for a feast,
and does not allude clearly to a punishing siege(3). We saw,
however, in chap.11 that leaders in Jerusalem regarded
themselves as the best pieces of meat protected by the pot.
Thus in a context where the poem is a parable directed at "the
rebellious house", where Yahweh orders that the pot be put on
after we hear that the king of Babylon has laid siege to
Jerusalem, it seems unlikely that the pot refers to anything
but the city. The good pieces of meat and the best bones
represent the people who are to be boiled in it by the siege.
    This much is made explicit in the passage, though possibly it
was made so originally in vv.9-10 which refer directly to the
poem, whereas vv.6-8 and vv.11-14 introduce the rust of the
pot, not referred to previously(4). But in vv.9-10, Yahweh
himself makes a big pile of wood (under the pot) which is
linked directly with the "bloody city"; indeed, a great many
logs are to be heaped on, the fire lit, the meat boiled well,
and (probably) the broth poured out. What some people in
Jerusalem had previously seen as a means of protection has
become a trap where they are "boiled" and finally "poured out
like scum". The ironic change of role for Jerusalem is not to
be missed by the exiles. Since Yahweh himself piles up the
wood, nothing but degradation remains for the city, now called
bloody rather than faithful.
    Some discrepancy between Ezekiel's vision and the way people
apprehended Jerusalem's destruction when it did come, is seen
in 24:6-8, 11-14. It seemed even worse to them then than
Ezekiel had predicted. The force of what he said was not fully
apprehended at the time (he was right to write down the date of
the day), but later some people did understand and express the
true extent of Jerusalem's guilt, which they could fully
appreciate only when the destruction had actually taken place.
The importance of the people's reaction is shown as their full
understanding comes only through a combination of prophetic
speech and events. The Book of Ezekiel adds extra details to
the description of destruction, not gratuitously, but to ensure
such an understanding.
    Since vv.6-8, 11-14 speaks of rust difficult to remove, and
uncovered blood, neither of which occurs in the poem, they are
probably later additions, expressing something of the tortured
realization of the meaning of events in Jerusalem. It is in
fact far worse than was imagined; their own realization of it
is worse even than Ezekiel's. The attention shifts from what
is put into the pot to the pot itself and the rust in it. The
city is the bloody city, a pot from which the rust has not been
removed (24:6). Jerusalem is therefore seen to be a place of
unresolved guilt, "for her blood is still within her".

Jerusalem has put the blood on the bare rock's surface and has not poured it out onto the earth so that it could be covered with dust (v.7). Anyone who believed that blood cried from the ground and needed to be covered (Genesis 4:10) would think bare rock a most unsuitable place to dispose of it. Jerusalem's guilt must be unresolved, since she shows no concern about blood on the rock. Her victims have been treated callously; therefore the same will happen to her: "To rouse anger, to take vengeance, I have shed her blood on the bare rock so that it may not be covered" (24:8) (5). The pot itself should be baked on the coals, its copper burnt, its uncleanness melted, and its rust consumed. But the rust stubbornly remains (vv.11-12).

What sounds like a harsh, even vindictive withholding of forgiveness, is a recognition that forgiveness without response is impossible. Any future response (the possibility of which is not entirely denied) can only come after the sufferings consequent on her lack of response have been felt. The unalterable necessity of people's response is emphasized finally (v.14), when Yahweh speaks and acts, does not relent, has no pity, and judges according to their conduct. God as inflexible punisher only makes the importance of human response all the clearer.

19. THE PEOPLE'S REACTION TO JERUSALEM'S DESTRUCTION:
    24:15-27

Thus though it is appropriate that this chapter comes back to the siege of Jerusalem, it is all the more so when the second part, in vv.15-27, relates the people's reaction to the impending destruction of Jerusalem, and to the consequences of knowing that "I am Yahweh". The people's reaction reveals the difference between railing at a catastrophic event and being prepared to find a creative relationship even in the midst of catastrophe. Ezekiel expresses this possibility in the culminating declaration, "Then you will know that I am Yahweh". In fact here there is a pattern of, first, the word of Yahweh; secondly, what Yahweh does, a happening; and thirdly, the people's reaction to it which leads to acknowledging that "I am Yahweh". It is repeated twice, emphasizing that the elements of the pattern which we have traced for ourselves in chaps.4-24 are in this last section made explicit.

The first instance of the pattern is in 24:15-18. The first element is "The word of Yahweh came to me" (v.15), followed directly by the second element, what Yahweh does. This is perhaps the most startling example of what "The word of Yahweh came to me" can mean: "Son of man, I am about to take from you the delight of your eyes at a blow" (24:16). Verse 18, which

120

reports the death of Ezekiel's wife shows what is meant by the expression "delight of your eyes". No reason is given for Yahweh to take her; just the way she is to die is expressed, abruptly, with one word in Hebrew, "at a blow". The third element, Ezekiel's reaction, already appears obliquely in the phrase used for his wife, "the delight of your eyes".

It would be going too far to infer from this probably common endearment that Ezekiel must have had an especially good relationship with his wife. An endearment is used however, and not just the term "your wife", with which she is mentioned for the second time in v.18 (1). What happens to her is indeed of more consequence to Ezekiel than what might happen to other people, so that it is all the more striking when he suppresses his natural feelings. This does not mean, however, that they were absent, nor that the events related here could not have arisen from his shocked realization that his wife was about to die, rather than from direct divine disclosure(2).

Ezekiel is commanded to respond in particular ways for reasons which go beyond private grief for his wife. Unexpectedly, he is not to mourn or weep for his wife (24:16), a command which seems alleviated at the beginning of v.17: he is allowed to groan - but only in death-like rigidity. In other words, he is told to repress his emotions, an unexpectedly harsh command in a culture where uninhibited emotional release was customary. He is distinctly told to hold no mourning, specifically, he is to bind on his headbands, not let his hair flow wild and free as mourners did; he is to put on his shoes, not go barefoot; he is not to cover his head to the moustache, a custom supposed to make one unrecognizable to the spirits of the dead; and he is not to eat mourning bread which possibly signified a recalling to life(3). The importance of the prohibition to mourn is shown by the fact that it is much more extensive than the sparse information about the death of Ezekiel's wife. The wife dies in the evening, and the very next morning Ezekiel does as he was told (24:18) - that is all. Thus the first instance of the pattern concludes laconically.

What Ezekiel does may seem callous, confirming the idea that when someone dies it is merely Yahweh taking him. Despite possible accusations of such rationalization, it must be said directly that death is not caused by God taking people. Death comes from various natural and accidental causes. God does not cause death directly, though it may be that something of significance to do with God is learnt through people's reaction to death. What is thus learnt of God may indeed be as significant as God's direct action has sometimes been seen to be. What people apprehend of God through their own realizations and reactions is as significant (or more so) than an apparently direct divine disclosure or action, because the people themselves are integrally involved, not mere passive recipients.

Since Ezekiel's reaction is extremely unnatural for a husband, and since the term "delight of your eyes" suggests that he would not ordinarily have regarded this reaction as natural, it must be a symbolic act with an importance going far beyond itself. Ezekiel is more personally involved than he was in the symbolic acts of the siege and the exile in chaps. 4 and 12. Whatever personal suffering he felt then has been greatly extended, since it is based on a real event involving his wife. Ezekiel may have felt the siege and the exile to be truly beginning in his previous symbolic acts, and he may also have felt some discomfort in his performance of them, but now his wife has died.

Ezekiel's personal involvement in his message reaches a climax then, in the last chapter of this section on the destruction of Jerusalem. The people's reaction to Jerusalem's destruction is so crucial that Ezekiel's reaction to his own wife's death is used to express what the nature of their reaction should be. In the structure as a whole, the word of Yahweh is what happens together with Ezekiel's reaction to what happens and its implications. The word of God means being convinced that something unconventional must be done, even in a situation of extreme personal distress. The word of Yahweh, with Yahweh taking Ezekiel's wife, expresses an absolute commitment to the situation as it exists. In complete integration with an individual and a people, the word of God shows not only the need for unconventional action in the determination to use even personal bereavement for something other than itself; but also contains the confirming knowledge that it is right to do so. This is why the term "word of God" can be applied here if the appropriateness of "God acts" might be doubted. "God acts" gives an impression of something isolated, but the word of God is in inextricable connection with human reactions, however different these reactions are from normal human conduct. Conviction about a happening, consequent determination to act in a certain way, and a knowledge of confirmation, add up to an experience of being addressed.

What happens next is that Ezekiel's reaction provokes a response from the people, which in turn initiates the second instance of the pattern: word, happening, reaction, acknowledgement. When Ezekiel does as he was commanded, "The people said to me, Won't you tell us what these things you are doing mean?" (24:19). Ezekiel's symbolic act is beginning to work. What the people say - and these are the first words of the happening because Ezekiel himself has made no audible reaction - indicates that they are now beginning to relate Ezekiel's behaviour to themselves. The supreme importance of the particular situation, even of its apparently trivial aspects, is seen when the symbolic act begins to tease people's curiosity. Such a "sign" by itself would be meaningless otherwise. The word of God as conviction and determination begins to affect other people, and may lead them to a knowledge of confirmation.

It is thus appropriate that Ezekiel answers the people's question in terms of Yahweh's word coming to him: "So I answered them, The word of Yahweh came to me ..." (The way it is put may indicate that the word-event formula originated in the way Ezekiel explained himself to the people(4).) The explanation, only to be communicated through himself, does not remain individual, but expands to inform the whole house of Israel: "... the word of Yahweh came to me, Say to the house of Israel, Thus says Lord Yahweh ..." (24:20-21). Ezekiel explains the coming to him of Yahweh's word by applying it to the people's situation. For Yahweh, having taken Ezekiel's wife, now profanes his own sanctuary, which belongs to both Yahweh and the people. The sanctuary is given the same name as Ezekiel's wife, "the delight of your eyes", as well as "the pride of your strength" and the "object of your desire". That the description is much more extensive for the sanctuary than for the wife indicates the importance of the people's reaction to the destruction of the sanctuary. To say that Yahweh profanes his sanctuary can only be understood as a much more far-reaching statement than Yahweh's taking Ezekiel's wife. She dies and that would (ordinarily) affect him. But the destruction of the temple undermines the whole people's existence. The temple was of course destroyed by the Babylonians, but to say that Yahweh profanes it means that they all have to face a completely new beginning, both in the religious and the personal sense: "... and your sons and your daughters whom you have left behind will fall by the sword". The last chapter of this section on Jerusalem's destruction is the first to mention that the exiles still have children left behind in Jerusalem(5). These people must therefore accept the necessity of and justification for the the destruction of their own children. They more than anyone are not permitted to say resentfully that it should never happen. The unconventional address connected with personal, political and religious life has broadened to its fullest extent.

The people must react by applying Ezekiel's reaction to their own situation. They must accept the rightness of what is happening by obeying the command to forgo even the comfort of mourning. What had seemed odd about Ezekiel's conduct is a sign to them: "So Ezekiel will be a sign to you: just as he has done so shall you do"(24:24). Ezekiel as a sign can achieve his purpose when the people react in the same way as he does.

Concluding this applied instance of the word, happening, and reaction pattern, the narrative next speaks of the consequences of acknowledging that "I am Yahweh": "When this happens, Then you will know that I am Lord Yahweh" (24:24). The whole matter will be confirmed when Jerusalem is destroyed, and in the people's reaction to its destruction. Knowing that "I am Yahweh" when this happens, follows immediately on saying to the people, "just as he has done, so shall you do". The knowledge that "I am Yahweh" appears in the combination of Ezekiel's reaction, the interpretation of Jerusalem's destruction, and the people's application of it to themselves. Conventional behaviour would leave unfulfilled the necessary purpose. The destruction of Jerusalem and what the people must do are now unavoidable. For those who do not shirk this, there is a possibility of restoration.

The second instance of "knowing that I am Yahweh" comes in an appendix added later (24:25-27), possibly in two stages, since v.26 speaks of a deportee on the day of Jerusalem's fall rather than of Ezekiel(6). But this emphasizes how important it is that the people continue to react properly over a period of time and so arrive at unexpected possibilities:

> Now you, son of man, is it not so, on the day I take from them their stronghold, their wonderful joy, the delight of their eyes and the object of their desire ... on that day your mouth will be opened [<to>? the deportee] (7) and you will speak and no longer be dumb - so you will become a sign for them and they will know that I am Yahweh (24:25, 27).

This passage appears prematurely, since Ezekiel's present intention is clearly to focus attention on the people's reaction to the destruction of Jerusalem. The addition has come about because of a subsequent insertion, the collection of the nations in chaps.25-32, and it is felt necessary to link chaps.24 where news of the fall of Jerusalem is given, with 33, where Ezekiel is free to speak again.

Placing this material here, however, does anticipate the result of the people's correct reaction over a period of time. There will come a time when Ezekiel reacts to Jerusalem's destruction not by restraining his mourning but by opening his mouth and speaking; and the clear implication is that he will speak restoration, not destruction. Ezekiel will be such a sign to the people that they will acknowledge that "I am Yahweh". This will entail their acknowledgement that destruction is legitimate, and also their realization that restoration is possible. There is after all a way ahead, become possible through an unnatural reaction to the destruction of Jerusalem. Thus the pattern of word, happening, reaction and acknowledgement that "I am Yahweh" has led to a very significant climax indeed. Based in what it is, the knowledge that "I am Yahweh" means not just hope, but confidence in renewal.

In the passage as a whole, knowing that "I am Yahweh" is mediated through the word of Yahweh. Conviction, determination, confirmation and confidence are experienced as a personal address, known through a person with special apprehension. People were not previously aware of the word of God in this way either in connection with themselves or with others. But now both personal and applicable to others, it leads to the crucial knowledge that a happening has its significance in the people's reaction.

124

For Israelites, Jerusalem was the supreme representation of a national confidence whose bankruptcy is easily recognizable now. But there are other matters which express a bankruptcy as serious, though more difficult to recognize perhaps, for the very reason that it does not have to be connected with places like Jerusalem, but can consist in particular attitudes. It is even harder for the people to see the significance of attitudes they regard as natural than the meaning of happenings imposed on them. One example is the robust, nonchalant confidence some peoples exude which causes others to believe themselves of little account. Such aggressive self-satisfaction can both consciously and unconsciously express a contempt of other peoples, and bring about a disregard for the future. When people whose vitality depends on such self-satisfaction, however, accept the denial by others of its legitimacy, that might denote their utter collapse. But Ezekiel's reactions in such a situation, where hope is unthinkable, imply that having self-satisfaction denied is itself the way to a new beginning. The greatest contribution to such a life is to admit that apparent catastrophe may lead beyond self-satisfied bankruptcy. The present state of affairs is never permanently determined. Ezekiel will be able to speak again.

The destruction of Jerusalem is not proclaimed gratuitously in chaps 1-24. It is primarily intended for the exiles, to prepare them for the possibility of <u>restoration</u>, and open up a way for the future. Chapter 24 establishes that the siege <u>is</u> taking place and will lead to destruction, but it also insists that the people must react in a certain (unnatural) way, not by mourning this catastrophic event but accepting it as right. Chapter 33 introduces restoration as its dominant theme: v.21, which announces Jerusalem's fall, indicates Ezekiel's change of emphasis from destruction to restoration.

What is the function of chaps 25-32 which come between? What has been said up to now concerns Yahweh, Ezekiel, the Israelites and the Babylonians. But many other peoples were involved in the great events of the time. A section on the nations here concentrates neither on the Israelites' own nation nor on the greatest power of the time, but acknowledges the realities of the interdependent life of all nations. Israel was surrounded by many other nations besides Babylon. Babylon was the most powerful, but what hope was there for restoration in the face of these other hostile peoples, especially if the other nations thought Israel's God was powerless to help her? To understand these chapters it is essential to grasp that the factor which weighed above all in the relation between Israel and the nations was their attitude to Yahweh. It was only to be expected that the Babylonian defeat of the Israelites would affect the reputation of their God - and many Israelites would have believed the ensuing contempt to be justified. Thus the realism of the Book of Ezekiel is complex: it recognizes the existence of other nations and acknowledges the effect their attitudes can have on Israelites. Further, if the Israelites are to be prepared to accept restoration, all their doubts concerning the other nations have to be eliminated. The realism appears in the varied form and content of the following passages, for these express many specific attitudes and reactions of different peoples.

1. A REACTION CONCERNING YAHWEH'S REPUTATION: 25

Chapter 25 deals not with Israel's most powerful enemies, but with her closest neighbours - Ammon, Moab, Edom and the Philistines - in separate units. These units are similar in form, all being introduced by the messenger formula "Thus says Yahweh", followed directly by the word "because" giving a

reason for the following threat, which is introduced by
"therefore". The conclusion is the formula of recognition,
"that they may know that I am Yahweh". The pattern "Yahweh's
word - because - therefore - know Yahweh" has been called a
word of demonstration(1), and may look stereotyped, but its
elements make clear that there are reasons for the threats
against other nations, that consequences are seen in worldly
terms, and that any theological conclusions will connect with
these worldly consequences, or not at all. Further, though
details are less specific in the case of some than of others,
all Israel's important neighbours, east and west, are listed.
The expression varies somewhat within the form. The reason to
repudiate Ammon and Moab lies in their own words, expressing
scorn of Israel in religious rather than in political terms(2).
    Ammon's words are directed against Yahweh's sanctuary: "...
because you said Aha over my sanctuary when it was profaned
..." (25:3), but the words of Moab, though at first appearing
more harmless, probably conceal a contempt that undermines the
basic foundation of Israel: "... because Moab [and Seir] (3)
said, the house of Judah is like all nations ..." (25:8).
These words impute to Moab a knowledge that Israel has a
special relation to Yahweh, a notion they totally reject. When
Yahweh's own sanctuary and Israel's basic relation to Yahweh
are subject to the contempt of other nations, Israel must
react, not only with reference to Judah, but also towards other
peoples. Much in Judah's own theology after all should have
forced her to agree with the words of Ammon and Moab; the fact
that she does not shows additional theological resources
equipping her to see beyond the destroyed sanctuary and the
querying of her relation to Yahweh. Modern readers must not
underestimate the significance of the ancient Israelites'
concern for Yahweh's reputation, a not entirely selfish concern
which allows them to appreciate the new historical situation.
    The consequences for both Ammon and Moab, though details
differ, are that Yahweh himself will deliver them into the
power of Easterners (25:4, 10) (4). These may have been
Aramaic desert tribes who were threatening settled
territory(5). Thus, the consequences of their scorn are seen
in Yahweh's action through other peoples. Those who gloat over
the destruction of Yahweh's sanctuary probably think there is
no future for Israel, and assume that nothing similar could
happen to them. But to say that they will know that "I am
Yahweh" when they are given into the power of Easterners (25:5,
11) means that such thoughts and assumptions will be shown to
be untrue. It is impossible to be silent about Yahweh's
reputation. As these passages demonstrate, it does not exist
in isolation, but it is closely connected with the present
situation of both Israel and other peoples. The restoration of
Yahweh's reputation (and given the facts, this is impossible
without reference to other peoples) must precede the
restoration of Israel. Without this there would be no inner
substance.

127

The units on Ammon and Moab are followed by a further pair on Edom and the Philistines. Though the basic form is the same, the reason for the charge against them is different: because they acted revengefully (25:12, 15) against Judah. The corresponding consequence is that Yahweh will act revengefully against them (25:14, 17), an important theme shown when the formula of recognition is adapted to it: "... that they will know my revenge ..." (25:14) or "... and they will know that I am Yahweh when I execute my revenge upon them" (25:17).

The units on Edom and Philistia differ from the first two because they are concerned with what the people do rather than their attitudes. At least for the Edomites it may be based on the knowledge, as Obadiah 13-14 has it, that at the time of Jerusalem's fall, Edom encroached on their territory and handed over the refugees to the Babylonians. Realizing that something like this did happen, perpetrated by a related people from whom some help might have been expected, modern readers can understand more easily (even if they cannot accept) why Israelites expressed the consequences as Yahweh's revenge. It assumes too much to think that revenge would be the main theme of any Israelite accusation against foreign nations, for this is the only place in all of chaps.25-32 where the theme is mentioned. These two units expressing revenge against Edom and the Philistines are arguably the most formal in the whole collection. The two previous units express the consequences in terms of Yahweh, but linked directly with what the Easterners do; here however, Yahweh first stretches out his hand against Edom (25:13), and only later is it added, after some detail, that he executes his vengeance against Edom by the hand of the people of Israel (25:14). How the Israelites are to do this is not made explicit; and the consequences for the Philistines are all expressed in terms of what Yahweh does alone, conveyed in well-used and rather lifeless formulae.

Such a critical view is necessary because there is much said elsewhere in the Old Testament about revenge. There is no point in trying to avert attention from its possible baleful consequences. On the other hand, it is only too easy to deny the theme of revenge any legitimacy at all. Today the word "revenge" is used in the sense of retaliation for the sake of personal satisfaction. The striking thing about the majority of references in the Old Testament, however, is that they leave revenge to Yahweh(6). Not only do a preponderance of passages deal with Yahweh's rather than human revenge, but also from earlier to later texts there seems to be a development away from the people exercising revenge themselves to relinquishing that right to Yahweh. Apart from the one reference to "by the hand of Israel" (25:14), the later sense dominates in this Ezekiel passage.

To speak of <u>Yahweh's</u> revenge is to acknowledge the need for justice where <u>people</u> are almost completely powerless to achieve it for themselves. It is also striking in these passages that from the outset Edom and the Philistines are spoken of as acting revengefully, without any mention of what in Israel's

conduct they are taking revenge for. The word used (nāqām) may
mean taking advantage of people in a situation of need, so that
to call on Yahweh to act in the same way is a cry for justice
to be re-established. "Yahweh's revenge" might be interpreted
by modern people as a god relishing his revenge; but revenge
truly belonging to God rather than to people could be seen as
an alternative either to human enmity against others or to the
endeavour to forget. That revenge belongs to God is a
particularly emphatic, perhaps emotionally necessary way to say
that it is pernicious for people to take revenge, but that to
forgive is not, however, to forget. To acknowledge that the
serious issues between peoples have to be balanced out may not
always be painless, but balancing is necessary and makes change
ultimately possible.

2. A REACTION TO TYRE'S PRIDE: 26 - 28.

The short units in chap.25 quickly dispose of Israel's closest
neighbours; the subsequent collection against foreign nations
has nothing more to say of them. Chap.25 stands then in great
contrast to chaps.26-28 and 29-32 which are almost exclusively
concerned with Tyre and Egypt respectively. Why was such a
disproportion of space given to these two countries? It is
especially striking since there is no condemnation of
Babylon(1), the enemy which was affecting Israel and all her
neighbours the most at that time, a sharp contrast with
Ezekiel's later exilic colleague, Deutero-Isaiah, who directs
himself almost entirely, if in different manner, against
Babylon.
  That most attention is devoted here to Tyre and Egypt may be
because they had no wish to attack Babylon. It was not Ammon,
Moab, Edom or the Philistines who were likely to offer any
serious resistance to Babylon, but Tyre and Egypt. It is
specifically said that Tyre and Egypt do not pose any threat
whatsoever to Babylon, because it was believed that Babylon was
the agent whom Yahweh used to effect his purposes in the world
at that time: these mainly comprised Israel's own defeat and
exile. By implication Yahweh's reputation is established in
this section in terms most unusual for the assumptions of the
time. His reputation is confirmed when the people accept the
Babylonian experience as the sole factor which gives them a
continuing life with Yahweh and each other in the future.
  The first part of the first passage against Tyre is, like the
units in chap.25, in the form of a word of demonstration,
though it starts here with a date: the word of Yahweh comes to
Ezekiel in the eleventh year (of the exile), either shortly
before the fall of Jerusalem or shortly afterwards, at a time
when other nations can see that Judah is destroyed. As with

Ammon and Moab, the reason for the charge against Tyre is given in their own words:

Son of man, because Tyre has spoken against Jerusalem, Aha the gate of the peoples is broken, turned over to me; <she that was once full>(2) is now laid waste ... (26:2).

These words do not relate to Yahweh's sanctuary or Israel's special relation to Yahweh, but most likely (depending on what the uncertain expression "gate of the peoples" means) to Jerusalem's central and strategic position for the forming of political alliances. It has been suggested that Tyre's joy at the breaking of the gate of the peoples means that she no longer has to share any political importance(3). The implication for Israel is that Tyre uses Yahweh's judgement on Jerusalem for her own benefit. The words differ from those of Ammon and Moab because here what Tyre can gain from Jerusalem's destruction is explicit. With no feeling for Jerusalem, she is a spectator waiting to grasp her own advantage.

Such self-directing aspirations cannot go uncontradicted in the state of the world of the time. Yahweh incites many nations against her, expressed in imagery which does not occur in chap.25. Yahweh incites the nations as the sea brings up its waves (26:3); Yahweh will wash away her soil and make her into a bare rock (26:4) - the Hebrew word for Tyre (ṣōr) means "rock", and Tyre was originally a small rocky island; thus she will become a drying place for nets in the middle of the sea (26:5). These images suggest a much more personal preoccupation with the nature of Tyre and its future than with the nations previously mentioned: they give a realistic impression of what is to be seen as the certain future of Tyre, more important than the agency of the judgement which was at first vaguely expressed.

Since the agents of judgement continually change in the passage as a whole, concern must lie more with actual judgement than with interpreting what did happen as judgement. That is, here too judgement entails the people's reaction to a complex process rather than to one external happening. Judgement presupposes people being able to convince others that the issue is significant; the others being free either to accept or reject it. This continuing process can be seen in the verses which follow 26:1-6, where - no doubt at a later time - the agent of judgement is named explicitly as "the king of kings", presumably Nebuchadrezzar, king of Babylon (26:7) (4): a clear indication of the way that an earlier conviction of the need for judgement can be connected with later events as they take place. Nebuchadrezzar did in fact begin a long siege of Tyre after his destruction of Jerusalem. Possibly some knowledge of the Babylonian methods of assault at Tyre was used in the further elaboration of 26:1-6 in vv.7-14 (5). These latter verses no longer have the full threefold form of the word of demonstration as in chaps.25 and 26:1-6, but concentrate on one element only: they describe the consequences of a particular nation's conduct.

That the destruction of Tyre is much more elaborately described than that of the peoples listed in chap.25 shows how much more personal is the involvement with Tyre. The vivid impressions, and the conviction that not even the might of Tyre will be able to withstand the power of the Babylonians are best summed up in v.11:

> He will trample all your streets with the hooves of his horses, he will slay your people with the sword, and the pillars in which you see your strength will crash to the ground.

There is no defence against the Babylonians, a truth emphasized in 26:12 which speaks of the Babylonians throwing the soil of Tyre into the midst of the waters, even though 26:4 speaks of Yahweh himself washing it away. The climax uses an idea found already in v.4, that it is Yahweh who makes Tyre into bare rock, a place suitable only for the drying of nets (26:14). Babylon never actually defeated Tyre so thoroughly, but certainly, confronted by Babylon, Tyre was unable to take the position of political pre-eminence that was evisaged after the defeat of Jerusalem (26:2). Israelites probably saw this much more realistically than Tyrians.

Having elaborated on the consequences of Tyre's self-centred political desires, the chapter proceeds to a matter which is not found in chap.25: the reaction of other peoples to the fall of the powerful nation.

> Thus says Lord Yahweh to Tyre, Will not the islands tremble ... at the sound of your fall? All the princes of the sea will step down from their thrones and remove their robes ... they will clothe themselves in trembling, sit on the ground ... and be appalled because of you. They will raise a lamentation over you ... (26:15-17).

Here the reaction of quite different peoples shows the realism of this collection. It sees the events of the time, not just as the private misfortunes of one nation, or the advantage one nation can gain from another, but as something which affects them all. Such a reaction differs from that of Tyre towards Israel's destruction: it is not primarily one of scorn, or relishing the chance to reap the benefits, but wonder and lament rather that such a misfortune could overtake such a great nation. While it is true that this lament is not one of sorrow, it is an effective expression of the conviction that the places will be destroyed. People do not sing a lament for no reason: the statement "How you have disappeared from the seas, O renowned city ..." (26:17) is reinforced by the image of Yahweh casting Tyre down with those who descend to the pit (26:20), a shadowy after-life from which there was no return to life. The lament demonstrates that it could not be taken for granted that the Israelites could envisage the end of a place of such renown as Tyre. If Israel had to acknowledge the reality about herself, she had to do so for other peoples as well, and so view the world and its future possibilities with greater realism.

The varied collection of charges against Tyre shows how difficult it was to acknowledge these realities. Chapter 26 began with the threefold word of demonstration familiar from chap.25, elaborated on the consequences of Tyre's behaviour, and passed finally to lament. Chapter 27, however, commences with the lament and makes it the framework for the whole:

> Then the word of Yahweh came to me, Now son of man, take up a lament over Tyre and say to her who dwells at the <entrance> of <the>(6) sea, merchant of the peoples to many coasts - thus says Lord Yahweh ... (27:1-3).

The importance of the lament is confirmed since it is expressed as the word of Yahweh: the reality of Tyre's destruction is sealed. To say at the outset that the word of Yahweh is a lament makes the matter emotional: it is no ruthless proclamation of Tyre's destruction, but a genuine feeling for what is being destroyed.

Tyre's own exalted estimation of herself is to be destroyed: "Tyre, you have said, I am perfect in beauty" (27:3). The reason for what follows is again given in the words of the people, with a change in emphasis. Ammon and Moab spoke in religious triumph; in 26:2, Tyre herself had spoken of acquiring political pre-eminence; but now what she says is totally self-centred, bound up with the perfection of her own being. A significant ambiguity is posed from the beginning: on the one hand, Tyre's self-preoccupation is exposed out of her own mouth; and yet on the other, in the description of her which follows, Tyre's success is portrayed in a way which only provokes wonder at its destruction. An image of Tyre as a finely built ship makes it all the the more effective. The narrator, even if he does not compromise with Tyre's own disastrous self-estimation, has to confirm her perfect construction: "Your builders made your beauty perfect" (27:4). These builders used juniper for the planks, cedar from Lebanon for the mast, oak from Bashan for the oars (27:5-6). Fine linen from Egypt was worked in colour for the sails, purple material for awnings (27:7). Tyre has drawn on many places to obtain the best they can offer(7), and it is said that Tyre is able to draw on the best people - the inhabitants of Sidon, and skilled men and elders from various places (27:8-9 and ff.) - for the running of the ship and its commercial enterprises. Tyre is supreme among her neighbours, but none of these resources is able to save her from the shipwreck which, in the original poem, followed soon after.

Once mention had been made of "bartering for your wares" (27:9), it was logical to make an addition listing the fifteen peoples (approximately) who acted as middlemen for Tyre in about eighteen different commodities (27:12-25). This is a prosaic, formulaic list clearly interrupting the poetic theme of Tyre as a ship which will be continued afterwards(8). Scholars disagree about the original (independent) purpose of this list, but perhaps it was meant to list the geographical and commercial spheres(9). In the context of a lament over the ship Tyre, it implies that not only the ship, but all these spheres of influence and traffic perish with her.

The wreck of this magnificent ship is now described: "Onto the high seas your rowers brought you - then the east wind wrecked you in the midst of the seas" (27:26). Even with the prosaic addition of v.27 included, this description of the consequences for Tyre is short in comparison with that elaborated in chap.26. The difference between the two accounts of Tyre's destruction is that the second elaborates on the reasons and then on the reaction of other peoples. The comparatively long description of the perfect ship after Tyre's own self-estimation of beauty (27:3-9), followed by a brief mention of the actual shipwreck, means the emphasis is on **what** is destroyed rather than on the destruction itself(10).

Much greater attention is paid to the reaction of other peoples than previously. When sailors of other ships hear the cry from the ship of Tyre, they are so appalled that they disembark to stand on the shore and observe the shattering event. They lift up their voices, crying bitterly, throwing dust over their heads and rolling in ashes as a sign of mourning. Their mourning is apparently sincere: they shave themselves bald, put on sackcloth and weep in wretchedness (27:28-31). The depiction of the people in full mourning rites makes clear how extraordinary, how incomparable this fall is: "... Who was like Tyre [...?](11) in the midst of the sea ... <Now>(12) you are wrecked on the seas in the depth of the water" (27:32, 34). There may seem to be an expression of scorn in the last verse(13): "Traders among the peoples whistle over you, you have become an object of terror, you are finished for all time" (27:36). But the whistling may indicate a protective gesture to ward off bad luck(14), and in any case, the climax is in the previous verse: "All the inhabitants of the isles are appalled because of you, the hair of their kings bristles with horror, their faces are convulsed" (27:35). Unlike the reaction of some peoples to the fall of Jerusalem, whether it is one of religious scorn, acquisitiveness or self-esteem, the reaction of these people is to realize that Tyre's fall closely concerns themselves. They know they cannot stand off as observers, but that they are participants who recognize the most difficult thing of all - that the same could happen to them. Not even Tyre can restrain the power of the Babylonians, which all peoples have to accept. Such is the realism which must influence Israel's present life within the world of nations.

The unending, deepening seriousness of the condemnation of
Tyre is shown by its variety. In 28:1-10 the lament is
abandoned completely, and the prince of Tyre is confronted with
direct divine address: "The word of Yahweh came to me, son of
man, say to the prince of Tyre, Thus says lord Yahweh ..."
(28:1-2). This is appropriate since, while Tyre's words quoted
in 27:3 ("I am perfect in beauty") show an attitude of exalted
self-esteem, the words of the prince of Tyre go even further:
"... because your heart is proud and you have said, I am God,
I live in the divine dwelling-place in the heart of the seas
..." (28:2). The claim of the prince of Tyre should be seen in
contrast to the words of Ammon and Moab in chap.25. They went
so far as to scorn Yahweh's sanctuary and ridicule any special
relation between Israel and Yahweh; but the prince of Tyre now
actually claims divinity for himself. Such a claim is probably
not personal hubris but derives from ancient oriental royal
mythology which saw a close connection between royalty and
divinity. All the more reason for Israel to reject such a
claim. Whatever individual Israelite kings may have tried to
put into practice, Israel always believed that even the
kingship was a historical institution subject to the authority
of Yahweh as much as any other human institution. So directly
after Tyre's claim, an immediate contradiction is made without
further elaboration:

> ... because ... you have said, I am God, ...
> when you are man and not God but only consider
> yourself to be divinely wise ... therefore thus
> says Lord Yahweh ... (28:2, 6).

Verses 3-5 must therefore be a later addition(15):
considering the immediate and direct contradiction in v.2, one
would expect the consequence also to be drawn immediately
(v.6). Further, having totally rejected Tyre's divine claim by
saying that he only considers himself to be so, it seems odd to
proceed to the statement in v.3, "You are wiser than Daniel, no
secret can puzzle you". This could be ironic, but since vv.4-5
say that Tyre has gained great riches through his wisdom and
that his heart has become proud because of these riches, it is
more likely that the intention is to show that such an
apparently wise king has only used his undoubted skill in
commerce as a ground for pride(16). The addition acknowledges
the doubts which even some of the Israelites might have had
about rejecting Tyre's claim: there was after all plenty of
evidence of his success. But even his success can be seen
ultimately to count against him.
The true state of Tyre is described again in 28:7:

> Therefore, thus says Lord Yahweh, because you
> consider yourself divinely wise, I am bringing
> against you strangers, the most violent of the
> nations and they will unsheathe their swords
> against the beauty of your wisdom and profane your

splendour.

This returns to the theology of Yahweh, using other peoples to execute his judgement, taking up the theme of the pit (28:8), already found in 26:20. Here though it is used much more pointedly to make clear that anyone cast down into the pit cannot possibly claim to be God!

> Will you still say, I am God, in the presence of those who slay you, when you are only man and not God (since you are) in the hand of those who wound you? By the hands of strangers you will die the death of the uncircumcised, for I have spoken, says Lord Yahweh (28:9-10).

The reality of Tyre's destruction means that she cannot possibly maintain her claim to divinity. Ezekiel counters this claim with real circumstances: the lie is given to Tyre in what can be seen happening. To say that Yahweh brings these violent strangers means that events are taking place which clearly demonstrate that Tyre is not God. Even if the Babylonians' long siege was not entirely sucessful, Tyre was not able to assert herself either, and was certainly unable to put any divine powers into operation. No mention of the reaction of other peoples is made here, for the terse presentation of claim, rejection and consequence more effectively reveals the facts of Tyre's humiliation. To re-establish Yahweh's reputation in the eyes of Tyre is to soberly present the facts of what Tyre really is against the myth of her divine superiority. The task of responsibility is not only to show Israelites, but also to show foreign nations her true nature. They belong to the same world where such unrealistic claims cannot be ignored.

When the last passage concerning Tyre is reached in 28:11-19, a good deal has been said about the consequences to be brought upon her and about the reaction of other peoples to her humiliation. So it is appropriate that these matters are finally dealt with, very briefly (vv.18-19), to bring everything to one last climax. The substance of the passage is an address to Tyre which brings out the reason for her destruction by a long description of what she is. The address to Tyre as "you" is not new, but is a persistent feature throughout, unlike the units in chap.25 where only the first, Ammon, is addressed in this way. Similarly the command to speak in the form of a lament, which is understood as the word of Yahweh (28:12), is not new. This way of introducing things, expressing the conviction that the form of lament is appropriate to the reality, is already to be found in the unit on Tyre as a ship (27:2-3). Nor is it new that 28:11-29 contrasts what Tyre claimed to be, what she once was, and what she is now.

What is new is that the contrast is brought to a climax by the use of mythological motifs. Repeating the substance of 27:3, it is said that "you were the signet of perfection, full of wisdom and perfect in beauty", and also, "You were in Eden, the garden of God, your garment was every kind of precious stone ..." (28:12-13). The placing of the king of Tyre in Eden(17) is followed by other echoes of Genesis 2-3, though the clothing in precious stones and other substances suggests that even more mythological features are preserved here than there. No cherubim guard against people, for God seems to place the king of Tyre alongside the guardian cherub(18) (though the text is difficult to understand) (19); he is on the holy mountain of God(20) and he walks among stones of fire (28:14). Since he inhabits the divine dwelling-place, perhaps the king of Tyre keeps company with other divine beings. In the next verse, 15, he is said to be blameless in his ways from the day he was created - until iniquity was found in him. This suggests that the king of Tyre is like the primal man in his first intimate relation with God(21). In such a description of the dignity of primeval beginnings, reference has commonly been seen to an actual myth(22), but recently it has been asked whether it is not rather that mythological as well as other motifs are being used here. Does the reference point to the celebration of the king as a divine manifestation rather than to his being primal man(23)? This would mean that v.16 is not secondary as some think(24), for to call violent commercial activity iniquitous entails decrying the king for Tyre's commercial self-esteem.

In any case, there is only one way to characterize him: "Your heart was proud because of your beauty and your wisdom corrupted for the sake of your splendour" (28:17). The consequences rapidly come to light: Yahweh casts him to the ground so that he is exposed in his true nature before other kings (28:17); and the reaction of the peoples who know him is to be appalled. At the conclusion of a scene where the king of Tyre has been seen in divine company and with divine attributes, his fall is the most disastrous possible; he has "become a horror and it is all up with you for ever" (28:19). To say - to some extent with wonder - that a (semi-) divine figure has fallen to the depths is to leave no doubt that even Tyre is human and must share the common fate of the other peoples of the time. No power on earth - or heaven! - can prevent it.

After this obvious climax it is an anti-climax to find another short indictment of another country. It is addressed to Sidon, perhaps more for the sake of completeness than anything else; it is natural to turn to Sidon after Tyre and together with the four countries in chap.25 (Egypt is still to come), Sidon makes a total of seven. The word itself is formulaic, including a formula of encounter(25) ("Behold I am against you Sidon") which introduces the significance of the relation between Yahweh and Sidon: it is that Yahweh's glory and holiness may be manifested in her (28:22-23). Since this is the main point, it indicates an editorial desire to summarize all that has preceded it, rather than to say anything particular about Sidon(26). While such an intention is almost concealed in the formulae, to say that Yahweh's glory and holiness will be manifested in connection with a specific people in fact accurately sums up the intention of the whole to restore Yahweh's reputation. The manifestation of Yahweh's glory and holiness will bring to light that which is peculiar to Yahweh; and ultimately it must be revealed. It is the final, comprehensive expression of the Israelites' belief that, without exception, no nation will ever see its own wishes realized in the present and future situation.

The preceding section was probably intended originally as a conclusion. A second conclusion considers the effect on Israel, which can be seen from the way 28:24 begins: "There shall no longer be for the house of Israel ..." Then an image is used which is not found elsewhere: "There shall no longer be ... a thorn to hurt or a briar to give pain among all those round about them who have scorned them". The image and statement show how deeply the Israelites felt the scorn of others at their defeat and exile. The manifestation of Yahweh's holiness entails gathering them from among the peoples where they have been scattered so that they will dwell securely and permanently in the land which is truly theirs (28:25-26). The secure permanence leads to the knowledge that Yahweh is their God, and makes plain that those who have been humiliated do not always have to remain so. At the time when it is uttered, scorn may seem the ultimate humiliation, but the restoration of Yahweh's reputation means a restoration which prevails even against scorn.

3. A REACTION TO EGYPT'S POWER: 29 - 32

One might expect the summarizing conclusions at the end of chap.28 to come at the end of the collection of accusations against Egypt in chap.32, rather than at an intermediate point. Perhaps there was once a collection which did not include Egypt. It is also possible, however, that the deliberate intention was to turn attention to Egypt at the very end of the collection, so that the last word would be about her. This would be understandable since, great though Tyre was in the commercial sphere, Egypt was undoubtedly the country which presented the greatest temptation to Israel in resisting inevitable defeat by the Babylonians, for she had long tried to bolster up her defences by alliances with Egypt. The temptation Egypt presented for Israel appears in the threat in 29:16:

For the house of Israel, they (the Egyptians) will

never again be an object of trust, a trust which
brings their (the Israelites') perversion to light
every time they run after them - then they will
know that I am [Lord] Yahweh.

It must be shown that this false object of trust will also
perish. It is just as necessary for Israel to accept Egypt's
defeat as inevitable, as it is to accept her own.

This must be done in connection with the particular events
relating to Israel's defeat. The reference in 29:16 already
indicates that Egypt is being specifically related to this in a
manner not evident with the countries mentioned earlier. The
first passage on Egypt also begins with a date, indicating a
series which has been calculated to extend for about a year
before and after the fall of Jerusalem(1). Because of the
extent of what follows (unlike 28:20-23), an effective
deliberateness in the collection of formulae introduces the
address:

> ...the word of Yahweh came to me, Son of man, set
> your face against Pharaoh, king of Egypt, prophesy
> against him and all Egypt, speak(2) and say, Thus
> says Lord Yahweh ... (29:1-3).

The imposing address against Egypt (powerful though she may be)
continues appropriately with the formula of encounter:
"Behold, I am against you, Pharaoh ...", which leads directly
into a characterization of Pharaoh as that "... great
crocodile(3) which sprawls in the midst of his arms of the
Nile, who says, My own Nile belongs to me, I made <it>(4)"
(29:3). Verses 3-5, a poem expressing an attack against Egypt,
picture the power of Egypt, but as a power which can be broken.
Pharaoh is a great crocodile sprawling over the delta of the
Nile, and it has been suggested that his claim that he owns the
Nile and made it could have been based in the successful
flooding of it(5). But as powerful a beast as the crocodile
can still be captured:

> I shall fix hooks to your jaws and cause the fish
> of your streams to stick to your scales. I shall
> bring you up out of your streams together with all
> the fish of your streams which stick to your
> scales. I shall cast you off in the wilderness,
> you and all the fish of your streams; you shall
> fall onto the open field, and not be gathered or
> buried. I give you as food to the beasts of the
> field and the birds of the air (29:4-5).

Pharaoh can be brought into an incompatible sphere where he
cannot survive. Further, whereas the previous chapters are
content to address the king of Tyre, those on Egypt explicitly
extend the address to the inhabitants of Egypt(6), for they are
the fish of the streams who stick to the scales of the

crocodile and thus share his fate. Not just Pharaoh but all
the Egyptian people are about to be brought down. There is no
help to be found, therefore, among the Egyptians, and the
formula of recognition shows it: "Then all the inhabitants of
Egypt will know that I am Yahweh" (29:6). Given the happenings
described, they must make this acknowledgement.

Note too the link with the reason in the following word of
demonstration:

> Because you have been only a reed staff for the
> house of Israel - when they grasp hold of you, you
> bend and wound all their <hands>(7); and when they
> lean on you, you break and make their loins tremble
> (29:6-7).

It is not necessary to wait until v.16 to see that the
accusation against Egypt is explicitly connected with the
present situation. It refers to Egypt's unreliability as an
ally - a matter of the greatest relevance during the period of
the Babylonian conquest of Judah. The power of Egypt is known,
but so are its weaknesses. This may also account for another
difference from the Tyre passage: the reaction of other
peoples to the fall of a great power is lacking. Israelites,
having intimate experience of the Egyptians' foibles, did not
necessarily consider that the fall of Egypt (despite the
crocodile) was cause for much wonder.

The second word of demonstration in 29:9b-12 uses the words
of Pharaoh from the poem (v.3) as its reason: "Because you
say, The Nile belongs to me and I made it" (29:9) - and goes on
directly to the consequence: "therefore I am against you and
your arms of the Nile ..." (29:10). This particular word of
demonstration expresses the utter and complete desolation of
Egypt, in a way which certainly bore no relation to the reality
of Ezekiel's · time or long after it. It is also expressed
stereotypically: "... her cities will be as a desolation
among ruined cities for forty years ...", and it even claims
that Egyptians will suffer the same fate of exile as the
Israelites: "... I shall scatter the Egyptians among the
nations and disperse them among the lands" (29:12). This
sounds like a desire to have the Egyptians endure the same
sufferings as the Israelites. Certainly the vivid challenge of
the original poem has been lost in this addition.

Just as these writers conceive of the Egyptians scattered
among the nations like the Israelites, however, so they imagine
them gathered and restored. This seems to be the only passage
in the Old Testament where restoration of another nation is
spoken of in the same terms as Israel - though ultimately with
a lowly result:

> For thus says Lord Yahweh, At the end of forty
> years I shall gather Egypt from the peoples where
> they were scattered, I shall restore the fortunes
> of Egypt and I shall bring them back to the land of

Pathros, to the land of their origin; and they
will be there a lowly kingdom (29:13-14).

While the Egyptians will return to Pathros (Upper Egypt, the
old heartland of their kingdom)(8), it is clear that their fate
will be lowliness, as is repeated in v.15. Just as humiliation
can be changed into exaltation so can exaltation be changed
into humiliation; even the great Egypt "... will never again
exalt itself above the nations ..." But on the evidence of
v.16, this passage had principally to do with Israel: she must
not be tempted to place her trust in such an unreliable ally.
The writers concern themselves primarily with this, rather than
with the somewhat unrealistic fate they envisage for Egypt
(even though, compared with her past, Egypt's future was rather
less than grand).

It is therefore necessary to face realities. To repudiate
Egypt as a reliable ally was to repudiate her primarily as an
ally against Babylon. But the most thoroughgoing commitment to
the current pre-eminence of Babylon is still to find expression
in the unit to come (29:17-20), the most extraordinary passage
of the whole collection. Dated in the twenty-seventh year of
the exile (571), it is the latest of all the dated units.
Sixteen years later than the only date to be found among all
the Tyre oracles (26:1), it evidently concerns the final period
of the Babylonian siege of Tyre rather than its beginning.

The word of Yahweh to the son of man here explains that
though Nebuchadrezzar made his army work hard against Tyre -
every head was made bald and every shoulder rubbed bare -
neither he nor his army received any reward for all their
labour (29:18). This is almost certainly a reference to the
inconclusiveness of the arduous siege from about 585-572
B.C(9). Tyre was not utterly destroyed in the way which had
earlier been envisaged, so that the principal difficulty for
the modern reader is that the prophecy seems to be wrong.
Notice, however, that there are no misgivings at the
incongruity, the principal concern being simply that
Nebuchadrezzar has not received his due reward. Modern readers
may think of prophecy in terms of exact predictions, whereas
Israelites were concerned with the relationships of peoples to
one another within the significance of the whole situation.
When it says that because Nebuchadrezzar received nothing from
Tyre he will be able to plunder Egypt as wages for his army,
modern readers will wonder whether it is not an attempt to
rectify a past mistake by postponing the outcome of the
prophecy. It is not known whether Nebuchadrezzar was any more
successful in his later campaign against Egypt than he was with
Tyre; and the prophecy may seem to be continually under
postponement.

Whatever the details of Nebuchadrezzar's fortunes against
Tyre and Egypt, however, there can be no question that in this
period of Israel's history Babylon remained the power which
effectively called the tune for all the surrounding countries.
Judgement consists not merely in exact details of particular

events, but the interpretation by the people of the significance of those events for them - which <u>includes</u> all the uncertainties of what is happening(10). Astonishingly, it envisages Nebuchadrezzar being given Egypt as his reward, because the Babylonians were working for Yahweh! (v.20). Thus - whatever exactly happened to Tyre or Egypt - commitment to the reality of the Babylonian dominance is paramount. If the Babylonians are working for Yahweh, there is no future of any kind for Israel unless they are prepared to accept the state of the world as dominated by Babylon. Within this acceptance, something entirely different from Babylon's dominance will become possible. The later addition in 29:21 (11), which speaks of a horn springing forth for the house of Israel and renewed prophetic speech, adds such a new dimension.

Unlike the other chapters in the series directed against Egypt, 30:1-19 contains no imagery for Egypt, but consists of a series of statements about judgement under the messenger formula(12). The first unit in vv.1-9, describing the nearness of the day of Yahweh and the sword, may take up the theme of chaps.7 and 21 and apply them to Egypt, including all who support her. It is not totally convincing, but it does show that what has happened to Israel can just as easily happen to Egypt. No combination of alliances whatsoever affects the situation.

The next section, in vv.10-12, shows that the present situation is placed under the hand of Nebuchadrezzar, king of Babylon, who will put an end to the hordes of Egypt (v.10). The word for "hordes" (hāmôn) is used twenty-five times in Ezekiel: of these sixteen are to be found in chaps.29-32, thirteen of them being directly applied to Egypt(13). Having these "hordes ", Egypt might reasonably think she has grounds for confidence, but not so. It is necessary to recognize that the Babylonians are the most violent of peoples quite capable of bringing about complete desolation.

Egypt was a country of many places and of great religious, political and human resources, which in 30:13-19 are listed(14) to emphasize the totality of her destruction. If everything is within the sphere of the God of Israel's competency, prevarication is impossible.

The same thing is expressed differently in 30:20-26. After the direct proclamation of judgement Yahweh tells the son of man of his dealings with Egypt and Babylon. This is a suitable form for narrating what was happening between these two countries around Israel, making clear the significance of the events for Israel. A new image is used, Yahweh breaking Pharaoh's arm (30:21). A broken arm can usually heal, but this arm has not been bandaged. These references are probably to Pharaoh Hophra's intervention in the Babylonian siege of Jerusalem about 588 B.C. But the Babylonians were able to quell him, which was important for the exiles to realize when they hoped about a year later (30:20) that Pharaoh might intervene again(15).

141

The principal subject-matter, again, is what is happening, and its interpretation: there is no hope of any further successful intervention. The arm is not bandaged for healing; further, Yahweh will not only break Pharaoh's good arm as well, but break again the one which had already been broken! (30:22). This means that one disappointing experience with the Egyptians does not preclude others. It is a cruel fact that the shattering of understandable hopes in a time of crisis may even be repeated. If both of Pharaoh's arms were broken, the sword could easily be struck from his hand (30:22), which could lead to the scattering of the Egyptians among the nations (30:23). The dominant, persistent factor in all these happenings is the military activity of Babylon, expressed in v.24 which says that Yahweh strengthens the arms of Babylon, in explicit contrast to breaking Pharaoh's arms. Appropriately, the element of reaction is now added - this time Pharaoh's own reaction. Previously just the passive object of all that was happening, now "... he will groan before him like a man mortally wounded" (30:24): even Egypt shows the emotional responses to defeat. Having spoken of the strengthening of Babylon and the reaction of Pharaoh, this then is the place to say "they will know that I am Yahweh" (v.25). This leads up to a repetition of the formula of recognition after another statement concerning the scattering of the Egyptians (v.26). The narrative of fact and its interpretation relentlessly drives home to the exiles their real situation year after year.·

The address to Egypt at the beginning of chap.31 contains something new: "Son of man, say to Pharaoh, king of Egypt, and to his hordes ..." (31:2). The addition of "hordes" (hāmôn) within the address itself brings out the difference between Egyptians and Israelites(16). This is their pride, which is hinted at in the very question addressed to them: "Who are you like in your greatness?"(31:2). Such a question might be addressed to God to express his incomparability (e.g Psalm 35:10). Addressed with at least a certain appropriateness to Egypt, it suggests the haughty eminence of one country over another.

Pharaoh has already been likened in chap.29 to the massively powerful crocodile (which can, however, be caught): now for the first time he is likened to a magnificent cedar tree (an image not used of Tyre, though there is mention of the garden of God in 28:13). This cedar of Lebanon is no ordinary tree for it encompasses everything: "... with beautiful branches ... of great height and its top extending to the clouds" (31:3). Nor is its source of water an ordinary one: "Water made it grow, the deep brought it to its height ..." (31:4). The word used for "deep" (tehôm) is also used in Genesis 1; thus nourishing the tree is the primeval deep itself. The cedar is tall, taller than other trees: "Therefore it grew taller than all other trees of the field, its boughs grew many and its branches long from the abundant waters ..." (31:5). It gives shelter and protection to all living creatures: the birds use it for nesting, the animals for giving birth, all

142

great nations dwell in its shade (31:6). It is in fact the cosmic tree around which is concentrated the cohesive totality of the whole universe(17).

No tree in the garden of God can be compared to her in beauty, not even other cedars, let alone other varieties of tree (vv.7-8). The whole world is implicitly concentrated around Egypt; little wonder that the end-result is, "[I have made it beautiful] (18) Because of the mass of its branches, all the trees of Eden which were in the garden of God envied her" (v.9). The hint of resentment at Egypt's eminence, present at the beginning, is now quite specific. The implicit question is: what can come out of such relations between peoples? Even an acknowledged pre-eminence can become a reason for resentment and rejection, although all the trees belong together as trees in the garden of God.

In 31:10 the messenger formula introduces an authoritative verdict. The height of the cedar, and its pride in its height are sufficient reasons for foreigners (the Babylonians) to cut it down (vv.11-12). Its proud height turns to desolation:

> Foreigners, the most violent of the nations, have cut it down and cast it on the mountains so that its branches fall into all the valleys, and all its boughs lie broken in the water-channels in the land.

All the peoples of the earth leave its shade. The birds and the animals live on the ruined tree rather than under it (v.13). The obvious moral is that no tree may come to such ascendancy (v.14). Mortality is common to all; all go down to the pit.

A wordy elaboration in 31:15-18 mixes deep mourning with a strong, final emphasis:

> Who are you like in glory and greatness among the trees of Eden? You too will be brought down with the trees of Eden to the underworld; you will lie together with the uncircumcised, together with those slain by the sword (31:18).

This same question is addressed to Egypt at the end as at the beginning, though with directly opposed implications. At the beginning, "Who are you like?" leads to a description of great pre-eminence; at the end it leads to the acknowledgement that the fate of the pre-eminent is no different from that of their inferiors. The example of great and powerful Egypt illustrates that, in relations between nations, the end is the opposite to the beginning. No people have the natural and legitimate right to maintain pre-eminence over other peoples.

In the charges against Egypt (chaps.29-32), the dating proceeds from the tenth to the eleventh, and now finally, to the twelfth year of the exile, after the fall of Jerusalem and probably a more threatening time for Egypt. The word of Yahweh comes to Ezekiel to raise a lamentation over Pharaoh, king of Egypt (32:1-2). With Tyre, the lamentation occurs in the middle of the charges against her (27:2); withholding it until near the end with Egypt makes the threat approaching even this great nation all the more immediate.

The threat applies even when Egypt is compared with a lion: "You consider yourself to be a lion of the nations ..." (32:2). But this was only what he considered himself to be; he is told rather anti-climatically that he is really a crocodile (as in 29:3), who troubles the waters with his feet and muddies the streams (32:2). The contrast between lion and crocodile may express the distinction between clear, natural leadership which all would acknowledge and follow, and something which is uninhibited, uncurbed, arbitrary - a plunging around in the morass of power. It is appropriate that, directly after this characterization which gives the reason for the accusation against Egypt, the messenger formula should be used to introduce the consequences. This uncurbed power will be checked: "Thus says Lord Yahweh, I will spread my net over you and I will haul you up in my dragnet" (32:3). Motifs already present in 29:4-5 and 31:12-13 are repeated but filled out in a way suitable to a climax. Chapter 29:5 speaks of Pharaoh falling on the open field and being given as food to the animals and the birds, but his fate in 32:4 is even more degrading: being flung on the field (that is, without decent burial) means that the birds settle on the carcass and the animals of the earth gorge themselves. It is total exposure to open disgrace.

That the flesh of this cosmic monster spreads out over the mountains, and the valleys are filled with his carcass (?)(19) (32:5), expresses the extent of the disaster. The earth is drenched and the water channels filled with his blood (32:6). It is not merely the death of an individual, but the destruction of a power having implications for the whole world. The extent of the destruction has cosmic significance, and so has its effect. The reaction of the peoples was a common motif in the passage on Tyre, but it has only been mentioned once in relation to Egypt (rather as an afterthought in 31:15ff.). The reaction is expressed in unique natural terms which show the magnitude of what is being destroyed:

When you <are>(20) blotted out, I shall cover the heavens and make their stars dark, I shall cover over the sun with cloud and the moon will not give its light. All the bright lights in the heavens I shall make dark over you, and I shall bring darkness on your land, says Lord Yahweh (32:7-8).

Pharaoh's fall will thus necessarily affect other peoples: "I shall trouble the heart of many people when I bring your <captives>(21) among the nations to lands which they did not know" (32:9). That Yahweh is said to cause this reaction brings to a climax the conviction that Pharaoh's uncurbed power will be checked.

The messenger formula introduces Babylon as agent: "For thus says Lord Yahweh, The sword of the king of Babylon will come upon you" (32:11). The prophet is convinced that what Yahweh does is happening through Nebuchadrezzar's conquests. The threats are now extended to all Egyptians through a direct confrontation with the prevailing military situation. The consequence of their pride is that Egypt's hordes will fall by the sword of the mighty Babylonians (32:12). With the destruction of Egypt's pride, nothing is left. Where power, in v.2, was expressed as the troubling of waters, in significant contrast it is said here that no man's foot will trouble them any longer; the waters will be settled and rivers flow like oil (32:13-14). This picture of undisturbed peace is to be set against the picture of the land of Egypt in desolation (v.15): this is indeed a lament over Egypt (v.16). Such a lament is not sung without cause. That Yahweh declares it means that the final obstacle to Israel's commitment to reality has been removed.

From the beginning of the final unit on Egypt (32:17-32), the Egyptian hordes are the explicit subjects of lamentation. For the first time too, the theme of going down to the pit is taken up at the outset. In this regard the Egyptians belong with other peoples, and do not hold a unique position (32:18). For a people to realize that they are not by nature on a higher plane than others is a most important insight. For the first time the theme of a common fate is combined with the question to the pre-eminent nation: "Who do you surpass in beauty? - Go down and be laid with the uncircumcised" (32:19). They are greeted by mighty heroes already there (32:20-21).

Next are listed all the great nations of the past who have already fallen into the pit and whom Egypt joins: Assyria and all her company are there, their graves in the outermost corners of the pit, humiliated even though they were once able to strike terror into the land of the living (32:22-23). Elam and her hordes also went down uncircumcised and bear their shame, even though they also once spread terror (vv.24-25). Finally there is Meshech-Tubal(22) (probably people from Asia Minor near the Black Sea) who, though they too spread terror in the land of the living, do not lie with the great heroes of the past (32:26-27). The original final verse (28) sums up the shameful fate of great nations of the past whom Egypt now joins.

In 32:29-32 are added Israel's present neighbours in the east and north, Edom and Sidon: not only past nations have been cast into the pit. Pharaoh will be somewhat consoled when he sees that the others share his fate. Egypt is finally laid with the uncircumcised (v.32), an ironic fate for the Egyptians did actually practice circumcision. But Egypt's present position in the world is a far more significant reality than the customs she observed. When Jerusalem fell, not one nation in the world could stand out against the power which caused it. Astonishingly though not a word is directed against Babylon, the nation which caused the fall of Jerusalem, and the very one which we would expect to see attacked first.

Direct theological statement is more restrained in the last unit than in some of the others; it gives the impression that a world order is being contemplated, a world directed by the Babylonians which now has to be accepted. Such is the framework for Ezekiel's preaching of responsibility (33:1-9) and restoration to the exiles (33:10-20), as he hears the news of Jerusalem's fall (33:21). Responsibility and restoration are introduced in a situation where military victory against the Babylonians is impossible, whether by the Israelites or any other country. Restoration can be achieved only by the exiled prophet's exercise of responsibility, and by response from the exiled people themselves.

1. RESPONSIBILITY FOR RESTORATION: 33

Restoration does not exist in itself, but only in connection with the various attitudes of the people. Thus one task of responsibility is to convince people of its necessity.

It cannot be taken for granted that the people want restoration: even in times of new hope, responsibility is needed to bring people to accept restoration. To accept it means accepting a need for it, which means admitting that things are not right as they are. Comfort may be gained even from loss and deprivation, and admitting that things are not right as they are puts such comfort into question. Restoration under responsibility may even amount to the restoration of reality, for example, in the uncovering of the pretence that misfortune is somehow good fortune.

Thus the task of responsibility, of convincing other people of the necessity of restoration, is to lead them to the recognition of their true nature and what they could be. They must be prepared to recognize and abandon present attitudes; above all, they must abandon the idea that they are doing everything possible. They must abandon the attitude that there is more comfort in accepting a known misfortune, than in an uncertain future. Restoration paradoxically entails hope renewed even in a time of hope; people prefer not to hope at a time of hope since such hope threatens as never before the present comfort of lethargy. A time of hope is not necessarily an agent of liberation but the builder of even greater resistance to anything new, let alone restoration in its many aspects. Therefore, it is above all in such a time that people must be brought to accept restoration; and someone must be ultimately responsible for the people who would rather remain without hope than accept restoration. Restoration is not something which has only to be offered to be taken. Responsibility for restoration then is prior to restoration itself.

This is the reason that in the Book of Ezekiel, where there is to be a particular restoration - the return to Israel after exile and the re-possession and restoration of the land - the prophet speaks first of all of his own responsibility (33:1-9) and only second of the people's responsibility (33:10-20). Responsibility for restoration is so paramount that the section apparently begins in complete preoccupation with Ezekiel. His brand of responsibility is thus revealed: in the time of hope when people prefer not to hope (33:10), the man who does hope will be held responsible if he does not offer others the possibility of a new way (33:8), even if he does not share the others' particular failings. Ezekiel is to be a watchman for the very people whose particular failing he does not share, understanding that his failure to exercise responsibility is at least as bad.

The coming of the word of Yahweh (33:1) is to be seen within this conviction of ultimate responsibility for others. To say that "the word of Yahweh came to me" cannot be separated from the conviction that if Ezekiel does not speak to warn the wicked, no one else will. It is an alternative between life and death, not only for the wicked but above all for himself. We saw in connection with 3:16-21 that "the word of Yahweh came to me" can be called "the word-event formula", and that it occurs some forty times in the the Book of Ezekiel, usually introducing a new section. Both the name of the formula, connecting "word" with "event", and the fact that it usually introduces a new section, show that the word of Yahweh was experienced as something which manifested itself to people at a particular time, to be communicated to other people: "The word of Yahweh came to me saying, Son of man, speak to the members of your people..." The coming of the word of Yahweh combines the time of hope to new possibilities of life.

People do not necessarily accept new possibilities (33:10), and Ezekiel knows that he and he alone is responsible for their acceptance, so responsible that he is prepared to communicate his responsibility to the people. The norm, especially in extremis is "devil take the hindmost". Even if in principle some responsibility for others is felt, it is normal to feel free of it when other people's conduct can be judged to be totally unreasonable. But the word of Yahweh to Ezekiel is immediately communicated, even though it may be of some advantage to him not to show how deeply he is committed. Here is the ultimate in responsibility which does not come about merely in one person's private thoughts but is disclosed only because of the rigorous conviction that ordinary people must be brought through him to accept restoration. Responsibility integrates what happens and its acknowledgement as judgement. Anything happening here is dependent on Ezekiel's conviction concerning the possibility of restoration; responsibility is still the necessary integration of restoration and the people's acknowledgement of it.

That "the word of Yahweh" can be used as a technical term suggests that there had already been some previous reflection that, although it is necessarily directed to people, it is not merely identical with their thoughts and speech. It is not just ordinary discourse - though it need not always be separated from such discourse - but expresses the conviction that what is now to be said to them has gone through the rigour of personal address to the point that it can no longer be called the people's word. "The word of Yahweh" is bound up with the responsibility which comes only in the starkest address to oneself. No longer the expression of normal reactions to people, reactions which might abandon them in disgust, but the expression of responsibility for them against all expectations of their being accepted and put into operation. The coming of the word of Yahweh is supreme confidence in the power of communication to create something new, even where people are still wallowing in the old, and even where he who is to speak the word has by no means a natural eloquence. This word can be effective even through those who are not eloquent but slow and hesitant of speech (Exodus 4:10), or through those who say that they are too young to know how to speak (Jeremiah 1:6). The word of Yahweh means that they are addressed personally over and over again on behalf of the persons of their community. Yahweh's word is not so much timeless or absolute as an awkward intrusion into a particular situation with particular people, bearing the last and fullest thing that could be said about and for them.

Ezekiel is the bearer of this word, which does not mean that he considers himself to be superior to the people to whom he speaks. In speaking of his responsibility, Ezekiel may be primarily speaking about himself, but saving his life (33:9) is the only possibility which others have of saving theirs; saving his own life entails exercising his responsibility for them. For this reason he is addressed as "son of man" (33:2). This one human creature, he, and no one else, is to be the watchman for the people. "Now you, son of man, I have made a watchman for the house for Israel ..." (33:7). This direct and personal statement contrasts with 33:2-6 which is in the form of a casuistic legal case, listing different cases impersonally and giving their legal decisions. A hypothetical case is being presented which could happen to anyone. Ezekiel, and through him the people, are asked to consider a situation where Yahweh "brings a sword upon a land". The last word, "land", comes first in the Hebrew, and this priestly, casuistic style emphasizes that it is the first entity to be considered: it marks the general sphere of operations before proceeding to particulars. Matters could become more specific, however, since Ezekiel has been directed to speak not just to "your people" but to "the members of your people" (33:2). The case is addressed to individuals, not vaguely applicable to the people as a whole, so that there is at least a hint of working towards a specific responsibility for others in the face of some disaster. Similarly, if the sword comes, the people choose one man and make him their watchman (33:2), which indicates that a particular person could be specially responsible. It is still hypothetical, however: the person is not named, and everything is contained in a conditional clause. One possibility appears in 33:2-5: the watchman, seeing the coming of the sword, gives warning, so that if anyone who hears does not take warning, it is entirely his own responsibility - "his blood being upon his own head" is the striking Hebrew way of making the point.

One side of the case is that the watchman does exercise his responsibility which throws the onus onto his hearers. Another possibility is that the watchman, this word now being the first in v.6 just as "land" had been in v.2, does not give warning,

so that anyone taken by the sword is taken in his guilt, with
Yahweh requiring his blood from the watchman's hand. Even
though the other person is guilty, the watchman is held
responsible.

With curious logic this passage makes the call to
responsibility more urgent than the accusation of guilt to
which responsibility is directed. This is analogous to a
situation where that part of the modern community which does
not come into the courts is faced with a more serious charge
than those who do. Those to whom the word of Yahweh comes,
those who are addressed, soon begin to know they cannot escape
it, because before the hypothetical case is established
(33:1-6), it proceeds to particular application (33:7-9) via a
transition (33:6). The person taken by the sword, it is said
impersonally, is taken away in his guilt; but now, quite
suddenly and for the first time in the case of the watchman, it
is said personally "I hold the watchman responsible", not "the
watchman will be held responsible"(1). Yahweh now appears as
the one who is involved, the one making the address who can no
longer be hidden. Progress to the particular application in
33:7-9 is inevitable.

The revelation of the one making the address also inevitably
reveals the one who is addressed. Up till now it has been a
general case of a watchman whom the people appoint in time of
war (33:2); now it is the particular case of a human creature
who knows that he has been personally appointed by Yahweh as
watchman: "It is you, son of man, whom I have appointed
watchman for the house of Israel..." (33:7). The specific
character of 33:7-9 contrasts with what precedes: 33:1-6 is a
word to the people, but 33:7-9 is addressed specifically to
Ezekiel: he knows that Yahweh has made him watchman(2). The
word "you" comes first in the form of a word of nomination(3),
which defines the office and its task and directly addresses
the particular person responsible for his people: "...whenever
you hear a word from me, you shall warn them from me" (33:7).
The new factor here is something happening to Ezekiel; his
reaction is to be responsible, bringing the people to an
acknowledgement of their godlessness. For Yahweh to make the
appointment implies that, while there are certain things the
responsible person cannot do for his people, they cannot do
without his help. There can be no restoration if the people do
not recognize what obstructs it within themselves. This they
can only achieve by being assisted through the responsibility
of another. His responsibility is indeed the integrating
agent.

In today's terms, such responsibility belongs to pastors, who
hear the word, but on behalf of other people - "... whenever
you hear the word from me, you shall warn them from me". At
the same time, however, pastors do hear the word for themselves
in hearing their responsibility for other people. It is the
difference between "every man for himself" and the conviction
of pastors that they share the responsibility, even though they
do not share a particular wrong. Verse 8 makes no suggestion

whatsoever that Ezekiel does share this wrong: it is simply that the responsibility of a pastor is entirely different:

> When I say to the godless, You are condemned to death, and you do not speak to warn the godless from his way, that godless man will die in his guilt, but I will hold you responsible for him.

The pastor's responsibility is to warn the godless; it might be called a responsibility of grace, because in battle the enemy does not give warning against himself: that responsibility belongs with those attacked. But here Yahweh actually gives warning against himself! This "irrational logic of God"(4) finds its incarnation in the responsibility of the pastor. In responsibility of grace pastors do not separate themselves from the people who do the wrong they do not share: they ask - they cannot avoid asking - how they can assist people to distance themselves from the wrong. They know further that, if this is not done, then theirs is at least as serious a wrong as the original, more serious perhaps.

It is in such deep knowledge and involvement that pastors know themselves to be fallible people, but in this very admission they experience more than fallible people, for they know they are addressed by God. This responsibility of grace is the primary concern in 33:8, not the fate of the godless (or "wicked" as the word is sometimes translated). No doubt the word means one who does wrong (33:15), but from 33:13 it is likely that it also means being one who trusts in his own righteousness, self-absorbed and with no concern for the source of what he is and does. It is in the hands of the pastor whether such a person "dies" or not. "Dying" probably does not mean literal death, but worse (33:10): continual separation from the God of Jerusalem, his whole people, and above all that hopeless lethargy unprepared for restoration.

When such a responsibility is placed squarely before pastors, they may fail - "... that godless man will die in his guilt, but I will hold you responsible for him" (33:8). The watchfulnesss or carelessness of pastors affects the life or death of the godless. That pastors may fail is not finally emphasized though. Rather they can succeed - even in failing:

> But if you do warn the godless man to return from his way, and he does not do so, he will die in his guilt, but you have saved your life (33:9).

Now the "you" of the watchman is emphasized in the same way as "land" and "watchman" had been previously (33:2, 6) - it is a question of how he can respond in order to evoke a further response. He must make the initial response - otherwise restoration is impossible for those who have no other response than heavy resignation. This is why the address is apparently preoccupied with Ezekiel: without the responsibility of the watchman-pastor, nothing will ever change, there can be no question of restoration.

This idea has already been emphasized since 33:7-9 are virtually identical with 3:17-19 (5). Additions to both sections contribute little to the meaning; thus the question arises which of the two is dependent on the other, and whether this contributes anything to our appreciation of the passage. Since it would be odd for the prophet to be solemnly invested as he is in chap.33 with the office of watchman as though it were something new and without any indication at all that it has been mentioned before, it is most likely that the passage originally connected closely with the fall of Jerusalem (33:21-22), and that 3:17-19 are dependent on 33:7-9 (6). This would mean, as pointed out earlier, that the passage from chap.33 was quoted at the beginning of the prophecy, because the office of the prophet as watchman provides an interpretation for the whole of the prophet's activity(7). As far as the prophet is concerned, nothing more can be said of him than that he is watchman for the people. There needs to be someone who, whatever the people choose, continues to offer pointedly the alternatives of life and death.

Though the watchman has the responsibility of making this offer, he cannot simply force them to accept it. They themselves have the responsibility to choose; indeed, it is part of the responsibility of the watchman to awaken the people's responsibility. This need not have been clear to the people from the way 33:9 ended, which, though ending on a positive note, is positive only for the watchman since the section is about him. In making that point, Ezekiel has spoken of the godless dying in his guilt, so that his hearers could possibly hear the word of grace about Yahweh himself providing a watchman, and yet prefer to go on dying in their guilt. Especially when it comes to accepting one's own kind of responsibility, it can give people a curious comfort to persist with their familiar behaviour. And so, if responsibility is not transferred, a potential positive can become a particular negative.

The argument must be directed positively for the people as well as the pastor, and this is the purpose of 33:10-20. The pastor cannot for ever skirt around the problem, but he and only he ("And you, son of man, say ...", 33:10) must directly attack the people as they are: "... say to the house of Israel, so you say..." The pastor must quote back to the people their own words to expose their situation, and to prepare the ground for a change - a true pastoral purpose. The people say, "Our crimes and our sins are upon us, and we are wasting away because of them, how then can we live?" The pastoral purpose may be found in the form of a word of disputation(8) (33:10-11), where a question from others is followed by a sharp contradiction. The purpose is positive: the offer of life rather than death. The prophet's responsibility is required to integrate what he believes can happen with the people's acknowledgement that it can. There can be no hope of restoration if people, far from exercising their own

responsibility of accepting its possibility, prefer to wallow
in things as they are.

The quotation from the people's own words suggests heavy
resignation, the sort of understandable but dangerous attitude
after the collapse of Judah before Babylon in 587 B.C. Its
real perniciousness is that it is a confession of sin; a
confession used to excuse a refusal to change, not a confession
which clears the way for something new, since it exhausts
itself in mournful lamentation. The people's words include,
notably, two of the Old Testament's three most common words for
sin, pešac and ḥattā't, the third, cāwōn, being used in 33:8-9.
These words can have their own particular meanings which to
some extent distinguish them from one another, but when used
together, they often lose their distinctions and refer to the
entirety of sins(9). This seems likely here because the verses
deal with a "confession" in which the people express a general
lethargy rather than a precise consciousness of particular sins
which have brought them into this plight.

The sorry condition of the people is that they accept a state
of complete paralysis - "a fate worse than death". They
neither exercise their own responsibility, nor are they
conscious of the possibilities of their responsibility. When
the people say they are wasting away and ask how they can live,
"die" is probably not meant literally. In exile, they were in
a sad plight, but rarely it seems in danger of literal death.
Rather, as I said before, to "die" means continual separation
from the God of Jerusalem and his people, and the hopeless
lethargy evidenced in the quotation, whereas to "live" means
the opposite: the acceptance of hope and a positive future
even within their sad plight.

"Living" is of the greatest importance for Ezekiel(10). Of
the approximately 205 occurrences of the basic form of this
verb in the Old Testament, no less than one fifth of them (43)
are to be found in Ezekiel. This is particularly striking if
compared with the mere nine occurrences, for example, in the
Book of Jeremiah. No less than ten instances of the verb occur
in 33:10-20 alone, plus one of the noun. The very next verse
(33:11) brings out the importance of "living" by its insistent
admonition to embrace it. The situation is sketched by quoting
what the people say; now the pastor will directly contradict
them, in the solemn terms of Yahweh's oath:

> As I live, says Lord Yahweh, I have no pleasure in
> the death of the godless but rather that he return
> from his way and live: turn back, from your evil
> ways, for why will you die, O house of Israel?
> (33:11).

Ezekiel makes an offer of life which the people can acknowledge
as a real possibility. Yahweh has no pleasure in the death of
the godless, but rather (using a strong adversative expression)
he wants the godless to turn from his way and live. His
insistent appeal implies that the people do have a response

they can make; in spite of what they say, something new <u>can</u>
happen. That Yahweh offers life means that even where people
wearily see only the negative, hope exists, the possible
release from the prison of their own wrong. People can now do
something new: the godless can turn from godlessness without
being trapped in previous godlessness (33:12).

The subject matter of 33:11, found in 18:23 and 32 as a
question and statement, here appears as a promise on oath(11).
Yahweh reaches out as far as he possibly can towards the
people. He insistently calls to the <u>people</u> to repent: "...
turn back from your evil ways ..." The double imperative leads
to the apparently absurd final question: "... for why will
you die, house of Israel?", which prompts the people's own
response. Since they wallow in their sin with no desire to
relinquish it, this promise and this call form the
indispensable foundation for change - restoration in and from
exile is impossible unless the people exercise their
responsibility in return. What is said is a thrilling
statement about the possibility of life which lies before every
human being. When God swears by his own existence and offers
life, it means that, even when deeply debilitated, one can know
a totally unexpected upsurge of energy which grants a new
departure from the point of death.

Verse 33:11 marks such a high point that it may seem
anticlimatic when Ezekiel continues in 33:12-16 with a didactic
passage, an instruction which may appear to offer less chance
for life(12). But it is not so heavily instructive as it first
appears. Rather than burdening the hearers with impossible
demands or unreasonable conditions, it demonstrates that the
godless individual can live, can now make his own response
which, because it is his own, makes him new and erases the old.
Anxious calculations as to whether the good outweighs the bad
become irrelevant. It is also done in relationship, for the
passage, though a learned exposition in legal style(13),
addresses the people through a human being, who communicates
Yahweh's direct speech to the people (33:13, 14) as well as his
attitude and action towards them (33:16). The offer of life to
these particular people is utterly genuine, and any
misunderstanding that righteousness can be aggregated must be
removed. An impression of unfairness might be gained from
33:13-16 which seems to select an arbitrary point in time, and
to leave the totality of a person's life out of account. But
it cannot be assumed that life, righteousness, a relationship
with God, are matters to be weighed mechanically, for and
against. Only a relationship with people <u>as they are</u> matters,
and what they are can only mean what they are <u>now</u>. There is no
question of saying: "At the moment I happen to be godless, but
if you look back you will find that I was righteous, and my
righteousness probably outweighs my godlessness". A
relationship with Yahweh cannot rely on such a calculation: it
arises out of the people's responsibility for themselves in
their present state. They cannot rely on past righteousness.

This is what the pastor has to say:

> You, son of man, say to the members of your people,
> the righteousness of the righteous will not save
> him at the time of his godlessness, and as for the
> godless, he will not stumble in it when he turns
> back from his godlessness (33:12).

The pastor speaks to the <u>members</u> of his people, to individuals,
showing again that here is no impersonal legalism. Once again,
as in 33:9, he emphasizes the positive: 33:12 may begin with
the case of the righteous who commits crime, but it ends with
the godless who can be saved by repentence(14). The next
verses, 13-16, also start with the case of the failed righteous
man, but by the far the greater part of the detail is devoted
to the case of the repentant godless. But if the righteous has
received the pronouncement of life from Yahweh and still trusts
in that righteousness, it will not save him - he will still
die:

> If I say to the righteous, He is to live, but he
> trusts in his righteousness and does evil, none of
> his righteousness will be remembered but he will
> die in the iniquity he has done (33:13)

The uselessness of resting on past merit is brought out more
strongly if these statements are linked with a cultic ritual
where the righteous actually heard the verdict of life
pronounced audibly on Yahweh's behalf by a priest(15). After
an impersonal expression in 33:12, verse 13 opens in a
personally direct way, "If I say to the righteous,
<u>He is to live</u>" - carried on in 33:14, with the next two verses
reverting to the impersonal style. Since the same direct
address with similar content is used twice elsewhere in the
Book of Ezekiel (3:18 and 33:8), it seems likely that it is a
form of speech taken from particular occasions in Israel's
cultic life when Yahweh, through the mouth of an authorized
spokesman, made the pronouncement over the wicked: "You are
condemned to death"; and likewise then over the righteous:
"He is to live". That is, a person's righteousness depends on
Yahweh's pronouncement, not on their own merit. The failure
described in 33:13 is not the main issue Ezekiel wants to
discuss:

> If I say to the godless, You are condemned to
> death, and he turns from his sin and does what is
> just and right, restores the pledge and makes
> restitution of what he has stolen, walks in the
> statutes of life without doing iniquity, He is to
> live, and will not die (33:14-15).

Instead a possibility directly opposed to what was said in
33:13 is brought out. The godless, who even though Yahweh has

155

pronounced death over him turns from his sin to do what is just and right, can still live.

One might ask why only these two examples of doing what is just and right appear in 33:15. It might be thought that there are more important and more centrally religious matters than giving back stolen goods and restoring the pledge (that is, surety for a debt, which might comprise a piece of property indispensable to a poor man, Exodus 22:26). Perhaps they give specific examples of a change in conduct, but they still do not seem comprehensive enough by themselves to motivate such a generous and far-reaching pronouncement of life. It is to be noticed, however, that 33:15 speaks not only of restoring the pledge and making restitution of what is stolen, but also of walking in the statutes of life, a summarizing phrase that may permit one to conclude that the prophet had at his disposal a whole series of sentences to describe the righteous, from which he has taken the two most suitable examples, which ultimately stand for a larger whole(16). Such a fuller series of "statutes of life" can in fact be found in chap.18:5-9. As in the decalogue, commandments on correct reverence to God are placed at the start, followed by cultic and ethical stipulations with regard to persons. Among them appear the two found in 33:15, whose character as quotation from a meaningful ordered whole is thus clearly demonstrated.

This form, the "guide for self-examination", ends in 18:9 with the pronouncement "he is righteous, he is to live". Again this may be a priestly declaratory formula, with the series as a whole originating in a gate liturgy (Psalms 24; 15; Isaiah 33:14-16) where the priest gave a decision, a torah, concerning admission to or rejection from the temple. "Life" or "death" must be granted, and granted in a manner which concerns the real life of the people. If one were to detect legalism in this passage, it would be necessary to see it in such terms. Ezekiel certainly does not imply that he considers the conditions of life to be burdensome, difficult, or anything to be proud of just by adhering to them. The people's responsibility is to see that they fulfil life rather than proving that they have done so. The statutes of life do not lead to a reputation, but to life.

We must now turn back to 33:10 which stresses that life is the very opposite of wasting away and enjoying the burdens of sin. Such an attitude is countered by the proclamation of Yahweh's will that people should live (33:11). What is given comes before what is required. The meaning of the words translated by "righteous" and "godless" (more often rendered "wicked") is indicated here. The state of the "godless" is expressed just as much by the attitude described in 33:10 as it is by evil deeds like failing to restore the pledge. Such evil deeds of course lead to death, where a certain kind of life is lacking, which goes beyond the mere doing of certain actions. Likewise though the "righteous" are people who do restore the pledge and so on, their lives are those which recognize and accept possibilities of change even in the most hopeless of circumstances. It is therefore a matter of relationship as well as of individual responsibility, so that it is better to speak of its negative side as being "godless" rather than "wicked". Neither "righteous" nor "godless" are satisfactory translations since, in modern understanding, they do not bring out the fact that it is not a question of single actions judged righteous or wicked in themselves, but rather one of total orientation: what one receives as well as what one gives in company with others.

The offer of life made so insistently in 33:11 is the primary factor to which the people must respond. An offer must be made, together with a response which no one individual can make for another. Together they make up "righteousness". Indeed the tension between them is the essence of the prophet's proclamation: life is something both given and accepted. The life of Israel, of every member of the people of God, is possible only by the free and incomprehensible dispensation of life from their God, a life to be grasped over and over again in repentance. God's will for life means that an offer is made to people, (usually through some human agent like Ezekiel), while the condition means that people must be prepared to accept that offer as an expression of a certain kind of life. The concept is simple, but its realization is not so easy. Since accepting life means admitting that radical change is needed, it is easier to remain with the status quo. "The way of Yahweh is not just" is the way in which Ezekiel's people put it (33:17). It is easier to postpone the decision, and settle for the chance that everything will be resolved if their righteousness and godlessness are weighed up. Ezekiel seems to fail as a pastor here because he does not attempt further explanation, he simply repeats the pronouncements he has already made (33:17-20). The pastor must be prepared to take up the same matters again and again for the very reason that the offer of life is not easy to accept. To be just, these verses are a shortened version of 18:25-30, and it is possible that they are secondary here since the people's statement about Yahweh makes more sense between 18:24 and 25 (18:24 ends with the negative dying and 33:16 with the positive living)(17). Also, more explanation is given in 18 than in 33. But, in any case, verses 33:17-20 are a useful reminder that the clearest of offers is frequently neither welcomed nor accepted. The best of pastors, with the best of intentions, is compelled to start all over again even though he thought what he had said could not possibly have been clearer or more acceptable. The task of awakening other people to responsibility is no sinecure and is never finished.

The unexpected and laconic message which follows is highly dramatic:

> In the <eleventh>(18) year of our exile, in the tenth month, on the fifth day, a deportee from Jerusalem came to me saying, the city has fallen (33:21).

157

Again the reader is prepared to be bored by the elaborate designation of the time (how heavy those numerals are, especially in Hebrew!), but then the mention of the deportee, a person direct from Jerusalem, quickens the interest. He then, in two simple Hebrew words, says enough to bring the whole structure of Israelite faith and politics crashing to the ground: the city has fallen!

This is what Ezekiel had been waiting for:

> Now the hand of Yahweh had been upon me in the evening before the deportee came, but he opened my mouth at the time he came to me in the morning; my mouth was opened, I was no longer dumb (33:22).

Not merely _waiting_; that the hand of Yahweh was upon Ezekiel the evening before and up to the time of the arrival of the deportee, indicates dumb apprehension that what is about to be announced is not merely a piece of information but the turning-point in the life of his people. It is some time since the fall of Jerusalem (587 B.C.) had taken place, and therefore it is likely that Ezekiel had a premonition of it. It may not, however, have been as long as 33:21 presupposes, in speaking of the twelfth year of the exile (i.e. from 597 B.C). 2 Kings 25:2 and 8 indicates that Jerusalem fell on the 7th day of the 5th month of the 11th year of exile, so the 12th year of Ezekiel 33:21 would mean that some one and a half years have gone by before Ezekiel hears the news. If the word describing the person who brings the news means a fugitive rather than a deportee, then it is just conceivable that it could have taken such a time, though it seems unlikely that Ezekiel would not have already heard by other means. In any case, the use of the same word in 6:8-9 (14:22) indicates a meaning of "deported prisoner" rather than "fugitive", that is, someone who·has escaped the sword rather than the victor. It does not seem likely that such people would take longer than a few months to reach Babylon, and textual evidence also suggests that the reading should be the eleventh year rather than the twelfth. This would date the deportee's arrival at 5.10.11, five months after the fall of Jerusalem. A further indication of the correctness of this dating can be found in the observation that, in the present order of the book, there is already a dating in the twelfth year in 32:17, so that subsequently it could have been found necessary to change "eleventh" to "twelfth" in 33:21 (19).

Thus some time has gone by since the fall of Jerusalem, during which Ezekiel has been waiting for this news. As the time draws near, he waits in great apprehension because weighty consequences will follow the news. The event announced is of unprecedented importance because, up till now, nothing has been narrated which did not issue in a word of Yahweh (compare, for example, 32:17) (20). For now, however, the fact of Jerusalem's fall is quite enough. The unprecedented nature of the event announced in 33.21 is confirmed by what happens in v.22 to Ezekiel. That the hand of Yahweh is upon him means that he is in a trance-like state, completely preoccupied with the will of Yahweh. This state is not of any value in itself, but with the coming of the message his mouth is opened and he is no longer speechless. The significance is seen in the body of Ezekiel, which is now released for something new (21). Both the events on which everything else depends - the fall of the city following the siege and what now happens to Ezekiel himself - mean that he has something which he wants to convey to his people.

If this is the passage which relates the event necessary for restoration, one might expect it to initiate the section whose main subject is restoration. Indeed the section in chaps. 25-32 on foreign nations is probably a later insertion, with the material now in 33:21-22 originally coming directly after 24:15ff., where the climax of Jerusalem's fall is spoken of. So why is 33:21-22 preceded by one passage on the responsibility of the pastor and another on the responsibility of the people if such responses only become possible as a consequence of the information given in these two verses? Placing these two passages first makes a direct address to the people in their present situation, and clarifies the context within which restoration can go forward: no restoration without responsibility. Furthermore it is within a combined context: the responsibility of the pastor combined with the responsibility of the people for whom he is responsible. Since this has already been made abundantly clear, the news of Jerusalem's fall cannot be purely negative, as it would be if it were related as an isolated fact. True, the outcome of that which is narrated in 33:10-20 does not sound promising, but the irremovable foundation of Yahweh's offer of life has been laid. Thus, for the very reason that 33:10-20 does not sound promising, together with the release effected in 33:20-21, no other possibility exists but to continue with the business of responsibility and restoration. That the responsibility of both pastor and people is so clearly presented means that the news of the city's fall as the release for the offer of restoration is not as callously mechanical as it sounds: up till chap.32, before the fall of the city, Ezekiel preaches judgement; from chap.33, when he hears the news, he preaches restoration. Restoration can never be entirely separated from judgement; as the present composition of the chapter shows, not only the news of the city's fall, but the question of the pastor's and the people's own responses are all relevant.

The necessity for Jerusalem to be destroyed before there can be any talk of restoration may seem to be expressed too much in terms of actual physical destruction; but if we remember that the fall of the city cannot bring about the people's restoration without their own response, we must also remember that, more than anything else, Jerusalem represented ancient tradition. It was the dwelling-place of Yahweh where nothing adverse, the people believed, could ever happen to them; where they would always be safe (see Jeremiah 7). In its negative aspects, therefore, the tradition of Jerusalem represented hope that the old ways would simply renew themselves, and make radical renewal unnecessary, a hope that had to be - and still has to be - destroyed.

Since the news of Jerusalem's fall (33:21-22) shattered ideas of automatic security, the next unit (33:23-29) appropriately concerns people who succumb to the piety of automatic trust in religious tradition. In the final two units of this chapter, Ezekiel shows his responsibility for the people left at home just as he does for the exiles. His responsibility for the Judaeans at home means ensuring that they see the unpleasant truth about themselves. Once again the address to the son of man appears as a quotation from the people in order to initiate discussion with them:

> The word of Yahweh came to me saying, Son of man, the inhabitants of these ruins in the land of Israel keep saying, Abraham was one man and yet he possessed the land; since we are many the land has been given to us to possess (33:23-24).

Here the pastoral discussion obviously takes place at some distance since the inhabitants of the ruins must be in Judah. Since Ezekiel must be taking up something reported to him at second hand, it shows the utmost in pastoral responsibility. He must ensure that separated members of his people realize that the destructive discrepancy between what they say and what they do cannot be condemned because of distance. Ezekiel is evidently no advocate of the philosophy of "out of sight, out of mind", but takes up almost all he hears for further investigation.

At first sight, what the people are saying appears to suit the spirit of its context: the need for their own responsibility in the new situation of hope brought about by the destruction of Jerusalem. The word of the people in Judah probably provided to some extent encouragement not to give up hope despite the ruins: they can repossess the land. Abraham was only one individual after all; why should not all of them together do what he did, especially as in exilic times one could evidently count on a widespread confidence that father Abraham was a sure guarantee of present blessing (Isaiah 51:2)?

The outcome is however an accusation against the people. Ezekiel evidently detects in what they say a certain false piety, an expectation of finding automatic support in religious traditions, coupled perhaps with superficial security in mere weight of numbers. The reaction to the destruction of Jerusalem cannot be a piety which has to be destroyed along with Jerusalem. This unit is placed after the news of Jerusalem's destruction and the corresponding change in Ezekiel, because if the people still remain unchanged there cannot be any automatic restoration. Restoration still depends on the people's response, and the very piety of the people's words is an obstacle to restoration.

160

Whatever the people say, their cultic and ethical behaviour
has not altered:

> Say to them therefore, Thus says Lord Yahweh, you
> eat together with the blood, you pay attention to
> idols and shed blood - and you will possess the
> land! You rely on the sword, you commit
> abominations, and you defile each one of you the
> wife of his neighbour - and you will inherit the
> land! (33:25-26).

As with other lists of commandments (eg. the decalogue) a
relationship with God and with other people is at issue. How
can people who eat meat with blood, worship idols, and commit
abominations (a word for all sins which make cultically
impure)(22), who shed blood, rely on the sword, and defile
their neighbour's wife, hope to possess the land? Conduct
incapable of furthering relationships with God and man can have
no basis in a pious hope. Ezekiel's responsibility is to spell
out that what people are and do cannot be hidden beneath their
religious beliefs and practices.

Most of the matters mentioned in these verses occur
frequently in the torah, i.e. in the Pentateuch, except for
reliance on the sword(23), which, since it is unique, seems
likely to be a direct reference to lawlessness in Judah in the
period shortly after the destruction of Jerusalem. To Ezekiel
there would be a logical connection between the evil that the
people were doing and their non-possession of the land. It is
not so logical today. We might well think that evil conduct
has some effect in people's lives, but people today act just as
reprehensibly as Ezekiel says, or worse, and still gain
possession of whole countries. This is not the point, however:
Ezekiel is not talking about people in general but about
particular Judaeans living in Judah at a particular time. As a
matter of fact, it was a long time before these people did
actually take possession of the land, and it was a tenuous
possession at that. Something similar will apply to the
consequence of judgement which Ezekiel draws from his
accusation:

> You are to tell them this: Thus says Lord Yahweh,
> as I live, those who are in the ruins will fall by
> the sword, and those who live in the open country I
> will give to the wild beasts for food, and those
> who live in the mountain strongholds and caves
> shall die by pestilence. I will make the land into
> a desolation and horror, and her proud might will
> be put to an end, and the mountains of Israel shall
> be desolate with no one passing through (33:27-28).

It might nowadays be argued that people are not punished so
drastically, and yet these verses may describe fairly
accurately what did happen in Judah about 582 B.C. after a

revolt against the Babylonians. Thus, as Ezekiel is very much concerned with the particularities of his own situation, so later interpreters have to be with theirs. Those who do not live in countries where military or natural catastrophes are common, may find it difficult, yet fruitful, to realize that particular judgement accompanies attitudes which bring on wars and famines and desolation. When people hear themselves addressed and see themselves involved, they are more likely to understand the direct confrontation with "I Yahweh" who makes the accusation and executes judgement. When people fail completely to comprehend the legitimate aspirations of others, they can be addressed in judgement: judgement is in the failure to exercise the responsibility which Ezekiel exercised even towards those members of his people separated from him when he drew their attention to their true state.

Just as Ezekiel says, "They will know that I am Yahweh when I make the land a desolation and a horror on account of all the abominations which they have done" (33:29), so a realization today of the complete lack of responsibility for one another, above all in unpleasant truths, can lead to the final goal of recognizing the necessity of the new address for all. When people recognize themselves as unhearing, unthinking embodiments of recurrent assumptions, sometimes pious but also sometimes arrogant, they know that recognition is itself judgement. The way Ezekiel expresses the formula of recognition with reference to Yahweh contains something demonic, yet at the same time purposeful and positive. The land was a desolation and a horror anyway. The address is directed towards people who see themselves involved in such desolation, but who then, in recognition, are freed from their guilt. They are thus open to a life so different that it is to know a God who is caught up with them as they are. The goal of the passage is judgement, but also a new and positive recognition which leads on from what is otherwise complete inaction. Such is the exercise of Ezekiel's responsibility.

Finally, Ezekiel exercises his responsibility towards the exiles with whom he is himself living in Babylon. The subject of 33:30-33 is the opposition to restoration which arises even from the people's admiration for the prophet. The reason that the units in this chapter are arranged together is now clear, and why to speak of restoration by no means eliminates all forms of judgement. In 33:1-9 appears potential opposition to restoration through lack of responsibility on the part of the watchman himself; in vv.10-20 through lethargic response of the people; in vv.23-29 even through piety; and now in vv.30-33 through the particularly insidious phenomenon of positive response for the wrong reason. These all show how much restoration has to do with the quality of the people's response. Here, on the surface, all sounds promising: the people treat Ezekiel as a sensation; Ezekiel has unexpectedly become something of a religious fashion. The first verse of the unit vividly conveys people's gossip:

> Now you, son of man, the members of your people are
> talking together about you by the walls and at the
> house doors, and everyone is saying to each other,
> Come and hear what the word is that is coming from
> Yahweh (33:30).

(Here incidentally is some rare information about the living
conditions of the exiles: evidently they had their own
houses.) Interestingly, what the people say to each other -
"hear what the word is that is coming from Yahweh" - resembles
the form of the call to attention ("hear the word of Yahweh"
6:3; 13:2) which is of course what the <u>prophet</u> usually says to
attract the people(24). Now, however, it is heard on the
people's own lips; they do not need calling but come running.
   Why this wonderful change? Sadly, 33:31-32 make it plain
that they come only for titillating entertainment.

> They come to you as people come, and they sit
> before you as my people ... and, for them, you are
> like a love song, with a beautiful voice and
> playing well; but, though they listen to what you
> say, they do not do it.

The people have evidently noted that something new has happened
to Ezekiel, but they do not make the correct response. What
Ezekiel says may be as attractive as a love song, but the
people do not feel bound by it. A response can be welcoming
but still not postively creative: Ezekiel's popularity is
actually a curious form of heedlessness(25). Further, this
heedlessness prevails among different groups of people in
different circumstances: this unit, as well as the previous
one, shows it as prevalent among the exiles as among those left
in Judah.
   It seems odd at first that Yahweh's word is directed to
Ezekiel since it concerns Ezekiel himself. Why does Ezekiel
have to be told? Surely popularity is a phenomenon of which
one becomes aware for oneself. But that is the whole point.
Hearing this as a word of Yahweh expresses the most difficult
of insights: that it is not at all the sort of thing of which
one becomes aware for oneself. Everyone is susceptible to
flattery and success. By being the recipient of an address
from outside, the prophet shows that he is realistic about and
responsible for himself. The quality of his response contrasts
with the people's response, for they absorb what they hear from
outside only in an inward direction. Ezekiel's response, on
the other hand, provides a check on what is happening, and
presents the possibility of using what is heard, not to confirm
the status quo - "though they listen to what you have to say,
they do not do it" - but to create a person capable of seizing
new opportunities. The passage is a necessary and effective
warning for the popular preacher, indeed for any popular
speaker. The warning is, however, not so much directed at the
speaker himself, as at the superficial response from his

hearers. Since the passage deals more with the listeners than with the speaker himself, it is primarily a reminder that the speaker remains responsible for his address even when it is popular. His responsibility is that it be genuine - provoking not only applause but a discerning, critical response. Applause is not necessarily bad, and those who are not popular are always in danger of being merely cynical about those who are. The point is perhaps that it must be asked of all speakers, popular or not, whether they speak realistically to people as they are, and say what ought to be heard, rather than what people want to hear; and whether they are really being attended to. If not, the result can be both popularity and indifference.

The ending shows that the passage is not primarily about the popular preacher but about a genuine address reaching the people, for it gives the preacher encouragement in the face of his popular reception: "When it comes - and it will come - they will know there has been a prophet among them" (33:33). "It" is vague, but in context it probably means both the restoration and the people's realization that they have not made the proper response to the restoration. Realizing that there has been a prophet among them encourages them to make that proper response. All parts of this chapter cohere, with a special connection between the first part and the last. The first (vv.1-9) shows that there can be no restoration unless the watchman exercises his responsibility, and the last that restoration depends on the quality of the people's response to the watchman. Restoration depends on the kind of person the watchman is - and the kind of person he is depends on the nature of the response he evokes.

2. THE RESPONSIBILITY OF LEADERS: 34

One may feel disappointed with this chapter in comparison with the previous one: it seems to lack its sharpness and direct address, which somehow span the centuries. But this new chapter makes clear that restoration cannot be seen in isolation: it must be viewed against present obstacles. The promises of restoration in 34:11ff., can only be seen in connection with the hindrances posed not only by the people in general, as in chap.33, but also by the leaders of the people themselves.

After the word-event formula in 34.1, v.2 describes circumstances which seem to arise from a familiar and specific situation:

> Son of man, prophesy against the shepherds of
> Israel, prophesy and say to them: Oh shepherds,

> thus says Lord Yahweh, woe shepherds of Israel who
> have been pasturing themselves! Should not
> shepherds pasture the sheep?

Who are the shepherds? There was an ancient oriental tradition
of calling the king shepherd. This had been done already by
the Sumerians, and the Babylonian king Hammurabi is called "the
salvation-bringing shepherd whose staff is just". The
Babylonian word re`u, related to Hebrew rācâ "pasture", became
a technical term for ruling. The ancient oriental conception
of kingship included power, but also the obligation to afford
protection, establishing pasture for the needy, providing them
with food and drink and places of safety. In the Old Testament
too, Yahweh can be called "shepherd of Israel" (Psalm 80:1;
Genesis 49:24), and his care for both his people (Psalm 77:20;
Isaiah 40:11) and for the individual (Psalm 23) appear in this
image. The rulers of Israel can also be described as shepherds
- the term is never used of a particular individual - an image
especially frequent in Jeremiah (2:8; 3:15; 10:21) (1). The
term "shepherd" would refer primarily then to kings, as 34:4 in
the main confirms, though v.3 could apply more widely to
include priests and prophets (cf. Micah 3:9-11).
   Against these leaders a devastatingly comprehensive judgement
is brought:

> You eat the fat and clothe yourself with the wool,
> you slaughter the fatlings but the sheep you do not
> pasture. You have not strengthened the weak or
> healed the sick; you have not bound up the injured
> or brought back the strayed, nor have you sought
> the lost, but have trod them down with force and
> violence (34:3-4).

The leaders of whom so much would be expected, far from showing
responsibility for their people, only exploit them. This is
what happens when the responsibility spoken of in 33:1-9 is not
accepted. Far from leading the people in the right way, these
leaders use the people's resources to lead reprehensible lives.
As John 10:10 would put it, these are not shepherds at all, but
thieves. The shepherd can be true only when bestowing fuller
life; these steal, kill and destroy. They are the complete
antithesis of the good shepherd described in John 10:11, who
will even give his life for the sheep. While not exactly the
same, Ezekiel's readiness (33:1-9) to recognize his guilt as
that which will require his life is strikingly similar. The
shepherd who gives his life for the sheep, in whatever sense,
differs from even the best leadership of past and present.
Usually the only leaders to give their lives are those who have
it taken from them by their own people. They are not the same
kind of leader as the Good Shepherd. What is said in John is
radical in the extreme.

The passage in Ezekiel is more limited than the passage in John. It does not demand that these shepherds give their lives for the sheep, but that they show responsibility for them. The last accusation - "You have not sought the lost" - is the most condemnatory, because it introduces the key idea of "seeking" (34:6, 8, 10, 11). The shepherd's responsibility goes beyond looking after the sheep in his immediate vicinity: he also has to go out after them, like the shepherd of Jesus' parable who, if only one of his sheep has gone astray, leaves the ninety-nine to look for the one (Matthew 18:12). If some go astray, the shepherd cannot leave them to their own devices, claiming that he is occupied enough with those that remain. Indeed, if the shepherd does not take ultimate responsibility for the sheep, all his work becomes meaningless. After saying that the shepherds have sought out the lost, but have trodden them down violently, 34:5 goes on to say that the sheep "were scattered without a shepherd, and became food for every wild beast". The result of the shepherd's lack of responsibility is that the sheep are without any goal except the meaninglesss one of being scattered:

> My sheep were scattered and strayed over all the mountains and over every high hill; my sheep were scattered over the face of the whole earth with no one to seek or search for them (34:6).

The meaning of "seek" alters in what follows. For, after repeating the accusations against the shepherds in 34:7-8, vv.9-10 draw the consequence, and speak now of Yahweh seeking his sheep from the shepherds:

> Therefore you shepherds, hear the word of Yahweh: Thus says lord Yahweh, See I am against the shepherds; I will require (seek) my sheep from them; I will stop them feeding the sheep. The shepherds will no longer feed themselves for I will rescue my sheep from their mouths so that they shall no longer be food for them.

Seeking the sheep now means that the shepherds are relieved of their responsibilities. That Yahweh rescues his sheep means that bad leadership is not automatically continued. What happens now is so radical that it is not bound to old structures. Leadership will be taken away - even when sanctioned by actual power. A modern example is Dietrich Bonhoeffer who, even though physically under the power of Hitler, (who was addressed as "der Fuehrer" - "the leader") was obviously led by him in no significant sense, so that the fact that his leader had the power to take his life was irrelevant. God had delivered him - just as he can deliver other sheep from other leaders. The passage shows how much is lacking when the leaders do not fulfil their responsibilities (v.4), and that they are dispensable (v.10).

The next section (34:11-15(16)) shows tht the main theme is not the deposal of the shepherds. The primary aim is to give a promise, a particular hope for the future. The climax occurs in 34:15: Yahweh himself will be the shepherd (an idea already anticipated in v.11 where emphasis is laid on "I will seek my sheep"). The same verb occurs here as above for the shepherd. The idea is confirmed by still another verb (biqqēr) which evidently implies the use of great care and concern. Leviticus 13:36 uses it in the sense of looking out for symptoms of sickness; it has been suggested that here in Ezekiel it is used for an inspection and counting of the flock, and a readiness to seek the lost (2). Chapter 34:12 reads:

> As a shepherd cares for his flock when he is among
> his scattered sheep, so will I care for my sheep
> and rescue them from all the places where they have
> been scattered on the day of the cloud and thick
> darkness.

Yahweh's sheep are lost in an exile from which his shepherding will deliver them. The theme of restoration as return to the land is thus struck, reversing the judgement for which cloud and darkness is a metaphor (both Joel 2:2 and Zephaniah 1:15 describe the day of Yahweh with the same two words). This judgement will be transformed into a return to their own land, with Yahweh's rich pasturing described in words reminiscent of Psalm 23:2:

> I will bring them out from the peoples, I will
> gather them from the countries and bring them into
> their own land. I will pasture them on the
> mountains of Israel, by the stream-beds, and in all
> the habitations of the land. I will feed them with
> good pasture, and their pasturing places shall be
> on the mountain heights of Israel; there they
> shall lie down in good grazing land, and they shall
> feed on fat pasture on the mountains of Israel
> (34:13-14).

The real climax follows in 34:15. Verse 16, summarizing v.4 and combining the shepherd theme with the next theme of the sheep in v.17ff., is almost certainly a secondary bridging verse between the two sections(3). The conclusive point is made in 34:15 with its double "I" and divine oracle conclusion formula: "I myself will pasture my sheep and I will cause them to lie down, says Lord Yahweh". Something new is indeed happening, and the reaction to it must diverge markedly from the way in which the shepherds behave.

The main intent is thus clear: in the face of the evil shepherds, the true shepherd is Yahweh. But what does it mean to say Yahweh is shepherd, that he restores the people to their land? Some think that the shepherd discourse in John 10 sees Jesus as the fulfiller of the prophecy(4). It is difficult,

however, to see that the author has this particular Ezekiel
passage in mind any more than a number of other Old Testament
ones which speak of God as shepherd(5). There are as well
important differences. The passage in John has complicated
imagery of a door as well as of the shepherd, and, as we have
seen already, a principal difference between the two passages
is that in John the shepherd gives his life for the sheep,
which is not suggested in Ezekiel. Some might want to say that
this is the very element which demonstrates the fulfilment of
Ezekiel in John, but it hardly does justice to the intention of
the older text, which plainly states that Yahweh is and will
continue to be the leader and sustainer of the people. In
John, a known individual, Jesus, is presented as the shepherd:
in Ezekiel there is no human embodiment of the metaphor.
Saying that Yahweh is the shepherd expresses mistrust of the
adequacy of human responsibility. It is tempered to some
extent by the challenge in 33:20, namely, that the people have
to exercise their own responsibility in accepting life.

Up till now it might sound as though the shepherds will
always be guilty, whereas the sheep will always be innocent.
But the people, the sheep, are in as much need of judgement as
the shepherds: "As for you, my sheep, thus says Lord Yahweh, I
will judge between sheep and sheep, between rams and goats"
(34:17). This section is probably later than the one
preceding(6). The latter stresses that Yahweh is shepherd, a
conclusion of such sublimity that it does not seem altogether
appropriate to proceed to the judgement of Yahweh's sheep. The
style, too, is more pedantic, as if a scribe working out of
another context was trying to adapt it to the earlier one:

> Is it too little for you that you feed on the good
> pasture, then trample with your feet the rest of
> your pasture, drink the clear water, then muddy the
> rest with your feet? (34:18).

A touch of pedantry appears too in v.19, a somewhat unnecessary
addition to v.18: "It is what you have trampled with your feet
that my sheep eat, and what you have muddied with your feet
that they drink" (34:19). An unusual extension of the
messenger formula (v.20) also changes the person - "Therefore
thus says lord Yahweh to them" - which could indicate a further
stage in the additions, and the verse also repeats v.17: "I
will judge between the fat sheep and the lean sheep" (34:20).
Another case is taken up in 34:21, with v.22 containing another
repetition of vv.20 and 17:

> Because you shove with side and shoulder and butt
> all the weak with your horns until you scatter them
> abroad, I will come to the aid of my sheep and they
> will no longer be a prey, and I will judge between
> sheep and sheep.

The passage is of course significant. Verse 18 pictures

clearly the "dog in the manger" attitude(7), which takes the best and spoils the rest. Such an attitude, sometimes regarded as being merely petty, is very serious. Far from contributing to restoration, health and general well-being, it abrogates all responsibility, preoccupies itself solely with personal welfare, and even begrudges to the needy what is left over. It is much more than petty - it can mean the death of others.

It the passage refers to the propertied classes' treatment of the unpropertied, then it is most likely that it best fits the time after Ezekiel, after the return to the land, when these fat "sheep" rather than the shepherds have become the problem. The point of adding the passage is this: the judgement which was appropriate for the shepherds is now valid for some of the sheep. For Yahweh to judge between sheep and sheep means that one of the most tenacious of all assumptions has been shattered, namely, that judgement may be applied to one kind of people, and not to another. To deny this assumption here is a positive and creative addition. If judgement is constantly applied to the same group of people, no matter how much they and the situation change, the truth will soon be missed. Verse 21 may possibly take up the same issue in another, later situation, when it speaks of jostling for the best places in the land. A situation after the return is again suggested, where the strong evict the others, and there is no consciousness of responsibility for others. People seek possession merely for their own sake, a manifestation of emptiness which is its own judgement. Though the whole passage speaks three times of Yahweh's judging between sheep and sheep, no further judgement is specified. The passage does not offer any clear solution of a difficult situation, but it does expose the fat sheep as aggressors, which is the most damaging judgement of all. We must be content with that.

Since sharp judgement between sheep and sheep was necessary, it is not surprising that the need was felt to go further and speak of an authoritative human leader: "I will establish over them one shepherd that he may pasture them, my servant David - he will be their shepherd" (34:23). Here is an understandable desire for a specific leader at the return. But, in the view of 34:15 which says emphatically that Yahweh himself is to be their shepherd, this is hard to comprehend. To say explicitly after v.15 that there is to be <u>one</u> shepherd (not Yahweh) could be regarded as a distinct provocation. Possibly David can be explained as one who is more intimately associated with Yahweh than any before; and all matters pertaining to deliverance by Yahweh are carried out by David, his servant, his earthly representative(8). But this has to be construed from such terms as "my servant David"; it is a secondary explanation rather than one which can be found in the fabric of Ezekiel 34 itself. If the chapter is taken as an original coherent entity the contradiction remains.

It is unlikely that a provocative contradiction to 34:15 was intended, so that the passage on David can be understood as an addition of a provenance different from that of the passage of

which v.15 forms the climax. It could be understood from
37:15ff. where (see v.24) the reunification of all Israel
takes place under one ruler(9). One expression of the union of
all Israel has presumably been used later as an expression of a
single, good leadership as opposed to the bad leadership
described earlier in the chapter. This consideration has made
the editor fail to recognize the logical contradiction between
34:15 and 34:23-24 - though it probably would not have been
natural for him to worry about it in those terms. The addition
expresses legitimate concern for the naming of a human leader
who can be trusted, because of his ancestry, to feed the sheep
rather than exploit them. This is the confidence of some that
what has proved itself in the past can again be of supreme
worth in the future. Just how strong this confidence is in the
past, without the modification often made elsewhere in the Old
Testament, is shown when the author speaks of a David to come,
rather than, for example, one from the stump of Jesse. This is
very unusual, occurring only twice outside Ezekiel, in Hosea
3:5 and Jeremiah 30:9. Both passages are probably additions,
thus confirming the judgement that this Ezekiel passage is
too(10). It is not very likely that a returning David would be
spoken of before the pardon of the Judaean king Jehoiachin in
561 B.C., and the last dated passage in Ezekiel is given as 571
(29:17).

Some scholars regard these verses on David as Ezekiel's
apparent accommodation to the traditional prophetic hopes of a
prince from the house of David, in spite of his own hope for
deliverance being fundamentally different. The prophet himself
would then have been responsible for the passage on David in a
sort of bureaucratic striving after completeness, a conforming
on paper to official requirements(11). But the commitment to
David in calling him Yahweh's servant, and prince (using in
v.24 a special word nāśî') does not sound like mere conformity.
Others deny the messianic character of the "servant David"
mentioned here, and maintain that all that is asserted is the
reinstatement of the old Davidic dynasty. But this is to
understate the case - after the destruction of Jerusalem and
the exile and imprisonment of the Davidides, it would have been
a momentous step to have reinstated them as kings of Judah in
Judah. If Ezekiel as the person mainly responsible for the
bulk of the material in the book had hoped for this, he would
have described it with far more care. It is possible though,
that a later editor could be wholly serious about the matter
without thinking it necessary to devote much space to it.

Others find in the word translated as "establish" (hēqîm) in
"I will establish over them one shepherd" (34:23) the idea of
David's resurrection from the dead(12). In Jeremiah 23:5,
however, the same word is used in saying "I will raise up for
David a righteous branch" where, since it concerns someone of
David's family, it cannot mean the resurrection of David
himself. The word certainly need not be used for resurrection,
and the Ezekiel passage does not require it. When it is
considered that the idea of resurrection from the dead is not

170

typical of the Old Testament, such an interpretation is extremely unlikely.

A writer after the pardon of Jehoiachin in 561 B.C., having the hope of an early return, might well have connected that with the hope that there would now be a direct descendant of the Davidic line, a true shepherd for a new united Israel. He would be David who, like Moses himself, would be Yahweh's servant, subordinate to him and doing only his work, but at the same time standing near him in a relation of privilege. The writer might have been more conservative than some others, since he thought it appropriate to imagine a direct descendant of David, rather than changing over to a different branch of the same house because of the limitations of the historical Davidic line. At the same time, he showed that he too wished for a genuine renewal, and thought of a messianic figure - not just a reinstated Davidic king of the old order - since he gave him the comparatively rare and prestigious title "my servant". He brought his office into close relation with the fact that Yahweh is their God, and called "[his] servant David" nāśî', prince, rather than melek, king: "And I, Yahweh, will be their God and my servant David will be prince among them ...", all emphasized as Yahweh's creative work by the final "I Yahweh have spoken" (34:24). It has been thought by some scholars that the use of the word nāśî' rather than melek represents a polemic against kingship as such, but this could hardly be so, if the one to come is to be of David's direct line. Others think that the use of the word is not so much polemic as the solemn use of an Old testament title, which at the same time avoids a worn-out international word(13). It is not necessarily lower in status than melek (as the unsatisfactory English translation "prince" might suggest); it is a title suggesting something new and with an honoured tradition(14). Admittedly, it is not entirely clear what nāśî' means or where it originates. It may be that the nāśî' was the tribal representative (one for each tribe - Numbers 2 - the word being translated "leader" in the R.S.V.) in a premonarchic confederation of Israelite tribes; it does seem clear that they were eminent in the tribe or other assembly (Genesis 34:2)(15).

These verses express the understandable desire to have a leader who is rooted in what is known (David), and also, because he is not called melek, is new. He will be the adequate leader in this new situation. Here it is at least a glimpse of the necessity of the new, though the question is whether it goes far enough. Is a restoration adequate which still retains strong elements of an old institution, even if its renewal is also envisaged? The old institution has proved its worth to a certain extent, but will an institution which was only partially successful even where it was more naturally at home be adequate in the new situation? Such questions cannot be answered from general argument but only from close reference to the particular circumstances. Even in the pre-exilic period of Israel the Davidic monarchy only partially proved its worth. David and a few others like Josiah showed they could usually adhere to the order of life set by Yahweh between God, king and people, and so were accepted as leaders by the people who trusted their reliability. But these two examples are significant since the military and political successes, which in all of Israel's history were most extensive under these two kings, partly account for such high estimation of their leadership. In the post-exilic period any reinstated Davidic figure would have had much less territory and political independence - a problem to which the author does not give any consideration. These deficiencies would have to be taken into account realistically when one considers any successful restoration of the Davidides.

The author of this passage may have glimpsed the necessity for the new - but he did not go far enough. If the majority of Davidic kings failed as leaders even in pre-exilic times, they would be even more likely to fail in post-exilic times. The Davidic kings must have been the chief target in the rejection of the shepherds earlier in the chapter. Despite the moving expression of hope, the writer is still trying too much to reform the old. In the present day it would be analogous to giving a political party another chance even though they are obviously bankrupt, and only because one has always voted for them.

Perhaps through defeat or being forced to operate in entirely different circumstances, a political party could be re-born. In Old Testament language, instead of "David", a "shoot from the stump of Jesse" could arise, based on the old, but through an experience of fundamental renewal become an adequate leader. If a political party is bankrupt at one time, it will not necessarily always remain so; to fail to recognize this is just as blinkered as failing to recognize the present bankruptcy. Likewise, to despise and reject the editor's hope in the David to come would be to assume simply that a completely satisfactory form of restoration cannot involve the old. The very expression of this particular Davidic hope, together with the more radical rejection earlier in the chapter, may itself test the hope in a way that will lead to a restoration, a restoration which goes beyond an overly unquestioning confidence in the old.

The following section (34:25-30) breaks with the shepherd theme to describe conditions in the land in terms of paradise(16), a theme made all the clearer when the shepherd theme returns inappropriately (34:31) after the concluding divine oracle formula, "says Lord Yahweh" (v.30), and after the conditions of the land (vv.25-30)(17). The final verse - "And you are my sheep, the sheep of my pasture ... I am your God, says Lord Yahweh" - evidently brought in as a unifying conclusion, attempts to link the theme of the land with that of Yahweh as shepherd. The editor exercises his responsibility to indicate that the land's restoration can only be for certain people, those who acknowledge their need to bow to the same kind of authority as that which stands over the land.

Restoration of the land is not something to be taken completely for granted. The whole section may address itself to the concerns of those closer to the return than Ezekiel. These were people who naturally wanted better conditions than those already obtaining. It is impossible to speak of restoration of the land and ignore its bad conditions; someone has to take responsibility for facing up to the problem. Here it appears as a confident assertion that there is a binding promise on Yahweh's part of good to his people:

> I will make to them a promise of security and prosperity and remove wild beasts from the land so that they may dwell safely in the desert and be able to sleep in the woods (34:25).

The word here translated as "promise" is berît, usually translated "covenant". But it is clear from this context that berît is a promise, for Yahweh says that he will remove wild beasts and the people will dwell safely; he lays an obligation on himself but not on the people, only saying what he will do for them(18). The use of this particular word lays an important emphasis on the binding character of Yahweh's promise to the people. To translate it by "covenant" is to miss the specific naure of Yahweh's binding promise to his people, just as translating the whole expression berît šālôm as "covenant of peace" or "covenant of salvation" also does. The way in which the berît šālôm is described in what follows makes clear that šālôm means security and prosperity, clearer concepts in the context than "peace". The expression is used only four times in the Old Testament (Numbers 25:12; Isaiah 54:10; Ezekiel 34:25; 37:26). All the passages say that such a promise is binding and lasting, and in the Isaiah passage its absolute irrevocability is manifest even when the mountains and hills pass away. Such a promise claims much. Ezekiel 34:25 starts by describing a place where all natural dangers are to be removed, and continues:

> And I will make them and the places around about my hill a blessing, and I will bring them down the rain in its season - they shall be showers of blessing. The trees of the field will yield their fruit, the earth will give its produce, and they will live safely in their land and know that I am Yahweh when I break the bars of their yoke and rescue them from those who keep them in service. They will no longer be plunder for the nations, the wild beasts will not consume them but they will dwell safely with no one to terrify them. I will provide for them a plantation of true renown so that they will no longer be swept away by hunger in the land, and they shall no longer bear the abuse of the peoples. But they will know that I, Yahweh, their God, am with them, and that they, the house

173

of Israel, are my people, says Lord Yahweh
(34:26-30).

The restored land will be an ideal place without natural dangers, and all this will be combined with a final deliverance from political bondage. Knowing Yahweh is closely connected with Yahweh's demonstration of himself in the world. Knowing him cannot be detached from what happens here. Such a reciprocal, mutually appropriate relationship between God and people is not theoretical, but based on the people's own recognition.

The principal legitimate concern that lies behind the passage is that the sheep themselves must be able to recognize what their leader is doing. It is all very well to speak of a return to the land, but unless the people make their own response, then "Yahweh" is a meaningless cipher. Under Yahweh, it is impossible to speak of a return to the land and yet ignore the conditions reigning there. Return to the land has no meaning in itself unless there is security and prosperity for the land. Acknowledging Yahweh as shepherd means a preoccupation with the realities of the situation, though not being content with them as they are. The passage is confident that transformation can come about.

We are faced with a dilemma, however, for while we know that some Israelites were able to return to the land, they certainly did not return to a secure and prosperous land. It is a reasonable and necessary wish to be confident of peace and security, but these never exist in a perfect paradisial sense. Peace and security, however, are to be found not only in outward worldly circumstances but also in human beings' attitudes to what is and what happens. The statements in this passage about the removal of wild beasts, or no longer being plunder for the nations, are insufficiently integrated with the statements at the end about Yahweh being with them and the people being his sheep (though the editor of the final v.31 was possibly trying to achieve this).

Responsible leaders accept and strive for better conditions; yet they will also find security and prosperity in working with what is imperfect and even with that which positively hinders them. Christ's words (John 16:33) express it more adequately: "In the world you have tribulation, but be of good courage, I have overcome the world". Here in contrast to confidence in paradisial circumstances, is a commitment to tribulation and a frank recognition of people's weaknesses. At the same time there is confidence that the real world of tribulation can be overcome because it has already been overcome. It has been overcome because the man Jesus has been prepared to accept and not to avoid what was coming to him, and far from resenting it was prepared to recognize its significance for himself and others. It is perhaps only when people are prepared to admit that they will be disappointed that, in this very admission, they can be confident of a life which is not overwhelmed by diappointment, and in doing so realize deliverance by God.

174

3. RESPONSIBILITY FOR ANOTHER NATION AND ONE'S OWN: 35:1 - 36:15

Since the last section in chap.34 speaks of the restoration of the land, the next appropriately speaks of the restoration of the land of Israel in the face of opposition from the land of Edom. It is realistic to insert a passage about Edom in the middle of this section on restoration: eloquent promises of restoration must take account of real enemies who might oppose it. A section on the mountains of Edom is necessary before speaking anew of the restoration of the mountains of Israel in chap.36.

It is certainly straining the concept of responsibility to use it of chap.35, which directs its harsh terms against Edom. It is possible too that only chap.35 was originally concerned with Edom, because chap.36 mentions Edom only once, in v.5, as a mere appendage to "the remnant of the nations". Otherwise it speaks of "the enemy", "the nations" and "the peoples"(1). In the present form, however, the words against Edom in chap.35 and for Israel (36:1-15) are evidently intended to be read together for there is no further instance of the word-event formula (35:1) until 36:16; they are strikingly linked, since chap.35 is directed against the mountain of Seir (Edom) and 36:1-15 to the mountains of Israel. The accusations made in both chapters are also basically similar: 35:10 speaks of Edom wanting to take possession of both northern Israel and Judah, and 36:2 of the enemy saying that the ancient heights have become their possession. Thus just as Ezekiel can quote his own people's words against them and be responsible for their replacement by truth, so can the words of other nations be quoted and issue taken with them.

Responsibility is exercised towards them at least to the extent that the truth of their iniquitous aspirations is revealed. It must be remembered too from the larger context that speaking in harsh terms against a people is not confined to foreigners; in fact the same threat of making the land a desolation and a waste which is directed against Edom for her confidence in possessing the land of Israel is also directed against Judah herself (33:23-29) for her confidence in possessing the land inherited from Abraham. Thus, while there is a contrast between Edom and Israel in 35:1-36:15, it is not exclusive: taking the passages concerning other peoples together also enables us to see that their aim is to express the truth to all, a truth which can be equally harshly expressed to one's own people as well as to others. Responsibility makes no distinctions.

The first address bluntly states opposition leading to a threat and a goal:

> The word of Yahweh came to me saying, Son of man,
> set your face against the mountain of Seir,

prophesy against it and say to it, Thus says Lord
Yahweh, Look I am against you mountain of Seir; I
will stretch out my hand against you and make you
into a desolation and a terror. I will make your
cities into a ruin and you will be a desolation and
know that I am Yahweh (35:1-4).

Seir stands for Edom, Seir being a mountain range of that
country and a name which could mean a wooded district, a rough,
wild land; it was the mountain country around the Arabah,
south of the Dead Sea(2). This word against Seir seems to be a
word of judgement without proper motivation: it starts with
the messenger formula in v.3, then merely states that Yahweh is
against Seir, and finishes in vv.3b and 4 with the threat. The
point of view of the writer is clear: all that Edom represents
cannot stand, which will probably lead to the confidence that
Israel can stand. But why? The absence of motivation up till
now serves to lead up to and give greater weight to the reasons
given in v.5(3). This section also consists of the form of a
word of demonstration, whose various parts are tightly
constructed together. It begins by giving a reason ("because
...", 35:5), continues with a consequence, an announcement of
punishment ("therefore ...", vv.6-9), and concludes with an aim
expressed as the formula of knowledge or recognition ("then you
will know that I am Yahweh", v.9b): the recognition of Yahweh
corresponds to his action in the world of people. The point of
the statement of recognition can be seen in such events as
those in Genesis 42:32-34, where the truth of what Joseph's
brothers say is to be demonstrated when they produce proof of
their integrity(4). This links with the way Yahweh is
understood here to act according to the circumstances of the
world of the time. "To know" means having gone through the
process of conviction as a result of something happening in the
present circumstances. Knowing Yahweh is possible only in
direct confrontation with the significance of such
circumstances, together with one's own and other people's
responsibility for their causes, and the willingness to face up
to the consequences of their effects.
   Knowing Yahweh can be illustrated by the comparison often
made between ancient oriental deities for whom one name is not
enough (Marduk, the principal god of Babylon, had fifty and the
Old Testament God who, even though other names are mentioned,
has them all subsumed under the one name Yahweh; a summary
appellation which seems to have something to do with the fact
that he is known entirely through human circumstances)(5).
Therefore these human circumstances, whatever they are, have to
be taken seriously - one reason for paying so much attention to
the Edomites who, it appears, did actually attempt very much
what is stated in 35:10 and 36:2. Obadiah 11-14 says that they
handed Israelites over to their enemies, and confirms that they
encroached on her territory and looted it. What appears to
modern readers to be an attack on Edom and support for Israel
represents the need to express matters as they really were

between Edom and Israel with regard to Israel's land. The expression is one-sided in that Edom is disregarded after desolation is called down upon her; but Edom's present claims on the land could not be ignored if it was to be returned to Israel.

The intrinsic reasons for the judgement against Edom are shown as very important, both in the way in which the first verses lead up to the word of demonstration and in the way the word of demonstration itself begins:

> Because you cherished perpetual enmity and delivered up the Israelites to the power of the sword at the time of their misfortune, at the time of final punishment ... (35:5)

This is the reason for the inevitable consequence: "therefore as I live says Lord Yahweh [I make you for blood and blood will pursue you], you are <guilty>(6) of blood and blood will pursue you" (35:6). This verse also shows the importance of the judgement residing in Edom herself, for it is not so much Yahweh as the "guilty" blood which invokes the judgement.

This has been called "the fate-effecting deed", or the "deed-consequence relationship", whereby in at least partial distinction to direct divine intervention, the evil deed itself brings on its own evil consquences(7). Blood is not neutral but can return the evil associated with its shedding to the perpetrator (cf. Genesis 4:10). Here, however, it is not isolated but combined with divine intervention as both other verses and this one verse itself would indicate, where everything comes about under Yahweh's oath. The formulation signifies that the Edomites' own evil creates their punishment. The deed-consequence formulation, it should be noted, makes this very point, though it could be thought, with some justification, that it presents a mechanical, even magical understanding of the connection between things. Such a view is obviously deficient if it means that for every evil deed there will be an automatic punishment. But as an expression of the conviction that deeds, and attitudes for the matter, do have consequences whether they are literally visible or not, this view is far more realistic than the idea that people can do what they like without suffering any ill-effects. It does not necessarily mean however (as the verses following 35:6 have it) that there will be a kind of reckoning made visible in the shedding of blood, (corresponding to blood shed previously by the one who has been judged), or that God himself will desolate the country of those concerned. It would be unfortunate if, because of this, the concerns which this repetitious passage is trying to express were totally rejected.

The next section begins (35:10) with a quotation from the people which exposes their attitude as one of brazen arrogance: "Because you said of the two nations and the two kingdoms, they will belong to me and we shall possess them - even though Yahweh was there ..." This quotation from their own words was possibly the starting-point of all that is now being directed against Edom. To say they have claimed that Israel belongs to them even though Yahweh was present is the most confident expression (on the one hand) that Israel does not belong to Edom in any real sense, and (on the other hand) of the knowledge that the Edomites are blithely but tragically unaware of the lack of foundation to their claim. It is impossible for the Edomites to offend more greviously. For this reason 35:11 expresses no petty revenge:

> ...therefore, as I live, says Lord Yahweh, I will act according to the wrath and jealousy you have shown; because of your hatred against them, I will make myself known against them when I judge you.

That the Edomites show wrath and jealousy cannot be ignored. The statement combines Yahweh's direct intervening action with the deed-consequence relation, and expresses the belief that Yahweh will make some visible judgement corresponding to their wrath, jealousy and hatred. In so far as it renders evil for evil and expects this to be seen, the statement is dubious. How the judgement is to be seen is left vague, though the kind of people they are does relate to the judgement under which they stand. It might be said now that this judgement would manifest itself in their relation to others, and in the way they reacted to Israel's desolation. Certainly their self-opinionated, unrealistic insolence is given abundantly clear expression: they make aspersions against the mountains of Israel (35:12), and apparently imagine that, in being able to take advantage of Israel, they can triumph in insolence over her God as well (35:13). The meaning of 35:14 is not clear, but it is evidently similar to v.15: Edom's joy at Israel's devastation inevitably finds a correspondence to her own devastation. What is happening now is that the land which gloated over another's devastation is to be devastated herself, while the devastated land is to be restored.

Thus, so far as devastation for Edom is concerned, the ending in 35:15 repeats v.9, while making clearer that such devastation is connected with the people's own expressed attitudes. The question now is whether self-opinionated, unrealistic insolence is not a sign of a more serious devastation than the merely physical. The statement relating to another people, "They are laid desolate and given to us to devour" (35:12), signifies the total removal of any possibility of living for and with others. Since this statement constitutes a desire to consume, it expresses merely a self-directed appetite. Once this attitude is understood in all its destructive capabilities, it is seen to represent not only retribution, but also the responsibility to draw the attention of those expressing it to its destructive capabilities. There are elements in this particular passage of too harsh a turning against Edom and of too favourable a turning towards Israel. But as has already been seen, there are now plenty of examples in the wider context of the Book of Ezekiel that show the need for judgement above all against Israel if she is to enjoy restoration. This shows that there could be no question of denying restoration to Israel just because it could not be granted to another nation. In the end, rather than being of any benefit to others, it may hinder sharing one's own gifts with them. There is no suggestion that Israel is to share her new fruitfulness with Edom (though one place in the Old Testament does say "You shall not loathe an Edomite" - Deuteronomy 23:7). But there is no pretence either that one party cannot prosper because another party cannot. Since Edom's attitude exists (35:10; 36:2), and is unchangeable, it is realistic to take it as it is. Israel therefore sees an instructive contrast between the two lands.

The theme of 36:1-15 is that in contrast to Edom's desolation, Israel is to be made abundantly fruitful (36:8). Just as the mountain of Seir has been prophesied against, so now there is a new commission to prophesy to the mountains of Israel:

> But you, son of man, prophesy to the mountains of Israel and say, Mountains of Israel, hear the word of Yahweh (36:1).

Here is a contrast not only with Edom but also with Israel herself, compared with what had been said against her earlier in chap.6. In 6:2 Ezekiel is to set his face against the mountains of Israel and prophesy against them, just as he must against the mountain of Seir in 35:2. In 36:1 he is to prophesy to the mountains of Israel. Prophesying against and to the mountains of Seir and Israel brings out in every case the importance of the land, so closely connected with the people that it can be addressed as though it were the people(8). From Israel's point of view this approach acts as a summary. For the mountains include not only North and South Israel as geographical entities, but there is also possibly a reference to the Israelites in earliest times inhabiting the mountains rather than the plains (eg. Judges 1:19). A matter is thus expressed which concerns Israel at all times, from the distant past to the present and into the future.

Desolation is called down on the altars of the mountains of Israel (6:4) just as in 35:1ff. the mountain of Seir is to be made desolate. Seir's mountains are to be filled with the slain (35:8), and so too Israel's slain are to fall in the midst of her mountains (6:7) (9). Those hearing the prophecy of fruitfulness to the mountains of Israel in 36:1ff. could be reminded of the previous prophecy of desolation to Israel. Such fruitfulness does not come to an Israel perpetually apart and innocent, but to a corrupt people who have to recognize its consequences themselves. The prophecy against the mountains of Israel in 6:1ff. is that Yahweh "... will bring a sword upon you and destroy your high places ... In all the places where you dwell the cities will be laid waste ... and the slain will fall in your midst that you might know that I am Yahweh" (6:3, 6, 7). That is, destruction will come on the whole land comprehensively: on cult, cities and people alike. The address to the mountains of Israel becomes a particularly appropriate address to the people because the cult to other gods was founded in the land, maybe on the very mountains themselves. As Edom made illegitimate claims politically on the land of Israel, so Israel herself had previously made illegitimate cultic claims on it. Chapter 6:1-7 expresses the divisive consequences, abhorring the break away from what is genuinely and significantly natural within the lives of the people to what is only apparently natural in the manipulation of supernatural powers within nature. Israel sought salvation in the religion of complicated paraphernalia: in high places, altars and incense altars, but Yahweh was to be found in their destruction. People like to manipulate power whether it be of the religious, political or any other variety: the promise of fruitfulness can be seen only in contrast to the forays which both Israel and Edom have made into the sphere of manipulation. And the contrast is a judgement - a judgement just as relevant for Israel as for Edom, indeed more so.

Despite first appearances there is thus a complicated background to the new commission and call to attention directed to the son of man and mountains of Israel in 36:1. The unity between land and people expressed in the new commission cannot be emphasized enough, for it shows the impossibility of a restored life without this land. This in turn prohibits anyone else from trying to appropriate it. Another quotation from the enemy illustrates this fact:

> Thus says Lord Yahweh, Because the enemy has said concerning you, Aha, the everlasting heights have become our possession (36:2).

Because of the brutal directness of most of this book, one would 'have expected that a consequence would have been drawn immediately, but in fact none is drawn until 36:7, where it is said that the nations round about will themselves suffer abuse (the aim of the word of demonstration with the formula of recognition does not come until v.11) (10). It is true that consequences seem to be introduced before v.7 with the word "therefore" featuring in vv.3, 4, 5 and 6; but there are so many that they are probably delaying additions to the original direct word of demonstration. The confusing abundance of commissions to speak ("prophesy", vv.1, 3, 6), calls to attention ("hear the word of Yahweh", vv.1, 4) and messenger formulae ("thus says lord Yahweh", vv.2, 3, 4, 5, 6, 7) confirms it. This abundance of formulas, which takes a long time to reach a definite conclusion, becomes all the more evident if the formulas of the first seven verses are isolated: "... prophesy ... and say ... hear the word of Yahweh(v.1), thus says Lord Yahweh, because ...(v.2) therefore prophesy and say, thus says Lord Yahweh, yes because ... (v.3)therefore ...

hear the word of Yahweh, thus says Lord Yahweh ... (v.4)
therefore thus says lord Yahweh ...(v.5) therefore prophesy ...
and say ... thus says lord Yahweh ...(v.6) therefore thus says
Lord Yahweh ..." (v.7).

Even in a Hebrew style known for its repetitiveness, this is
very unusual. Readers only have to go as far back as 35:1-9 to
compare it with the clear progression there from reason to
consequence to aim. The logic of 36:1-11 has therefore been
broken up by a plethora of later additions, whereas the
original sequence began with the reason quoted in the enemies'
words in v.2, which lead on to the direct consequence in v.7.
This was followed by the detailed, but clear word of salvation
in vv.8-11. Thus vv.3-6 is later exegesis - the work of weak
souls wallowing in moral indignation. It does, however, show
that they found it difficult to accept the brazen attitude of
another people towards Israel's land. The expression "Yahweh's
zeal" (36:5) emphasizes this, qin'â being a word often
translated by "jealousy". But it is not the kind of jealousy
directed towards the possession of something belonging
rightfully to somebody else: it is the realistic reaction of
one who knows that something is being taken away which
rightfully belongs only to him. Likewise in 36:6 Yahweh speaks
in his jealous wrath because Israel has borne the illegitimate
abuse of the nations, whereas it is legitimate that those who
pour out abuse should themselves suffer it (36:7). It is here
that a definite consequence is finally drawn, providing an
immediate contrast to the salvation offered Israel.

The word of salvation appears in 36:8-11 (11). The first
verse indicates that it originated not very long before some
Israelites did in fact return home in 538 B.C.(12).

> But you, mountains of Israel, you will put forth
> your branches and bear your fruit for my people
> Israel because they have joined together to come
> home.

This prophecy is an expression of hope, understandable at a
later time, that the land will again be fruitful for the people
of Israel, and that its meagre population will be multiplied,
as vv.10-11 conclude:

> I will multiply men upon you, the whole house of
> Israel, the cities will be inhabited, and the ruins
> rebuilt. I will multiply men and cattle upon you
> [and they will multiply and be fruitful](13), and I
> will re-inhabit you as in former times and treat
> you better than ever before. Then you shall know
> that I am Yahweh.

This prophecy has not yet been fulfilled. While it is dubious
to enlist the aid of God for material prosperity, one realizes
that the Israelites would not have understood "material"
prosperity as it is understood today. The way in which Yahweh

addresses the land directly shows it. Just as men, animals and plants can be fruitful in direct relation to the ground, so the land is directly dependent on the life-giving word of Yahweh. The Israelites did not see the land as something removed from their faith. The prophecy functions legitimately not so much in the predictive sense of the term, but as a statement that, though Israel is separated physically from her land, she is not separate from her God. This word of salvation witnesses to the Israelites' conviction even in exile that the exile is not the end, that return is possible. The circumstances of the return are painted rather too extravagantly, but the conviction that they will be able to move out of present hopeless circumstances and to work through conditions not as favourable as expected, is vital. Yahweh coming to them (36:9) even in exile affords the knowledge that life can be fruitful even when old convictions are shattered.

It seems probable that 36:12 is a transition to a related but different theme (14): "I shall cause men to walk upon you, my people Israel [they will possess you and you will be their inheritance, and you will no longer bereave them of their children]" (15). It is probably a transition because 36:11 ends with the formula of recognition, v.13 begins with the messenger formula, and (within the square brackets) proceeds to address in the second masculine singular, whereas the second masculine plural had been used before. It also introduces the theme of bereavement, the principal and detailed theme of 36:13ff. This effective transitional verse shows that the land needs a possessor, and the possessor needs to know that he will not be swallowed up by the very thing he possesses:

> Thus says Lord Yahweh, because they say of you, You are an eater of men and you go on bereaving your people of children, therefore you shall no longer eat men and you shall no longer <bereave>(16) your people of children, says Lord Yahweh (36:13-14).

To eat your own children was the worst action of all, since childlessness was a deep disgrace in Israel (eg. Genesis 30:23).

This is a secondary conclusion to the address to the mountains of Israel for, apart from the first "you" in v.13, the address is now in the second feminine singular, to the land as such, a feminine word in Hebrew. This shows that something secondary is not necessarily inferior: it is a necessary conclusion because it can well be imagined that the exiles, having been promised a return, would then fall into the debilitating despair of thinking it was no use, since the land devoured its children. Since Israel was a harsh land always prone to famine, the prophecy hardly came true in a literal sense. Once again though, it is not so much a question of literalness as of disgrace:

> I will no longer let you hear the abuse of the

nations and you shall no longer suffer the scorn of
the peoples [and you shall no longer bereave your
people of children](17), says Lord Yahweh (36:15).

The greatest responsibility of all for nations in disgrace with
others is to communicate that because they have been disgraced
once (and maybe with good reason), that is not itself a reason
why it always has to be so. It is possible for a disgraced
nation to rehabilitate itself in relation to its fellows, and
to deny this would be a disgrace in itself.

4. RESPONSIBILITY FOR GOD AND THE RENEWAL OF PEOPLE: 36:16 -
38

The end of chap.34 emphasized the necessity of not being
overwhelmed in tribulation. The person who can do this is
provided for in 36:16-38 which presents the necessity of a
radical and inward renewal. Without it, there can be no
restoration of any sort; indeed, recognizing the need for
responsibility for inward renewal is the ultimate
responsibility, and the basis for restoration. It is also
necessary that this should come after the first part of the
chapter, for there is no future in the renewal of the land and
its population without an inward renewal of people.
  To convince the people of this possibility was not an easy
task. Considering their state, the natural reaction would have
been to believe that nothing more could be done for them. That
real and threatening state of affairs could not be ignored, and
hence the sombre description in 36:16-20 of the physically
revolting, apparently inevitable state of sin. A plain address
about the people's past conduct, unequivocally stating its
consequences, has the ultimate aim of presenting the
possibility of a new address to the people which will bring
about a different response. Such a reversal has to be
energetically worked for, because if the reality is faced and
the people's sin mercilessly exposed, one is left with the
serious question: it is all very well to say the people will
return home and the land be fruitful, but how is such a thing
possible in view of their sin? The usual view of judgement as
a conclusion and not as a necessary confrontation for a
positive end has to be taken into consideration. The prophet
himself has to be sure of it first, and for this reason, he is
first addressed: "The word of Yahweh came to me..." (36:16).
The word-event formula comes to him first so that he can be
sure that the state of the people's sin is indeed the basis for
a complete change of attitude. He who knows more about the
people's sin than any Israelite still has to confront it so
that he will seek no other solution. He must be addressed with

a double truth: that present circumstances obtain but that even they can be reversed. The people were wallowing almost physically in their sin, as it states in a characteristically priestly way in 36:17:

> Son of man, when the house of Israel dwelt in their own land, they made it unclean by their conduct and evil deeds; their conduct was before me like the uncleanness of menstruation.

Not just a few more or less serious individual misdemeanours have occurred: the whole land is infected and the people unable to be approached, like a women who in her menstrual period was ritually unclean (Leviticus 15:19ff. though cf. vv.2ff.): all blood was taboo. Such an accusation levelled against them by Yahweh could only have one result:

> Then I poured out my anger against them for the blood which they had shed in the land and for the idols with which they had made it unclean (36:18).

The result is punishment in accordance with their faulty ethical and cultic conduct:

> I scattered them among the nations and they were dispersed through the lands; I judged them according to their conduct and their evil deeds(36:19).

Since the people had defiled their own land, it was only right, so the argument goes, that they should be scattered throughout other (unclean) lands. But this brings with it further and more serious implications. The people not only sinned, but even involved Yahweh in their sin:

> But wherever they came to the nations, they profaned my holy name in that it was said of them, These are the people of Yahweh and yet they had to go out of his land (36:20).

They defile their own land, they profane Yahweh by including him in a judgement which does not apply to him. It is a sobering thought that a people's conduct can affect the reputation of their whole religion. This means that they even have a responsibility for God. Thus more is at stake here than mere human misfortunes(1). There could hardly be a more devastating way of presenting the sin of the people.

That is one aspect of the issue. But being responsible for God means being prepared, even in the most hopeless of circumstances, to accept the possibility of change. There is a second, almost incomprehensible truth that despite the people's sin, and even despite their implication of Yahweh, Yahweh will still cleanse and renew them. In 36:21 the possibility of reversing the previous result of scattering and dispersal is introduced. In the face of the people's sin and its particular consequences, Yahweh could only have concern for himself: "But I had concern for my holy name which the house of Israel profaned wherever they came". The insistence that Yahweh will still act for Israel though it provides absolutely no justification for doing so, is expressed in this harshly provocative way. Of many comparable addresses in Ezekiel, it is probably the most provocative of all:

> Therefore, say to the house of Israel, Thus says Lord Yahweh, It is not on your account that I am acting, house of Israel, but on account of my holy name which you have profaned among the nations where you have gone (36:22).

Up till now the address had been to Ezekiel alone; the address to the people has a new impact. That the only reason for restorative action lies in Yahweh himself causes the words of 36:21ff. to be expressed in such a way as to seem that Yahweh is concerned only for his own reputation, to the exclusion of caring for the people at all. It is the ultimate provocation to the people's complete hopelessness which - it must be said - is expressed in such an extreme manner that it runs the risk of removing a holy God beyond their reach, of separating Yahweh from his people.

To point out that this kind of argument is not peculiar to Ezekiel, but occurs also in Isaiah 43:22-28 only emphasizes the point. The most relevant verse in Isaiah - "I, I am he who blots out your crimes for my own sake, and I will not remember your sins" (v.25) - is mild compared to the harshness and coldnesss of Ezekiel(2). On the other hand, what is said may just have the opposite effect as an ultimate provocation can do: make people realize that it is their own complete lack of merit which is the very factor that can remove the last barrier of prevarication. Yahweh acting on his own account, and not on account of people, means the final rejection of the typically human, piecemeal solution, but it does not mean the end of all solutions for human beings. It is apparently curious that the God who says he is acting not on account of people but on his own account, speaks only of what he will do for the people! For, within the whole context of the Book of Ezekiel, Yahweh's acting for the sake of his name could only be for the purpose of offering Israel life; and it could only be assumed that Yahweh's name means "the God of Israel", the God involved in a series of relationships with his people(3). The present context bears this out. When Yahweh speaks of vindicating the holiness of his name, he immediately speaks of doing something for the people:

> I will vindicate the holiness of my great name profaned among the nations, which you have profaned in their midst so that the nations will know that I

am Yahweh, says Lord Yahweh, when I prove myself
holy through you in their sight (36:23).

Yahweh can only prove himself holy through them; the harsh new
address leads now to a reversal of the old result:

> I will take you from among the nations and gather
> you from all the lands, bringing you to your own
> land. I will sprinkle clean water upon you so that
> you become clean of all your uncleannesses, and I
> will cleanse you from all your idols (36:24-25).

It is sometimes thought that the last clause refers to a ritual
introductory act to remove old impurity, particularly that of
idols (see Numbers 19)(4). The point in any case is that
however great the sin of the people, they cannot block
restoration. For Yahweh to act for the sake of his name means
that there is nothing which cannot be changed, a proposition
argued by Paul in somewhat similar terms (I Corinthians 6:9-11)
when he demonstrates to his readers that they had been in a
state of the deepest immorality and yet were washed,
sanctified, justified(5). For Ezekiel in 36:25-27, where the
climax is reached in an expression of complete inner renewal,
Yahweh outbids anything he has done for Israel before(6):

> I will give you a new heart and I will put a new
> spirit in you, removing the heart of stone out of
> your flesh and giving you a heart of flesh. I will
> put my spirit within you and cause you to walk in
> my statutes and carefully observe my ordinances
> (36:26-27).

The new things which are happening reach right into the inner
nature of people. In comparison with 20:9, for example, where
Yahweh leads Israel out of Egypt - doing something for them -
here he does something to them that produces a complete inner
transformation; of necessity, for Israel has become incapable
of obedience. For Yahweh to give them a new heart and spirit
(comprising the intelligence and emotion) means that what is
necessary now cannot be done by an act of the human will, but
can only be brought about by a complete change, as something
given and received. The change can come about only in
recognizing that such a change of life must not be taken for
granted, but is a wonder - especially when seen against the
background of a recognized need for judgement.
   That God gives a new being, that he can make the supremely
unresponsive wholly responsive, means first of all, that no one
can dwell on the thrill of the promise in isolation, but must
see it within the human situation, which is something more
mundane and challenging. This is the reason that the people
are at first shown to be wallowing in a state of sin. God's
gift of a new spirit means, paradoxically, not escape from this
world but complete commitment to it. It means rejecting the

most universal of all human attitudes, summed up in the faulty grammar of "who, me?"

God's gift of a new spirit presupposes that one is needed; in Ezekiel's terms its purpose is not to reveal a diseased mind, but to expose reality in a provocative way. For Ezekiel and Israel, it leads to the description of Israel scattered among the nations, that is, being in unclean lands, just as they had made their own land unclean. Today it might mean, since Ezekiel is speaking of Israel and the nations, that compared with the others, some peoples consider themselves cultural voids. They may possess a culture without being able to recognize it. The judgement, if they are capable of thinking about it at all, is that they cannot see themselves as anything but culturally empty: ironically, this situation can exist in the presence of a culture which they have trivialized as a show for tourists.

But if God's gift of a new spirit means the acceptance of people in their worst state, it also means the apparently impossible: the courage to grasp that even those in the worst possible state do not have to remain in it. If it is difficult to take the step beyond the plausible excuse that things are not as bad as they seem, how much more difficult is it for the ingenious human being not to give way to the false comfort that, if things are so bad, then there is nothing to be done about them, making any response unnecessary. But, notwithstanding the infinite variety of human excuses, God's gift of a new spirit means that even to such ingenuity a further address can be given: namely, "It is not on your account that I am acting ..."

Once he has cleared the grounds, the new address in terms of inward renewal is appealing and intimate. The obvious comparison with the new covenant passage in Jeremiah 31 shows this. There v.33 speaks of Yahweh putting his law within the people; but here Ezekiel is more intimate, for he speaks of Yahweh putting a new **spirit** within them: that is, Yahweh himself is made to participate more directly in the people's new response(7). The new spirit may be partly understanding, but it is also the strength providing the capacity for what is new. The Jeremiah passage uses the term "covenant" but Ezekiel, strikingly different, does not. This suggests that, while the term could have a particular theological effect (a new covenant is something to which the people are bound), it is not absolutely essential. Indeed it might be said that Ezekiel is intimately human for not using it, which more than compensates for his coldness in 36:22. Verse 28 ends with the so-called covenantal formula - (8) "So you shall dwell in the land which I gave to your fathers, and you will be my people and I will be your God" - but as can be seen here the formula is not necessarily connected in an explicit way with the use of the term "covenant". It is a binding statement of reciprocal relationship - in Ezekiel's terms the necessary offer of life and the necessary responsibility of accepting it.

It seems at first surprising that, having spoken in such a way of inward transformation, the passage should go on to speak of material plenty:

> I will deliver you from all your uncleannesses, and summon the grain, multiplying it, but not laying hunger upon you. I will multiply the fruit of the tree and produce of the field in order that you might no longer suffer the disgrace of hunger among the nations (36:29-30).

Old Testament people, however, could not separate the "spiritual" from the "material". Rightly, they did not tend to say that the material is of no real consequence. As the comprehensive expression here puts it, a theology of renewal means the giving up of mere party interests: renewal is not religious or material, individual or communal; renewal is not the gospel versus feeding the hungry, the past versus the present - it is the recognition of the simultaneous and necessarily complementary need of all these together. Renewal reveals the partial nature of our own particular interest, though at the same time providing people with the grace not to give up that interest.

While we may not want to connect God so directly with the giving of material increase, it is still true that people who are inwardly transformed will be concerned with material prosperity as well. Even if they are inwardly transformed, it does matter whether or not they and their fellows are starving, just as the people who are satisfied still need to be inwardly transformed. It is impossible ever to complete this transformation; indeed, transformed and returned to their land, the people must remember their evil ways and therefore loathe themselves: "You shall remember your evil ways and your deeds which were not good and be disgusted at yourselves for your perversions and abominations" (36:31). Finally we hear that it cannot be on their account that Yahweh has acted:

> It is not on your account that I am acting, says Lord Yahweh; let that be known to you. Be ashamed and confounded at your ways, O house of Israel (36:32).

This may seem to be over-emphatic. Yet this reaction of self-loathing does not provide justification for punishment (as in chap.6) but the foundation for a totally new inner transformation. These final words are not spoken in order to humiliate, but so that people might be delivered from that continually re-assertive self-confidence which, however much it might have been transformed in the past, is always in danger of bringing matters to a standstill again(9).

It seems likely that the final two units in 36:33-36 and vv.37-38 are later additions expressing a more mundane matter(10): a marked and continued preoccupation with the repopulation of the land. It is one thing to integrate inward transformation with material prosperity, as in vv.26-30, it is another to concentrate solely on the latter. Formal matters also indicate a later addition. Verse 33 speaks of "on the day when I cleanse you", so could well be a later elaboration of v.25, and one which, unlike v.25 itself, is much more concerned with repopulation and replanting than inward transformation:

> Thus says Lord Yahweh, On the day when I cleanse you from all your perversions, I will cause the cities to be reinhabited and the ruins will be rebuilt. The devastated land will be tilled instead of being a desolation in the sight of all who pass by. They will say, This devastated land has become like the garden of Eden ...

The word for "this" in the phrase "this devastated land" is not found anywhere else in the Old Testament in the form used here(11). Finally, the way in which 36:37 starts with "this also", a convenient additive formula, makes it look like a further addition to that which preceded it:

> Thus says Lord Yahweh, This also I let the house of Israel ask of me to do for them: I will increase their people like sheep ...

While the additive nature of these units is clear, the longings expressed are completely understandable. It was one thing to go back to the land; another to face up to it on arrival.

5. RESPONSIBILITY FOR LIFE: 37:1-14

The unusual vision of life here is all the more striking since it takes its origin from observation of ordinary life. When the vision is interpreted in 37:11-14, there comes a quotation from the people themselves. Ezekiel is to listen to them saying, "Our bones are dried up, our hope is gone, we are cut off from life" (37:11), showing the down-to-earth origin of Ezekiel's highly unusual vision of a miracle of life. The background shows too that this vision is not an expression of faith in resurrection from the literal dead, but of something far greater than that, of faith in life for people who want to die. Since what the people say expresses resigned lethargy with no hope in the possibility of life, it means that Ezekiel's vision of life must contend with impossible odds. The cry of despair makes it likely that it dates from soon after the fall of Jerusalem, probably before what is now to be found in 36:16-32; it seems more likely that the latter belongs to a time closer to the return(1). It could be that, just as the insistent offer of life in chap.33 begins this section on restoration, so this striking visionary experience of confidence in life is deliberately set towards its end. The framework of belief in life at impossible odds is necessary before the true state of the Judaeans and the exiles is exposed even after the fall of Jerusalem (33:21-33), as well as after the promise of restoration and inward renewal (34-36).

In this situation of destruction and despair Ezekiel knows that "The hand of Yahweh came upon me ..." (37:1). The terms "hand" and "spirit" used together in this verse have been mentioned before, but their combination in this most striking of all visions demands detailed commentary. About 200 passages in the Old Testament speak of the hand of Yahweh, particularly in statements referring to special deeds of power by Yahweh. For example, he carries out the Exodus with a mighty hand (e.g. Deuteronomy 26:8)(2). The hand of Yahweh can be said to lie heavily upon people, afflicting them (I Samuel 5:6), as well as having a protecting power (Isaiah 49:2). In the prophets it can be an expression of authorization by Yahweh (Isaiah 8:11), and certainly in Ezekiel 37 this vision issuing in a promise is given strong authorization when the hand of Yahweh comes on the prophet.

In the Book of Ezekiel there are seven instances of the expression: in 1:3; 3:14, 22; 8:1; 33:22; 37:1; 40:1. Thus it is to be found in the introductions to all four of the great vision reports: in 1:3 introducing the call vision; in 8:1 the vision of the abominations in Jerusalem; in 37:1 the vision of the valley of dry bones; and in 40:1 the vision of the new temple. All of these visions are connected with a definite message, each with a particular content, so that the expression "the hand of Yahweh" must be associated with the message. On the other hand, the expression cannot simply be identified with a message because 33:22, for instance, is a narrative which does not lead into a word of Yahweh's. The hand of Yahweh is therefore not connected with any particular message, but seems to express a state of complete devotion to Yahweh, in which reception of the word can take place. It can also (3:14-15) include a week-long state of dumbness as its consequence, though significantly a consciousness still remains of the presence of the hard people to whom he is to deliver a hard message (3:15; 7-9). That "the hand of Yahweh" is not identical with "the word of Yahweh", is shown in the fact that word-events without visionary features are never introduced by a reference to the hand of Yahweh.

Thus the use of the phrase here clearly indicates a supra-normal experience connected with the content of a particular message, but not to be simply identified with it. Ezekiel, far from merging with the deity, is convinced of a source of life other than (though inseparable from) himself - "the hand of Yahweh came upon me". Ezekiel is caught up in an encounter where he will be convinced of something which, by himself, he would not be capable of grasping. Something new

190

happens to him. He personally confronts the complete opposite of that which is expressed by the people in 37:11, something so overwhelmingly different, such a conversion of the impossible to the possible, that he needs time to surrender himself completely to it, time between himself and God only.

All this appears when, the hand of Yahweh having come upon him, "... he brought me out in the spirit of Yahweh and set me down in the middle of the valley ..." (37:1). The reference to the "spirit" is striking, for such references are rare after the early prophets and before Ezekiel. It seems strange too to use the phrase "spirit of Yahweh" when "Yahweh" is the subject of the sentence(3). But possibly the phrase came to be used in order to place special emphasis on an uncommon experience so intense that it was natural and appropriate to use it. Ezekiel, presented as a visionary, sees himself in a valley, and the way he expresses this "vision of transport" in terms of spirit demonstrates again his knowledge that it does not originate in himself, however much it might be bound up with him and his world. The spirit of Yahweh differs completely from Ezekiel's world, which in many ways is the same as that into which he is put, for the valley is full of bones:

> The hand of Yahweh came upon me, and he brought me out in the spirit of Yahweh and set me down in the middle of the valley - it was full of bones! (37:1).

The "introduction" to the passage is very literal within the context of the supra-normal vision; he is "introduced" into a particular place, the word for "valley" meaning the valley plain in contrast to the mountains, probably the broad alluvial plain of Babylon, that of the river Kebar(4). Particularly apt to his own and his people's situation is that the valley is full of bones.

The "introduction" is emphasized by the next verse; "He led me right among them - they were very many there upon the valley, and they were very dry" (37:2). Ezekiel is left in no doubt about what he is up against; he sees this death, he is led around in the midst of it, and is made aware of its reality(5).

In an effort to elicit a response, there follows an address in the form of a macabre question:

> Then he said to me, Son of man, can these bones live? I answered, Lord Yahweh, you know (37:3).

The answer "Of course not" might have been expected, but Ezekiel, while not prepared to commit himself to saying that these bones can live, indicates that he is prepared to reckon with the possibility. The answer is full of reserve, revealing the consciousness mentioned before that human beings are not their own source of life(6). Ezekiel does not present himself as any kind of expert "man of God", but understands he is the "son of man". The son of man knows himself to be addressed, does not jump to the conclusion that things will always have to be as they are, and exemplifies that attitude responsive enough to discover a relationship within circumstances which can change them. Thus the macabre question elicits a response which, cautious though it may be, makes possible a command to the son of man which will eventually lead to a new result. Seen in this light, the command is not nearly as bizarre as might appear:

> Then he said to me, Prophesy to these bones saying to them, O dry bones, hear the word of Yahweh (37:4).

Ezekiel hears a command which anybody who jumps to conclusions could only consider absurd: he is to prophesy to the bones; the dry bones are to hear the word of Yahweh! The implication is that even people as dead as Ezekiel's people can receive words, can take in a new content. Those who respond as Ezekiel does are those who are prepared to accept the challenge, who can comprehend a command promising life to the dead: "Thus says Lord Yahweh to these bones, I am about to bring breath into you so that you may live" (37:5). Even the "dead" can have "breath" put back into them, and how "dead" the heavily resigned can be. The breath of life in the bones is the most important, as the fact that it is mentioned here, before the sinews, flesh and skin in v.6, shows. The breath recurs at the end in connection with the word of recognition itself:

> I will lay sinews upon you, and bring flesh over you and cover you with skin. I will put breath in you that you may live and know that I am Yahweh.

The recognition of Yahweh comes with the realization of new life. New life does not come of itself, but from a source. The source is bound up with giving a promise to those who are prepared to listen to it. The promise, we must remember, comes through the son of man, whose responsibility for life goes so far that he has been prepared to answer an absurd question and obey a bizarre command.

The next stage is the execution of the command:

> So I prophesied as I was commanded: then there was a noise as I was prophesying, a rattling as the bones came together. Then I saw sinews upon them, flesh came upon them and skin covered them from above. But there was still no breath in them (37:7-8).

The breath is vital. After the grotesque details of the rattling of the bones coming together with the sinews, flesh and skin upon them, it is said that there is still no breath in them, the word for "breath" being placed emphatically in the

sentence. The execution of the command has led to a result
without fulfilment. A renewed command follows, which is
especially directed towards the breath:

> Then he said to me, Prophesy to the breath,
> prophesy, son of man, and say to the breath, Thus
> says Lord Yahweh, come from the four winds, O
> breath, and breathe upon these slain that they
> might live (37:9).

The fresh command brings out the decisiveness of this
moment(7), filled with unexpected possibilities. The breath
(unlike that in Genesis 2:7, though a different word is used
there) does not appear to come directly from God (though it
does have to be prophesied for at his command), but is a
possibility existing throughout the world, there to be
summoned(8). It is also the same world in which the lethargic
exiles live: realization of life is possible in the most
hopeless of circumstances; Ezekiel's responsibility for life
goes so far that he is not put off by despair. The fresh
command leads now to the fulfilment of life;

> So I prophesied as he commanded me: the breath
> came upon them and they lived; they stood upon
> their feet, an exceedingly large number (37:10).

These bones were very dry. The wonder of life can be and is
realized. What has already happened to Ezekiel can be
transferred to the people.
Ezekiel is supremely responsible for the life of his people.
The opening of the interpretation of the vision in 37:11 is
immediately focused on Ezekiel's people, on their present
situation and attitude:

> He said to me, Son of man, these bones are the
> whole house of Israel: listen to them saying, Our
> bones are dried up, our hope is gone, we are cut
> off from life.

Life does not come automatically from the people themselves,
which is emphasized, curiously, by Ezekiel never actually
telling the people about his vision as such. His vision was
necessary for his own private conviction, since responsibility
for life cannot be exercised merely from congenital optimism.
He who is responsible for life must be faced with the sober
reality - in this case that "these bones are the whole house of
Israel", and in this stark confrontation may be private
elements he can never share with others. He who is responsible
for life can and must communicate the substance of his
conviction in terms perhaps more intelligible than those of his
private vision. There can be no retreat into privacy, no
question of the vision being interesting only for its bizarre
nature. This is now shown in the new confrontation with the

people, in the extreme form of a word of disputation where their own words are quoted and then contradicted. The conviction behind the vision makes Ezekiel into the kind of person who can speak even to these people. The image used changes from bones to grave, which may have been thought more natural in answering what they were saying. It does not necessarily indicate that the vision and its interpretation did not originally belong together, as is often held(9).

> Therefore, prophesy and say to them, Thus says Lord Yahweh, I am about to open your graves, and I will raise you from your graves [my people](10), and bring you to the land of Israel (37:12).

The promise explicitly applies to these despairing people in terms of a return to their land, probably the last thing they were expecting to happen. Their lack of expectation was understandable, and without the theological promise:

> You will know that I am Yahweh when I open your graves and raise you from your graves [my people]. I will put my spirit within you and you will live, and I shall set you down upon your own land so that you will know that it is I, Yahweh, who have spoken and acted, says Yahweh (37:13-14).

The ultimate goal of the promise has finally been reached. Startling in its theological arrogance, it is the recognition of Yahweh. The recognition of Yahweh could not, however, be divorced from the statements on opening the people's graves, putting his spirit within them, and setting them down upon their own land. Nothing like this is possible by itself, but only in relationship.

6. RESPONSIBILITY FOR SEPARATED BRETHREN: 37:15-28

Though the vision of the valley of dry bones in 37:1-14 is striking, the final unit of this section in Ezekiel 33-37 is in a sense the most striking of all. It is concerned with restoration as reunion, the reunion of Northern Israel with Judah(1). Considering the emphasis on the "house of Israel" in Ezekiel, on the restoration of people to their land, the most fitting climax for the last section is indeed the reunion of the two parts of the people, separated for so long. Those who live in divided countries today, like Germany and Korea, know how strong aspirations for reunion can be, at least to some, but they also know how difficult it is to achieve once new and separate structures have developed and hardened. They also know how the desire for reunion can soon begin to fade. None of these factors would have been any less significant in Northern Israel and Judah in Ezekiel's time; so the fact that the desire for reunion occurs again now is all the more striking when we realize that some 350 years of separation have passed, in which the North seems to have been more or less repudiated in the South. Aspirations for reunion need not have died out completely, however. Indeed, that they are present, and given such pronounced expression by Ezekiel, suggests a strong memory of common faith. Perhaps Judaean exiles met with descendants of Northern Israelite exiles of the 8th century, who could easily have come down to the southern part of the then Assyrian Empire - but we do not know. Possibly the Judaeans, perhaps to their surprise, found they still shared the same faith with these brothers and sisters. Common ground would have been all the more noticeable given their differences from the Babylonians and other exiles living there.

In some ways, then, the possibilities were right before the people's eyes, and Ezekiel's responsibility was to draw the people's attention to them as vividly and forcefully as he could;

> The word of Yahweh came to me saying, now you, son of man, take one stick and write upon it, Belonging to Judah and the Israelites associated with him, and take another stick and write upon it, Belonging to Joseph, the stem of Ephraim, and the whole house of Israel associated with him, and join them together into one stick that they may become one in your hand (37:15-17).

In a symbolic prophetic act, Ezekiel is to take one piece of wood to represent the South and another to represent the North. Since the general word for "wood" is used, it is difficult to know exactly what is meant(2). Some might think of a wooden tablet, but it seems more natural to imagine a stick, especially if it were like a staff inscribed with the owner's name. The reason that the North is referred to as "Joseph" (or, possibly as an addition, as "Ephraim", the kernel land of the Northern kingdom) is that Ezekiel wants to use "Israel" to represent the whole of the people(3). These two sticks, so long broken apart, are then to be joined together. The question from the people in v.18 indicates that it is not a matter to be taken for granted. Because of the length of the separation and the magnitude of the task, their preoccupation is comparable with the modern ecumenical movement(4).

> When the members of your people ask you, Won't you tell us what you mean by these ... ? (37:18) -

The reaction of the people is integrated with the prophet's interpretation, which can now be offered to them directly:

> ... speak to them, Thus says Lord Yahweh, look I
> am about to take the stick of Joseph which is in
> the hand of Ephraim) and the tribes of Israel
> associated with him, and I will join [them](5) with
> it the stick of Judah; I will make them one stick
> and they will become one in my hand (37:19).

Yahweh's interpretation is the same as his commission to the
prophet (vv.16-17). In prophetic symbolism, what was done
would happen even as it was done, not magically but bound by
interpretation and understanding. Reunion has not yet taken
place (it never did on any scale) but it is first recognized
against many odds as a possibility by one person and then
offered to others for their acceptance. Such are the
consequences that the new happenings are having, not only for
the inward life of the people (chap.36), but also for their
outward organization and public attitudes. For though it is
impossible to view this promise as though it were fulfilled, it
is still a significant indication of having rejected the
attitude that what has been done cannot be reversed, or the
less neutral attitude which often goes with it: that those who
have been separated are becoming more and more alienated from
each other and can only be actively opposed. All this is
strongly countered by the promise given here, so much so that
Ezekiel sees it in terms of being reconciled again:

> When the sticks on which you write are in your hand
> before their eyes, then speak to them, Thus says
> Lord Yahweh, I am about to take the Israelites from
> among the nations where they went and gather them
> from round about and bring them to their own land
> (37:20-21).

That is, reunion connects with the promise of the return. Part
of the significance of the return itself - the dominant theme
in Ezekiel's presentation of restoration - is that it takes
place with a reunified people. Reunion consists in a gathering
of all Israelites from their exile, their being brought back
together to their common land. It naturally strengthens their
unity to say that they will be under one king:

> I will make them into one people in the land on the
> mountains of Israel and one king will be king for
> them all; no longer shall they be two nations and
> no longer divided into two kingdoms (37:22).

One of the features of the disruption of North and South was
that the monarchy was divided. It is interesting too that the
word melek for "king" is used here and not nāsî' as in 34:24,
and that no attempt is made to say who this king is to be. The
aim is to express reunion in terms which come to mind naturally
and immediately rather than be particularly concerned with the
literal significance of the detail. The aim is not to identify

David as in 34:23 and later in this same chapter (37:24-25).
Matters could have been brought to a conclusion before v.24,
with the typical statement about purification and the
"covenant" formula in v.23:

> They shall no longer defile themselves with their
> idols, with their abominations and all their
> crimes, but I will deliver them from all their
> backslidings in which they have sinned, and I will
> cleanse them so that they shall be my people and I
> will be their God.

Reunion combines with the return, and leads to the inner
renewal of people. The last chapter of the section (33-37)
contains all the themes of restoration mentioned elsewhere:
return, inner renewal, David, covenant, with the addition of
the sanctuary. By concluding with restoration as reunion, this
chapter certainly presents a climax.

It is only after the conclusion of 37:23 and the use of the
term "king" within the theme of unity, that the need was
apparently felt to stipulate who the king is to be. (By v.25
he becomes nāśî' again).

> My servant David shall be king over them, and they
> shall all have one shepherd; they shall walk in my
> ordinances, and keep my statutes and do them
> (37:24).

Since v.22 leaves the king unidentified, it sounds as though an
interpolator wants to make quite sure that he can only be one
of the Davidic line. The Book of Ezekiel speaks in one place
of the kingship of Yahweh (20:33)(6), so that, even if all the
"king" passages in the book were attributed to Ezekiel, they
still could not be reckoned as central. The important facts
about reunion have already been stated, except that it was
logical to mention David, as he was the only king, apart from
his son Solomon, under whom there was a united kingdom.

A new theme is now taken up, that of permanent validity:

> They will dwell in the land which I gave to my
> servant Jacob where your fathers dwelt; they and
> their children and their grandchildren shall dwell
> there for ever, and my servant David will be prince
> over them for ever (37:25).

It has often been remarked that the figure of David is never
given fuller expression in the Book of Ezekiel, which remains
far behind the luxuriant expression of Isaiah 9:6-7; 11:1-5;
Micah 5:2-4, or Zechariah 9:9. "David" has something of a
timeless cypher about it here(7). The theme of permanent
validity takes over, culminating in the much more important
theme in Ezekiel of Yahweh's sanctuary which has no necessary
relation with reunion:

> I will make a promise of restitution (covenant of
> peace) to them; it will be an everlasting promise
> [them, I shall give them](8), and I will multiply
> them and set my sanctuary in their midst for ever
> (37:26).

Yahweh promises again material and spiritual benefit, the
latter in the form of the permanent establishment of Yahweh's
sanctuary among them. This entails Yahweh himself dwelling
among them, which goes far beyond the re-establishment of the
Davidic monarchy. "My dwelling place will be with them and I
will be their God and they will be my people" (37:27) (9).
Above all the conviction of Yahweh's presence will cause the
nations to acknowledge him: "The nations shall know that I,
Yahweh, am sanctifying Israel, when my sanctuary is among them
for ever" (37:28). In as far as this happened, it was through
a conviction of God's presence among them rather than the
re-establishment of the Davidic monarchy or even the reunion of
the people, for these last two simply did not come about. Some
Judaeans undoubtedly aspired to reunion (see also Jeremiah 3
and 30-31). Not all took it for granted that the Northern
Israelites - and only they - were impenitent syncretists (see
also Ezekiel 16 and 23). Hope for reunion could have been a
necessary creative element in their relationship in Ezekiel's
time. But in the end this hope, like the re-establishment of
the Davidic monarchy, came to nothing. The re-establishment of
the sanctuary both in material and spiritual terms in
post-exilic times was the true creative focus of Israel. The
later interpretation of this passage was necessary. True
restoration eventuates when a tradition is created freed from
the old irrelevant models. Restoration is freedom for the new
expression to speak creatively to people now.

APPENDIX: THE RESTORATION OF ULTIMATE REALITY: 38 - 39.

After the call vision in chaps.1-3 where the source, medium and
goal of Ezekiel's vision are shown, chaps.4-24 reveal how
important it is for the exiles to hear what is said about the
judgement of Jerusalem. If they do not understand its
implications, they will not realize that the possibilities for
restoration actually lie with themselves. To do so, they also
must realize that the other nations should not be regarded as
obstacles to restoration (25-32): they must see the obstacles
within themselves. The contribution of chaps.33-37 to the
composition of the book as a whole is this: the fall of
Jerusalem is announced, without presupposing that either the
prophets of the people will necessarily exercise their
responsibilities, or that at home or in exile they will

necessarily respond appropriately (33). Nor are the leaders
any guarantee that the new happenings will be interpreted
correctly (34); the exiles themselves must recognize the
contrast between the surrounding desolation and the restoration
promised to their land (35-36). The return and
re-establishment of life there is worth nothing, however,
unless accompanied by an inner renewal (36:15ff.); new life is
offered to them in their present state of death, along with a
possible reunion(37). In this pattern of restoration the
exiles are continually faced with the real world, in terms both
of their response and of outward circumstances.

Is a settled peace to be the _final_ reality? People must look
beyond what is most immediate(1); what then is restoration of
the _ultimate_ reality? We can therefore understand the
following semi-apocalyptic presentation of the coming of a
mysterious prince, of the shaking of the world, and in general,
of the final denouement. It expresses the fear of the unknown,
the presentiment that there is still a threat unresolved, still
much of a decisive nature to come. Restoration cannot be taken
for granted: just as the election of a new government does not
solve everything, so the introduction of a new order does not
automatically fulfil everything. This reservation must be kept
in mind when the restoration of the temple and the land is
described in chaps.40-48. Chaps.38-39 are the boldest
expression of the creative freedom afforded by restoration, for
they will neither give up what has been promised nor pretend
that it has already been effected.

As early as the second verse of this section (38:2) there
appears an obstacle to the promise in the form of Gog, the
chief prince of Mesech and Tubal (northern peoples in the area
now known as Asia Minor). Gog has been identified with Gyges
of Lydia in Asia Minor, which leaves Gog's relationship with
Mesech and Tubal uncertain. "Gog" is more likely to be an
intentionally unknown and mysterious figure with great power as
the leader of numbers of peoples(2). (This is the only place
in the whole book which addresses such an unknown figure)(3).
But even this threat can be destroyed: Yahweh is against Gog
(38:3). Countries which have recently re-established peace
(often by independence from a greater power) may brood
fearfully over what can still be done to them, and be uncertain
about the intentions of greater powers. But the form of
address to Gog implies that even a figure such as he does not
hold ultimate power. By 38:7 it is clear that Gog and all the
powers over which he has authority are actually being called up
in the service of Yahweh.

It is not clear when this will happen; 38:8 says "after many
days", and sees the attack taking place in a land which has
become peaceful:

> ... a land restored from the sword, gathered from
> among many peoples onto the mountains of Israel
> which had long been desolate - a land which has
> been saved from the peoples where all are living

without care.

That the attack comes like a storm spreading over this land
(38:9) does not mean that the peace is invalid, but emphasizes
the tension between peace and threat, and shows how exposed the
restored land is. Restoration is not something static. What
is promised in chaps.33-37 must be seen within a continuing
reality even if it cannot be defined exactly. Restoration is
not yet restoration if it is thought to have found a perfect
end for all time.

The material in 38:1-9 probably began a basic text(4) which
originally continued in 39:1-5, where Gog's swift destruction
is described. The material in 38:10-13 must be additions
because of the unexpected and unusual attention directed
towards Gog's own self-consciousness(5):

> ... I will go to the open country, I will come
> upon those living peacefully and without care, all
> of them living without wall and fortification
> ...(38:11).

The first person style lends the presentation a great
liveliness, with Gog's own words expressing guilt at having
attacked the unfortified settlements of Israel. In the basic
text, Yahweh simply calls up Gog and then destroys him. It is
"objective"; 38:10-13 show that human reaction to what people
are told to do is essential, and that nothing arbitrary can
happen outside of that. The destruction of the threat has more
dimensions than might be thought in the transition from 38:1-9
to 39:1-5. The establishment of security cannot be taken for
granted. Plans can be made even against the "navel of the
earth" (38:12), the centre of the universe. The dramatic and
lively potentiality of the situation appears in the quotation
from other peoples (38:13):

> Sheba and Dedan and the merchants of Tarshish and
> all its traders say to you (Gog), Are you coming to
> take plunder and mustering to get booty, to carry
> off silver and gold, to take cattle and possessions
> in order to take great plunder?

It is characteristically human that the conclusion of this
section brings out the commercial possibilities of the whole
situation. Such a dimension of guilt, must not be left out of
account; it is significant for human beings in general, not
only for business people, that guilt, when explicitly
discussed, emerges in a commercial setting.

The style of addition (38:14-16) is questioning
reflection(6):

> ... is it not so, on that day when my people
> Israel are living in peace that you will bestir
> yourself and come from your place ... and go up

against my people Israel like cloud ... and that I
bring you up against my land in order that the
peoples may know me when I sanctify myself through
you before them, O Gog? (38:14-16).

Yahweh in sanctifying himself through Gog, uses him to make
himself known to the nations. When this happening takes place
before the eyes of the nations, they as well as Israel are
drawn in as direct witnesses(7). The destruction of the threat
is not a private matter between Israel and another power but a
universal recognition. The greatest power cannot control the
ultimate outcome of its deeds, and the people who strive to
retain their peace have the support of other nations who know
as much as they do.

The first verse of the next section (38:17-23) uses
deuteronomistic rather than Ezekielian language(8):

... you are the one of whom I spoke in former
times through my servants the prophets of Israel
who prophesied in those days ... that I would
bring you against them.

Even if this did not form part of the basic text, it probably
defines the basic motivation of the text: to doubt whether, in
the context of peaceful re-settlement, such prophecies as
Jeremiah's (4:6) of an enemy from the north, had as yet been
fufilled(9). Once this doubt has been expressed, the
fulfilment can be seen in cosmic terms different from those of
the basic text: world-wide convulsions. Israel is caught up
in a great earthquake (38:19) which then extends to universal
world judgement. Unusually it speaks of the quaking of fish,
birds, animals, insects and people along with the collapse of
mountains and walls (38:20), that is, the whole world, natural
and constructed, together with every kind of living creature,
shakes in the catastrophe. This cosmic judgement sweeps away
Gog himself in panic and storm (vv.21-22), the passage
culminating in a statement of universal recognition (v.23).
Though not set logically in the composition as a whole, this
section attempts to express the world-wide effects of the final
destruction of the last threat to Israel. We cannot see this
as the literal means of establishing peace; but we must
understand that the progression towards it involves all peoples
in more fundamental ways than simply being aware of what is
happening.

The main theme, that of bringing Gog to the peaceful land
where he is quickly destroyed, is to be found in the basic text
38:1-9; 39:1-5, and 39:17-20. The basic text is filled out
with material on Gog's guilt, the exposed situation of Israel,
and the world-wide witness and significance of the destruction.
Not all these issues lead logically to the original account of
Gog's destruction, but the additions certainly provide a more
meaningful inner structure. All danger is to be destroyed:
this is made clear by the close connection between the account

of Yahweh's bringing Gog against the mountains of Israel and the first mention of Yahweh himself being the direct agent of Gog's destruction (39:2-3). In the duel set up between Yahweh and Gog (v.1), Yahweh strikes the bow from Gog's left hand and the arrows from his right; this great force will be rendered powerless. The end is a shameful one (39:4-5). Gog is given to birds and animals of prey for food; he falls on the open field unburied. When one nation's power over another is appreciated by both sides as shameful, an opportunity arises to grasp some control over the fundamental changes which are taking place, so that what is truly fitting may finally be established.

Since 39:1-5 ends with Gog becoming food for the birds and beasts, the original continuation probably appeared in the address to these creatures in 39:17-20. Before it the utter destruction of Gog is expressed in an additional way, by fire (39:6). The destruction is extended to the Greeks, who are the ones now said to be living securely. The destruction is understood to mean that the time for desecrating Yahweh's name is over (v.7); such desecration entailed the opposite of recognizing Yahweh and his holiness, so that what is taking place is appropriate. As an interpolation, 39:6-8 shows how positive and universal is the destruction of the threat.

The next addition in 39:9-10 draws the consequences of the destruction: the Israelites burn the armaments for seven years. No need for ordinary firewood! A practical act, which shows how a powerful threat has been completely destroyed and (though it is probably not intended) it reminds the reader of a time of peace where the means of war have been destroyed (see Isaiah 9:5).

Just as it takes seven years to burn the armaments, so it takes all the people seven months to bury the dead of the conquered and so to purify the land - so many dead have there been. Since some men are especially commissioned to go through the land and bury those remaining (39:14), the land will be totally purified. This priestly interest connects with chaps. 40-48, and logically contradicts the activity of the birds of prey. It shows that there is no point in averting the threat if nothing acceptable can be put in its place. The people's preparation is so important that they are even said to reflect something of Yahweh's glory (39:13).

Thus, in these additions between 39:1-5 and 39:17-20, Gog's shameful destruction in being given to the birds and animals as food has universal significance with two consequences: the destruction of weapons of war, and the purification of the land. This leads back to the original argument in 39:17-20 where the feast described is a sacrificial meal at Yahweh's own invitation. Not only all people but all animals are witnesses and participants, so that the destruction of the threat in the face of peace has a truly cosmic and religious festive significance. It is even said that the birds and beasts will eat the flesh of heroes and drink the blood of princes (39:18). This expresses the conviction that, far from the heroes and princes constituting an obstacle to peace, their destruction brings about a satisfying conclusion (39;19-20). Indeed, in eating fat and drinking blood, the animals participate in what would normally be reserved for Yahweh (Leviticus 3:16-17). No one goes away from Yahweh's table unsatisfied. The defeat of the warriors means that it is no longer necessary to fear the superiority of other peoples.

In 39:21-22 the recognition of Yahweh both by other peoples and by Israel indicates that the established peace for all will last. In 39:23 appears a completely new thought, which has to do with the people's acknowledgement of the connection between the guilt of Israel and their exile. This has no concern with Gog, but means, as elsewhere, that their guilt should under no circumstances be forgotten. Not forgetting is indeed the very thing which ensures a genuine transformation to a new life, when the Israelites recognize Yahweh not only in being exiled but also in being brought back to their land (39:28). Further, the pouring out of Yahweh's spirit over Israel, when he no longer hides his face from them, expresses the guarantee of the continuance of life in their land (39:29). This passage had nothing to do with Gog originally, but now it performs the necessary function, through the emphasis on the continuance of life, of linking the restoration of life in chaps.33-37 with the planning of the central agency to this end in chaps.40-48. The elaboration of the most important medium is still to come.

1. THE PLACE: 40 - 42 (1)

Once again Ezekiel is brought in divine visions to Israel
(40:1-2). Once again a particular date is given: "In the
twenty-fifth year of our exile ..." Scholars have suggested
that the figure "25" might deliberately represent the middle
point on the way to the year of release, which was supposed to
take place at the year of Jubilee every fiftieth year
(Leviticus 25)(2); certainly the figure "25" or multiples
thereof appear prominently in the following measurements of the
temple. If so, it indicates a confidence that already half the
time has elasped before the return of the exiles to a restored
place. Significantly, another reference by date is given, "in
the fourteenth year after the city had fallen". The fallen
city contrasts with the city-like structure which Ezekiel now
sees on the very high mountain on which he is set. Clearly he
is brought to a place built up from that which had fallen.
     Thus these first two verses insist on the importance of the
restoration of place to this concluding section of the book.
The place to be restored is of the greatest significance for
the life between Yahweh and the people. The restoration of the
sanctuary expresses the faith that the people do not return to
their country with a totally broken relationship with what had
sustained them before; they find that it is possible for this
relationship to be renewed in an unexpected way. The sanctuary
expresses the need for both continuity and renewal in the
passing from one country to another, with all the upheaval and
opportunity which that brings. Chapters 40-48 are (loosely)
the other side of the vision of the abominations in Jerusalem
in chaps.8-11: the re-ordering of disorder(3). The theme of
the sanctuary occurs too in chaps 20, 24 and 37, so that 40-48
bring to a culmination what has already been in large measure
introduced(4). In 11:16, the surprising statement is made that
Yahweh himself has become something of a sanctuary for the
people in exile. This means that the continuation of life is
not bound to one place, but the reticence of the statement also
means that the most adequate restoration of the sanctuary will
be found elsewhere. Yahweh as sanctuary in exile is
encouraging but still provisory. Later, 20:32 says the
Israelites will not become like the nations, and (implicitly)
it will be possible to re-establish the sanctuary in Israel.
The need for it to be re-established is clear from the end of
the section on judgement in 24:21 where people must accept that
Yahweh himself profanes the sanctuary. The sanctuary shows the
need for a new beginning in both the religious and personal
sense. The profanation of the sanctuary is the very

circumstance which advances matters for by 24:25 it is said
that the day when Yahweh takes away the delight of their eyes
will be the day of release.

This reference to the sanctuary in 24:25 links chaps.25-32
with the chapters on restoration in 33-37. This important
section ends, crucially, in 37:26 with the re-establishment of
"my sanctuary" along with the promise of permanent restitution.
When it comes to the promise (berît) of restitution (šalôm)
which is to be permanent (côlām), it is given substance through
the sanctuary; the word for "permanence" is also explicitly
used with it. Indeed, Yahweh's dwelling place among the people
(v.27 - a different word is used from v.26) is so important
that it is spoken of in connection with the formula of
belonging together(5): "I shall be their God and they will be
my people". Thus the most appropriate and full life for Israel
is promised through the sanctuary, something which will last.
More, such life emanating from a specific relation is visible
to others. The last verse in the restoration section (37:28)
takes on a universal aspect:

> Then the nations will know that I Yahweh am
> sanctifying Israel when my sanctuary is to be found
> permanently in their midst.

To say that other nations witness the permanent
re-establishment of Israel's life is to express confidence that
it really will be so. It also underlines how indispensable the
physical location is. People who move from country to country
look for both continuity and renewal, and really do need such
locations. How little embarrassment is felt about the
importance of physical place is shown in the present
composition of chap.37, which implies that the future is in
neither re-unification nor the re-establishment of the
monarchy, but the sanctuary. Then, just as the end of chap.24
links by way of 25-32 with 33-37, now the end of chap.37 links
by way of the appendix (38-39) with the fulfilment of the
promise of the sanctuary given in great physical detail in
chaps.40-48 (6).

After Ezekiel has been set on the very high mountain(7) where
there is a city-like structure, he immediately sees a "man"
whose appearance is like bronze (40:3). A heavenly figure is
thus to act as a guide for Ezekiel through the vision"; and
the motif of guidance is one of the prominent features of the
basic text(8). At the same time, the man has a down-to-earth
function since he is immediately described as having a linen
line and a measuring rod in his hand. He stands ready at the
gate. Measuring also plays a dominant role in the basic text;
the measuring procedure is described there nineteen times(9).
The correct physical dimensions of the sanctuary which provides
the means of life are thus of the greatest importance.

Ezekiel is to make an attentive response since there is only
one reason for his having been brought here. He must see - and
then he is to communicate everything he has seen to the house

of Israel (40:4). That one man as an eye-witness is able to inform everyone emphasizes that the re-establishment of the sanctuary and all that it entails for the life of the people can be regarded as a fact(10). As in the call vision in chaps.1-3, form and word belong closely together, expressing the factual nature of the conviction. The sanctuary exists, and its significance can be communicated. Nor does the communication concern something which the people cannot see for themselves. Ezekiel is the responsible medium between form and word, with the goal that the people themselves become involved in every dimension.

With this commission before him Ezekiel then **sees**. The commission and its significance must be kept in mind when reading details which modern readers might regard as boring. In the remainder of the first part of the basic text (40:5-37), the reader is systematically guided from the outside to the inside, from the outside wall through the outside east (40:6-19), north (vv.20-23) and south gates (vv.24-27), to the inner gates (vv.28-37)(11). This guided tour with its measurements, pressing on directly to the centre of things, is interrupted in 40:38-46 by specific details concerning the equipment of the inner north gate. The visionary element is to be found only fleetingly in v.45a, and the motifs of measuring and guidance are not to be found at all(12). The material clarifies details about the slaughtering of sacrifices, (vv.38-43) and determines the distinctions in service of different classes of priests in the temple generally and at the altar in particular (vv.44-46).

Thus 40:38-46 do not belong to the basic text, which is taken up again in 40:47 - 41:4 (13). This resumes the measurements, first of the inner courtyard; then the temple house, described in its three parts: hall, temple room and holy of holies. When in 40:47 the position of the altar is mentioned (nothing more is said about its function), we press towards the essentials of the temple building itself. In 41:4, where discussion of the ark might be expected, it is not even mentioned; we are given rather the external dimensions, confined to the most important proportions(14). In 41:4 the "man" speaking for the first time to Ezekiel shows that the goal of the whole basic text is reached: "Then he said to me, This is the holy of the holies!" At the beginning Ezekiel had been told to see, and now he is taken beyond the act of seeing with the first words of explanation. This emphasis implies that the holy of holies (even though they may not enter it) is the place of the greatest significance for all Israel, the place which is the central focus on the renewal of life(15). All who return will need this place. It is there.

This passage (40:1-37; 40:47 - 41:4), with its features of guidance in the vision and its measurements all leading to the goal of the holy of holies, formed the basic text to which later additions were made. The first of these in 40:38-46, concerning the slaughtering of sacrifices and the distinctions in priestly service, has already been mentioned. The second,

in 41:5-15a, gives the outside measurements of the temple and
the way these fit into the whole temple area. Within this area
the western side seems to be closed off. It has been argued
that this enclosure suggests that God cannot be approached from
behind, but only face to face (from the east)(16). Then in
41:15b-26 occurs an unexpected reversion to the interior
decoration of the temple(17). Special attention can be drawn
in this case to 41:22 where a further description of the altar
appears: "Then he said to me, This is the table which stands
before Yahweh". Again this expresses the conviction, perhaps
from a later time and in connection with a part of the temple
which was closer to the people than the holy of holies, that
the whole people have access to Yahweh and to renewal of life.
The movement from country to country has not blocked the
channels.

In 42:1-14, verses about the priest's sacristies, occurs a
different emphasis which clearly separates priest and people,
especially in the last verse. It is the opposite of the
devaluation of the holy in chap.8 (18), but it is unwise to put
more emphasis on the distinctions between people than on the
service to be done by one group to another.

Finally in 42:15-20 the measurement is comprehensively
described. This ends in v.20 with a statement relating to the
outside wall, which has the function of separating the holy
from the profane. The result could be to make the
re-established sanctuary too remote from the people. On the
other hand, since it is the medium of life and something
special happens there, its own special character must be
recognized and accepted if its benefits are to be received.
The responsibility connected with the place is to ensure the
preservation of its special character and its continued benefit
for the whole people.

2. WHAT HAPPENS IN THE PLACE: 43 - 46

The guidance through the temple and its description in
chaps.40-42 show that this new temple is to be a real place,
with a significance to be communicated to other people. What
follows now, however, demonstrates not only that the place
exists and has a communicable meaning, but also that something
new happens there, essential to the people returning from one
country to another. A totally new element suddenly enters, a
dimension made immediately clear in 43:1-2 where, as soon as
the "man" has led Ezekiel to the east gate, the prophet sees
the glory of the God of Israel coming from the east, the glory
which the reader knows has left the temple as the climax of the
abominations described in chaps.8-11. Here it is clearest that
40-48 form the counterpart of 8-11.

Something of the greatest significance is happening for the people, because the glory of the God of Israel comes. This glory represents a dimension of life totally different from anything they have ever experienced; for it is said that the sound of it was like the sound of many waters and that the land shone brightly with its splendour (the same word - kābôd - that is used for "glory"). That which had departed from them before "comes back with a vengeance", it might be said. The comment in v.3 that the appearance (of this glory) was like the appearance which Ezekiel had seen at the destruction of the city and also like that which he had seen at the river Chebar seeks to make clear that this present experience is not isolated from those related in chaps.8-11 and in 1. Judgement in Jerusalem, continuance of life in exile and the future of the return form a continuing integrated experience, of which no one part would be possible without the other. Those who look forward to a future in the new land cannot cut themselves off from either their past or their present.

The glory of Yahweh having now proceeded into the temple, the spirit lifts Ezekiel and brings him into the inner courtyard, where he sees that the temple is filled with the glory of Yahweh (43:4-5). Though this chapter begins with the guidance of the "man" he soon recedes, and the former expression of the spirit transporting Ezekiel is used again(2). This is all the more notable since this expression is to be found only here in chaps.40-48. The spirit taking over from the man emphasizes that something special is taking place in the new temple, something of crucial importance for the people.

In 43:6-7 the "man" loses both his role of guidance and his explanatory speech. Now Ezekiel hears someone speaking to him from inside the house: it is not the man he hears, for we are told explicitly that the man is standing all the while beside Ezekiel. What Ezekiel hears is this:

> Son of man, this is the place of my throne and my footstool where I shall dwell in the midst of the Israelites permanently ... (43:7).

The references to throne and (literally) the "place of the soles of my feet" derive from traditions concerning the presence of Yahweh expressed through ark and footstool(3). They do not necessarily limit the presence of Yahweh finitely to one human place, though they certainly establish a very close connection between him and this particular place. The final emphasis, however, is not on Yahweh's dwelling in the temple but his dwelling among the Israelites(4). This central reference to people has to be kept in mind amid all the details of place in chaps.40-48, for it is similar to what is said in 37:26-28 about Yahweh setting his sanctuary among them permanently and his dwelling place being with them(5). The return of the glory of Yahweh to the renewed temple can be regarded as the fulfilment of Yahweh's promise to dwell among his people, the reason for the temple's existence. But this means in turn that Yahweh's dwelling place among his people must be expressed in appropriate conduct by the people. The demand made in 43:7 indicates that neither the temple nor even Yahweh's dwelling in it can be contemplated by the people as independent facts but must be connected with the whole direction of the people's lives.

The people who have sought to manipulate everything for their own well-being (the opposite of Yahweh dwelling in their midst) receive a prohibition: "The house of Israel shall no longer pollute my holy name - neither they nor their kings through prostitution and through the memorials of their kings <at their death>"(6) (43:7). This statement refers to the previous close proximity of the temple to the royal palace - they were separated only by a wall (v.8). The separation is the most revolutionary element of the new temple(7). It implies that God's sphere is separated from human, even from kingly claims, though within the context of his dwelling in the midst of his people. It prevents people, even kings, from presuming that they can exercise arbitrary influence in all spheres of life. It brings the full possibilities of life as close as possible to all people whoever they are.

The people must not forget that they too have exercised their own "prostitution": the ninth verse says that they are to remove both this and the memorials of their kings from Yahweh that he may dwell permanently among them. The demand not to pollute the name of Yahweh, far from being other-worldly, increases, not diminishes, the responsibility of the people themselves; and it must be remembered that in chap.24 Yahweh himself could be said to profane his sanctuary when necessary. Ezekiel is also involved in the extension of responsibility. In 43:10 he is directed to describe the plan of the temple to the house of Israel - literally to "tell the house of Israel the house". This takes up the original commission of 40:4 where he is told to tell the house of Israel everything which he sees(8).

Thus Ezekiel is not only responsible as a medium between form and word. He is not just responsible to communicate what he sees, but also to make a particular application: "... so that they become ashamed of their perversions". It is notable in the Book of Ezekiel, that being ashamed is not part of judgement, but of salvation(9). Here it appears in connection with the plan of the temple which means much that is new for them. Being ashamed opens up the way for recognizing what the new can do. The specific architectural plan (the form of the house, its exits, and all the instructions concerning it - 43:11) is implicitly a proclamation of salvation which must be made known and written down. The new temple is not merely a place, but a whole new mode of existence to be put into operation and used, an idea which provides the background to the summary direction, torah, of 43:12: "On the top of the mountain all its territory round about is most holy"(10).

A detailed central example is given in 43:12-17, 18-27, with the measurements and consecration of the altar for burnt offerings. The culmination of the first part is to be found at the end of v.17 where it is said that the steps turn towards the east. This would mean that the altar itself was orientated towards the temple, the implicit opposite of 8:16 where Ezekiel sees men worshipping with their backs to the temple(11). Clearly the new place is established for legitimate worship in the light of past experience. Concern for legitimate worship is also obvious in the passage about the consecration of the altar in 43:18-27. The capacity to offer acceptable worship is regarded as something given, for here Ezekiel becomes (like Moses) the medium between God and the priests of the ritual prescriptions(12).

Ezekiel is now brought back to the east gate which he finds closed (44:1). He is told it must remain closed with no one going through it; the reason being that Yahweh, the God of Israel, has entered through it (v.2). Evidently the closed door is a reminder of the unique and indispensable return of the glory of Yahweh. Even the special privilege granted the prince of sitting there to eat his sacrificial meal (v.3) suggests the function of a cultic place and not of a gate(13). Among all the regulations of this section the striking description of the closed gate keeps alive what has happened in this place with the return of the glory of Yahweh.

The motif of the glory of Yahweh also introduces the next section on the priests (44:4-31)(14). The event of the coming of the glory is changed to a state, since Ezekiel sees the glory filling the house of Yahweh (v.4). The judgements and regulations concerning the priests (v.5) have been subsumed under the same authority as the description of the temple and its significance for Israel(15). This claim must be viewed critically since, in what follows, judgements are made concerning the priesthood which have no foundation either in chaps.1-39 or in the basic text of 40-42 (16); the discrimination which lies behind them would find litle favour with many people today. In the first place, in 44:6-9, the abominations of the "rebellious house" (the only place in 40-48 where this term is used)(17) turn out to be the fact that Israelites have allowed foreigners to serve in Yahweh's sanctuary. The reference is not clear: it has been suggested that there were groups of non-Israelite origin living in Israel who were drawn into temple service (Joshua 9:27; Ezra 2:43ff.), or that they were foreigners who might have gained admission during the reigns of Manasseh and Amon(18).

Whatever the allusion, in Ezekiel 1-39 the Israelites themselves are obviously seen as involved directly in the abominations. There could be no question of weakening the charge by shifting the attention to foreigners, nor, in what follows in vv.9-14, by singling out one group of priests, the Levites, as those who turned away from Yahweh to follow their idols. The Levites are therefore allowed only a lower order of service in the temple, and are thus contrasted with another group of priests, the Zadokites, who are said (vv.15-16) to have maintained the service of Yahweh's sanctuary and are uniquely allowed to perform the legitimate priestly function of sacrificial service. No evidence survives for such a difference in conduct; indeed it could be assumed from chaps.8-11 that the Zadokites, the Jerusalem priests, were the ones primarily implicated in the abominations described there. The authors of this passage are firm, however, in their partiality for the Zadokites, because the regulations for the sanctity of the priesthood which follow (44:17- 31) apply to them only, with no further attention being paid to the Levites at all.

It is difficult to say what attitudes, circumstances and conduct stand behind this presentation(19). No doubt the Levites received a great deal of unpleasantness and injustice, and therefore one might want to condemn the passage for being inconsistent with other parts of the Book of Ezekiel, and to regard its claim to the same authority as the description of the temple as spurious. We cannot whitewash the Zadokites, but equally we cannot ignore the consideration that, for a period, the Zadokites were a prominent and influential group through whom (we know) the life of the temple functioned. To condemn them is to overlook the more comprehensive fact that the restoration of life occurs through the medium of groups of people, who always, in one way or another, present an ambiguous front, and are never selflessly attuned to restoration alone. Especially in a section like 40-48 where there is a "specific" presentation of restoration, which bears dangers of elitism, it is fitting to have a reminder that restoration is possible only through circumstances and people as they are(20).

The theme of land (dealt with in more detail later)(21) is suddenly introduced in 45:1-8. Without a reallocation of land, there could be no restoration for people, and, characteristically, land is connected with the detailing of various groups of people. The opening verses (vv.1-5) deal with the land specially allocated to Yahweh, the place of the sanctuary, which also serves as a place for the priests. Alongside is another section of land, the property of the city, which belongs to all Israel (v.6). Finally, as the climax of the present form of the passage (vv.7-8), comes a realistic appreciation of princes as they were in the past, for, after the allocation of the land to them in the same manner as to the others, it is said they will no longer oppress Yahweh's people but allow them to have their own land. All the people in their various ways have rights to the restored land.

An exhortation to the princes(22) in 45:9-17 begins by calling on them to relinquish violence and practise justice, proceeding (vv.10-12) to a statement about the correct use of weights. The remainder of the passage concerns correct quantities in the offering of sacrifices, and since vv.16-17 say that the people bring the material to the prince, who bears the responsibility of arranging the offering for the atonement of Israel, it is likely that vv.13-15, relating to the

211

quantities, were originally addressed to the people. The present composition probably envisages the restoration of a ruling class which, rather than practising oppression, established order(23). In the all-important matter of atonement, people and princes have interlocking parts to play; even the prince does not actively participate in the practice of the cult, though his is the final non-priestly duty(24). It is noteworthy that now it is the prince who has a responsibility to exercise, not the "man", nor even Ezekiel, nor the priests. In a context of atonement the prince is closer to the people than the priests, and remains for them a continuing and responsible representative. It is also the prince's responsibility to provide for himself and the whole laity(25) ("the people of the land" - 45:22) the sacrifices at the times of the great festivals of passover and tabernacles (45:21-25)(26). It was believed, that without these sacrifices the festivals would not fulfil their function for the people, so that the prince's responsibility is crucial. Following a section on the purification of the sanctuary (45:18-20) where the sacrifices would have been made, the implication of the passage is that the service at the sanctuary will be effective for that renewal of life represented by passover and tabernacles. All is now the exact opposite of the former state of affairs, where destruction has to begin with the sanctuary itself (9:6).

In 46:1-15, containing ordinances for the sabbath and new moon, the prince clearly has certain privileges. He is the first to be able to take up his stand by the part of the inner western gate which is open only on the sabbath and new moon (it is the outer eastern gate which is closed all the time, 44:1f.); and in doing so he worships with the sacrifices which are brought, as the people do (46:1-3). However v.10 says explicitly that the prince both comes in and goes out among the people. Thus the prince's privileges (referred to again in v.12) are continually integrated into the common worship of all people.

When 46:16-18 goes on to speak of the land of the prince and his family, we find that only they possess the land permanently (v.16); if the prince gives a servant land, it reverts to the prince in the Jubilee year (v.17). On the other hand, v.18 goes on to stipulate that, whatever privileges the prince might have with regard to land within his own family, they cannot be extended at the cost of the people's land. Even the first representative of the people in the cult has no right to take another's land by force. He is responsible for the land in the sense that, neither on his own behalf nor on that of the other people, does he have the last say; "Yahweh's people" are not to be dispossessed (v.18).

(This section ends with another addition in 46:19-24 on the priestly sacristies, where the portions of the sacrifices to be eaten are prepared. One would expect to find this rather in connection with 42:1-14)(27).

3. THE LAND SURROUNDING THE PLACE: 47 - 48.

This section begins appropriately in the style of the earlier
vision (chaps.40-42), with Ezekiel being led back to the place
where he was told to write down his vision(1). But now he sees
something different: water flowing eastwards from the
threshold of the temple (47:1). The "man" begins to measure,
and Ezekiel is taken in four stages with the progress of the
stream: at the first stage, the water is only up to his
ankles, at the second to his knees; at the third, to his hips.
At the fourth (the number of completion), the waters are so
deep that he can no longer wade through - it would only be
possible to swim (vv.3-5). This vividly demonstrates the power
of the water, which is to transform. It flows eastwards, not
to any easily transformed place, but to the driest place of
all, into the desert of the east and into the salty waters of
the Dead Sea, which it will purify (47:6-8). Where this stream
goes (coming from the restored temple) everything, anything
will live (v.9). On both banks of the stream, fruit trees will
appear whose leaves will not wither and whose fruit (fresh
every month) will not come to an end (v.12). The vision
effectively expresses the conviction that the restored medium
of life will make something happen in the everyday world of the
people. The restored temple does not stand apart as something
holy, but transforms the most unpromising spheres of life.

The restored temple is placed rightly within the land as a
whole. The boundaries of the land are given in 47:15-20, a
list placed within the framework (vv.13-15, 21) of a command to
distribute the land(2). The land belongs to the people: they
have a right to possess the land, of which the temple forms the
centre. The boundaries given, extending from a point far north
to one far south, are probably intended as the ideal extended
boundaries of a "greater Israel". Strangely, however, there is
nothing said about the East Jordan territories. Perhaps it was
felt that the people formerly living there had never been
properly integrated with Israel, and that only the West Jordan
country was the subject of promises to the patriarchs(3).

Before proceeding to the description of the territory
allocated to each of the twelve tribes in chap.48, there is an
important addition (47:22-23): the only place in the Old
Testament to stipulate that sojourners who have sons are to
gain possession of land among the native Israelites(4). This
may bring out the great importance of the land, for it appears
that dwelling in the land itself confers this status, and
overrules earlier ethnic disabilities(5).

Thus the present understanding of the land witnesses to a transformation in Israel's life. The possession of the land was seen to be deep-rooted. In the distribution of the land, Israel is spoken of as "the tribe of Israel", a designation not used in the rest of the book, which may here establish a relation with the original possession of the land. In 48:1-29 the distribution of land for each tribe is elaborated from north to south, giving each tribe a strip of land stretching from west to east. Between the 7th and 8th tribes lies the special "tribute" (terûmâ) of land (already mentioned in 45:1-8) for the temple, priests and Levites, city and prince. Seven tribes to the north and five to the south, an arrangement which does not correspond to any historical reality since some of the earlier northern tribes are even placed in the south(6). The arrangement establishes a balance between north and south while also preserving the memory that, historically, the north was larger than the south. The most curious feature of the arrangement is that Judah is placed to the north of the special territory and Benjamin to the south, a complete reversal of their historical geography. The reason is probably that Benjamin had a historical connection with the city of Jerusalem, which is now placed in the southern part of the special territory, and perhaps also because of a desire to place Judah in as close proximity as possible to the stronger full-blooded tribes Manasseh, Ephraim and Reuben, which are located directly to the north(7). One obvious principle of the arrangement is to place the tribes stemming from Jacob's concubines at the extremities of both north and south. The apparent intention is to place the restored sanctuary in the situation where, far from resting as an entity in itself, it will produce the greatest possible benefit for the people to whom the surrounding land is allocated. Such realism goes beyond mere sentimentalism.

There was some danger (particularly in chaps.43-46) that the temple would become a holy place set apart from its own purpose. The final addition to the Book of Ezekiel in 48:30-35 suddenly focuses attention on the city (not the temple which up till now had been at the centre)(8). This section integrates with those preceding it by naming the twelve gates of the city after the tribes, but when it is said that the name of the city from now on is "Yahweh is there", all that had been claimed for the temple to which the glory of Yahweh had returned is transferred to the city as a whole(9). The superlative claim for the city places the restoration of the medium of life into a wider, more specific and earthly context, itself transformed by the restoration within it.

CONCLUSION AND SUMMARY:
THE INTEGRATION OF RESPONSIBILITY AND RESTORATION

The Book of Ezekiel shows that people do not necessarily want restoration. Indeed, until a crisis has been reached, they may have no idea that restoration is necessary, but assume (or hope) that they will simply be able to return to their past existence (1-24). Then when such a return is obviously no longer possible, people may reject restoration, preferring to remain where they are, in every sense: resignation can be the means of trying to escape necessary restoration, which entails a realization of how much has happened, how much must be done.

Responsibility integrates with restoration when it is realized that restoration is not merely offered for the taking, but can only be achieved through people's attitudes. Responsibility means recognizing that people must be convinced of the need for something they do not want. Responsibility involves the delicate task of defining the true needs of people before trying to meet those needs. If the exercise of responsibility leads to the conviction that restoration will at least partially meet these true needs, restoration becomes one goal of responsibility. Restoration is not therefore possible without responsibility, and responsibility therefore precedes restoration. Responsibility is fundamental, and will almost certainly turn out to be demanding.

Since responsibility for restoration means recognizing that attitudes of other people must be considered, it is clear in general (and illustrated by Ezekiel in particular) that any religious experience connected with responsibility cannot be private. That Ezekiel sees his divine visions among the exiles, in full consciousness of his people and their situation (1:1), shows the nature of responsibility. What happens to one person must, through his reaction, be transferred to other people. The reaction is primarily one of responsibility, and since responsibility needs to find its fulfilment in the response of others, and since the people are said to be exiles, there is already a hint that this response will have something to do with restoration. The experience of responsibility can also involve the realization that responsibility has a source (1:1) which provides the ability to persevere. Responsibility with a source, with restoration as a goal, has the resources of the past at its disposal, which Ezekiel's call vision with its traditional elements demonstrates.

A further aspect of responsibility with a source is accountability, vividly expressed (in the addition in 1:18) when the rims of the four wheels are said to be full of eyes. Responsibility involves a subject observing an object, where the subject also knows himself to be under scrutiny. This accountability leads to the ultimate consequence that, as the responsible subject, Ezekiel knows he has to offer the people restoration whether they want it or not (33:10-11).

Responsibility drives towards restoration against the stream. Responsibility with a source also finds expression in being addressed: the end of the call-vision issues in an address to Ezekiel (1:28 - 2:1). The person addressed is accountable for more than that which the people, on whose behalf he is addressed, want. Responsibility for people in this sense means awakening a response for something which they do not want to hear (3:7). Responsibility means that its bearer knows he alone is chosen (either Ezekiel speaks or no one does). This very consciousness of having to speak contains the knowledge that something is lacking which could be present, and it may thus lead to speaking of restoration. True restoration, however, demands free acceptance: another aspect of responsibility is allowing people the freedom to hear or not to hear (3:22-27).

The primary aim of responsibility however is to bring such people to hear what must be heard. If terrible things happen and Ezekiel believes the people must face up to their consequences, he cannot avoid telling them the truth. In such a situation, responsibility means primarily judgement, without which responsibility would not be possible (4-24). Without judgement, people will always be seeking explanations outside themselves, and so will never see the need for restoration. Here the closest relation between responsibility and restoration becomes visible, for responsibility integrates what happens with its acknowledgement as judgement (4:8). Only this may lead to restoration. Because of this goal, judgement is not proclaimed in any merely vindictive or light-hearted way; indeed for such proclamation to have any chance at all of being successful, the person responsible (the watchman) will himself have to be personally involved (4:4; 5:1-2).

If what is happening and the need to accept it as judgement are taken seriously, responsibility means being prepared to go to any lengths to achieve the aim of restoration (6:1ff.). It must develop into a concentrated responsibility, which over time can lead to a reaction of revulsion at oneself, laying the ground for restoration (6:8-10). The responsibility prepared to go to any lengths will not only declare what is about to happen, but will go so far as to declare what is happening in terms of the people's conduct (7:4-5), the blooming of their own unrighteousness (7:10). Responsibility means not sparing any detail which can bring on a reaction involving all the people (7:22-24). Only such a responsibility leads to restoration, not in the sense of some people managing to escape, but in the full appreciation of possibilities for good and evil in present events (9:5-6). This responsibility leads to involvement, and to personal pain (9:8). The seeds of responsibility lie in one responsible person who cares, and they may be handed on to those who recognize the hopelessness of Jerusalem, and the possibilities even of exile (chap.11). A reaction both from the prophet and from the people is required. Previously the main reaction was expressed through Ezekiel's - responsibility integrating what happens with its acceptance as

216

judgement (4:8). Now it is clear that the complementary reaction of the people in the process of integration must be understanding (12:3), which is necessary to make them recipients of restoration.

Since responsibility means being prepared to go to any lengths, it also means a dogged adherence to reality - as it relates to people as well as to events - and the attempt to bring others to recognize their true nature (e.g. the prophets in chap. 13). When confidence in the leading classes, simply because they are leaders, has broken down (prophets and elders in chaps 13-14), it becomes easier to realize that all people are responsible for themselves (14:12ff.), especially when the negative conduct of some can be used for the benefit of others (14:4-11). Responsibility means having to realize, for example, that the survivors of the fall of Jerusalem only demonstrate that its destruction was not without cause (14:22). The change from external happening to the people's own conduct leads, first, to a conviction that the conduct of some can be used for others' benefit. The emphasis changes again to the people's own nature (chap. 15), leading in turn to a definition of responsibility which goes so far in judgement as to acknowledge that one's own guilt is greater than that of others (16:51-52). Responsibility means drawing attention not only to other people's guilt but even to one's own. Indeed reaction to one's own nature as the worst can even take on a universal regenerative aspect (16:51). There is no more adequate position from which to make a new start for restoration (16:52-53)! Restoration can arise even out of the recognition of the worst.

No new generation, if it makes its own creative response, need have its life cut off by the legacy of a previous generation (chaps 17-18). Here responsibility is democratized, for the potential of the people does not stand or fall with that of their leaders. Such a responsibility demands so much of people, however, that they can prefer not to take it up (18:19, 25). As an alternative to their refusal, the restoration of life is offered to people (18:27-28). Restoration demands a totally new start (chap. 20), proceeding from their extreme revulsion at themselves. Such revulsion can assume a highly individual form, as when the death of Ezekiel's wife is used as a symbol of the necessity of the destruction of Jerusalem (24:15ff.); but this ultimate involvement of the responsible subject has an application to the necessary reaction of the people as a whole. From such a reaction people may become recipients of restoration.

Not every aspect of the situation has been exhausted yet, for responsibility and restoration must take account not only of the people who are primarily addressed, but also of the people who surround them. These others prove scornful obstacles to restoration. Responsibility is concerned to show, not only the nature of one's own people, but also that of other peoples, and their situation (chaps 25-32). Once this responsibility is exercised, it is obvious that these other peoples are also part

217

of a real, not mythical world, and that they therefore provide
no obstacle to restoration. Thus, for Ezekiel and the exiles,
responsibility and restoration are expressed in a situation
stripped of any hope of military victory against the
Babylonians - indeed the acceptance of this very situation is
the indispensable foundation for restoration.

Within this situation, the responsible person does not
withhold his responsibility, ensuring first that everything
turns out as predicted, but communicates his own responsibility
as the foundation of his warning to others (33:1-9). He is not
relieved from his responsibility when the conduct of other
people does not seem to deserve it, but is prepared to take the
risks of exposure, risks which must be taken if one's people
are to be brought to accept restoration.

Since this is so, the only goal of such responsibility is to
awaken in others their own responsibility for themselves, as is
expressed in a much more tautly integrated way in the
composition of 33:1-9 together with 33:10-20. The prophet is
convinced of the possibility of restoration - based in the new
occurrence of the fall of the city - and he is responsible for
integrating his conviction with the people's acknowledgement
that restoration can eventuate. They may to some extent
recognize the truth about their own piously selfish aspirations
(33:23-29). Restoration depends on the recognition of such
things, but faces potential opposition. Opposition may result
from a lack of restoration on the part of the watchman
(33:1-9); from the lethargic response of the people
(33:10-20); from misplaced piety (33:23-29); or even from a
positive response for the wrong reason (33:30-33). Once the
interlocking relationships of these various aspects have been
demonstrated, responsibility is seen as directed towards people
in their need, not towards their exploitation by their leaders
(chap.34). Something new is happening with the breaking down
of old structures, when (one aspect of restoration) leaders can
be dispensed with, and replaced.

Another matter can be taken a stage further here. When the
evil aspirations of another people are revealed (35:10), to
direct responsibility against them (35:15) does not mean that
responsibility for one's own people should be neglected
(35-36:15). Responsibility demonstrates that no disgraced
nation must remain so for ever (36:15). Indeed, the new things
which happen reach into the people's inner nature: the
ultimate responsibility of recognizing the need for, and
possibility of, inner renewal presents itself as the
fundamental basis for restoration (36:16-38). The overriding
implication is that being prepared to accept the possibility of
change leads to being responsible for God; and the conduct of
the people can affect the reputation of their whole religion
(36:20).

A responsibility to restore life to people who want to die
(37:1-14) forms the climax: it even means being prepared to
listen to absurd questions and bizarre commands (37:3-4). The
possibility of life realized by Ezekiel can also be transferred

to other people. The offer of life can be expressed as restoration to the land (37:12), as reunion of the people (37:15-28), and as (again) inner renewal of the people (37:23). Such are the multifarious consequences of the new happenings.

Restoration is finally expressed neither in terms of reunion nor, for example, in terms of the re-establishment of kingship, but rather as the re-establishment of the sanctuary (37:27-28; also chaps 40-48). The glory of Yahweh returning to the sanctuary grants a totally different dimension of life (43:1-3). Within the responsibility, which means above all to communicate reality (a concern continued into the last section of the book - 40:4; 43:10), restoration neither gives up what is promised, nor pretends that it is already in place (chaps 38-39); it does not find a perfect end for all time (38:8-9). Though restoration does not cling to old irrelevant models, it offers the freedom of a new expression of what is partially old but which is renewed in speaking creatively to people.

Baltzer   Ezechiel und Deuterojesaja: Dieter Baltzer,
             Ezechiel und Deuterojesaja. Beruehrungen in der
             Heilserwartung der beiden grossen Exilspropheten,
             Walter de Gruyter, Berlin, 1971

Boadt   Ezekiel's Oracles: Lawrence Boadt, Ezekiel's
             Oracles Against Egypt. A Literary and Philological
             Study of Ezekiel 29-32, Biblical Institute Press,
             Rome, 1980.

Carley   Ezekiel Among the Prophets: Keith W.Carley, Ezekiel
             Among the Prophets. A Study of Ezekiel's Place in
             Prophetic Tradition, SCM Press Ltd, London, 1975

Carley   The Book of the Prophet Ezekiel: Keith W.Carley,
             The Book of the Prophet Ezekiel, The Cambridge Bible
             Commentary, Cambridge University Press, 1974

Childs   Introduction: Brevard S.Childs, Introduction to the
             Old Testament as Scripture, SCM Press Ltd, London,
             1979

Eichrodt   Ezekiel: Walther Eichrodt, Ezekiel. A Commentary,
             tr.by Cosslett Quinn, The Old Testament Library, SCM
             Press Ltd, London, 1970

Fohrer   Ezechiel: Georg Fohrer, Ezechiel, Handbuch zum
             Alten Testament 13, Mohr, Tuebingen, 1955

Garscha   Studien: Joerg Garscha, Studien zum Ezechielbuch.
             Eine redaktionskritische Untersuchung von Ez 1-39,
             Herbert Lang, Bern, 1974

Gese   Verfassungsentwurf: Hartmut Gese, Der
             Verfassungsentwurf des Ezechiel (Kap.40-48)
             Traditionsgeschichtlich untersucht, Mohr, Tuebingen,
             1957

Gowan   When Man Becomes God: Donald E.Gowan, When Man
             Becomes God. Humanism and Hybris in the Old
             Testament, The Pickwick Press, Pittsburgh, 1975

Herrmann   Heilserwartungen: Siegfried Herrmann, Die
             prophetischen Heilserwartungen im Alten Testament.
             Ursprung und Gestaltwandel, Kohlhammer, Stuttgart,
             1965

Hossfeld   Untersuchungen: Frank Hossfeld, Untersuchungen zu
                Komposition und Theologie des Ezechielbuches, Echter
                Verlag, Wuerzburg, 1977

JBL   Journal of Biblical Literature

Keel   Jahwe-Visionen: Othmar Keel, Jahwe-Visionen und
                Siegelkunst. Eine neue Deutung der
                Majestaetsschilderungen in Jes 6, Ez 1 und 10 und
                Sach 4, Verlag Katholisches Bibelwerk, Stuttgart,
                1977

Lang   Kein Aufstand: Bernhard Lang, Kein Aufstand in
                Jerusalem. Die Politik des Propheten Ezechiel, 2nd
                ed., Verlag Katholisches Bibelwerk, Stuttgart, 1981

LXX   Septuagint

Levenson   Theology of the Program of Restoration: Jon Douglas
                Levenson, Theology of the Program of Restoration of
                Ezekiel 40-48, Scholars Press, Missoula, 1976

Noth   Gesammelte Studien: Martin Noth, Gesammelte Studien
                zum Alten Testament, 2nd ed., Kaiser, Munich, 1960

Pennacchini Temi Mitici: Bruno Pennacchini, Temi Mitici in
                Ezechiele 28:1-19 Studio Teologico "Porziuncola",
                Assisi, 1973

Raitt   A Theology of Exile: Thomas M.Raitt, A Theology of
                Exile. Judgement/Deliverance in Jeremiah and
                Ezekiel, Fortress Press, Philadelphia, 1977

Schulz   Todesrecht: Hermann Schulz, Das Todesrecht im Alten
                Testament. Studien zur Rechtsform der Mot-Jumat
                Saetze, Toepelmann, Berlin, 1969

Simian   Die theologische Nachgeschichte: Horacio Simian,
                Die theologische Nachgeschichte der Prophetie
                Ezechiels. Form- und traditionskritische
                Untersuchung zu Ez 6; 35; 36, Echter Verlag,
                Wuerzburg, 1974

VT   Vetus Testamentum

von Rad   Gesammelte Studien: Gerhard von Rad, Gesammelte
                Studien zum Alten Testament, Kaiser, Munich, 1958

von Rad   Old Testament Theology 2: Gerhard von Rad, Old
                Testament Theology, vol.II, The Theology of Israel's
                Prophetic Traditions, tr. by D.M.G.Stalker, Oliver
                & Boyd, Edinburgh & London, 1965

221

Wevers   Ezekiel: John W.Wevers, <u>Ezekiel</u>, The Century Bible,
              Nelson, 1969

<u>ZAW</u>   Zeitschrift <u>fuer</u> <u>die</u> Alttestamentliche Wissenschaft

Zimmerli*   <u>Ezekiel</u> <u>1</u>: Walther Zimmerli, <u>Ezekiel</u> <u>1.</u> <u>A</u>
              <u>Commentary</u> <u>on</u> <u>the</u> <u>Book</u> <u>of</u> <u>the</u> <u>Prophet</u> Ezekiel,
              Chapters <u>1-24</u>, Hermeneia, tr. by Ronald E.Clements,
              Fortress Press, Philadelphia, 1979;

              <u>Ezekiel</u> <u>2</u>: Walther Zimmerli, <u>Ezekiel</u> <u>2.</u> <u>A</u>
              <u>Commentary</u> <u>on</u> <u>the</u> <u>Book</u> <u>of</u> <u>the</u> <u>Prophet</u> Ezekiel,
              Chapters <u>25-48</u>, Hermeneia, tr. by James D.Martin,
              Fortress Press, Philadelphia, 1983

Zimmerli   <u>Gesammelte</u> <u>Aufsaetze</u> <u>I</u>: Walther Zimmerli, <u>Gottes</u>
              <u>Offenbarung.</u>   <u>Gesammelte</u> <u>Aufsaetze</u> <u>zum</u> <u>Alten</u>
              <u>Testament</u>, Kaiser, Munich, 1963

Zimmerli   <u>Gesammelte</u> <u>Aufsaetze</u> <u>II</u>: Walther Zimmerli, <u>Studien</u>
              <u>zur</u> <u>alttestamentlichen</u> <u>Theologie</u> <u>und</u> <u>Prophetie.</u>
              <u>Gesammelte</u> <u>Aufsaetze</u>, Band II, Kaiser, Munich, 1974

*It should be noted that though reference is now
made   to the English translation of Zimmerli's
commentary I worked with the German of both volumes,
since the translation appeared at a later stage.
This accounts for the differences of wording in my
work as compared with the translation.

    Full information about the above books is also
given the first time they appear in the notes.

INTRODUCTION

1. More information is given in the notes as the book proceeds.
2. For example, Walther Eichrodt, Ezekiel. A Commentary, tr. by Cosslett Quin, SCM Press Ltd, London, 1970, p.1.
3. Eichrodt, Ezekiel, p.7. It is possible that initially some readers will find some of the material which now follows too daunting; but there may be some point in returning to it after reading the book.
4. G.Hoelscher, Hezekiel, der Dichter und das Buch, Toepelmann, Giessen, 1924. For a fuller survey of the history of criticism, see Walther Zimmerli, Ezekiel 1, tr. by Ronald E.Clements, Hermeneia, Fortress Press, Philadelphia, 1979, pp.3-8; also Eichrodt, Ezekiel, pp.7-11.
5. V.Herntrich, Ezechielprobleme, Toepelmann, Giessen, 1933; see Horacio Simian, Die theologische Nachgeschichte der Prophetie Ezechiels. Form- und traditionskritische Untersuchung zu Ez 6; 35, 36, Echter Verlag, Wuerzburg, 1974, pp.21-24.
6. W.O.E.Oesterley and T.H.Robinson, An Introduction to the Books of the Old Testament, S.P.C.K., London, 1934.
7. See Eichrodt, Ezekiel, p.8.
8. K.W.Carley, Ezekiel Among the Prophets. A Study of Ezekiel's Place in Prophetic Tradition, SCM Press Ltd, London, 1975, p.2.
9. Zimmerli, Ezekiel 1, p.6.
10. C.C.Torrey, Pseudo-Ezekiel and the Original Prophecy, Yale University Press, New Haven, 1930.
11. J.Smith, The Book of the Prophet Ezekiel. A New Interpretation, S.P.C.K., London, 1931.
12. G. Fohrer, Die Hauptprobleme des Buches Ezechiel, Toepelmann, Berlin, 1952; Commentary: Ezechiel, Handbuch zum Alten Testament 13, Mohr, Tuebingen, 1955.
13. J.W.Wevers, Ezekiel, The Century Bible, Nelson, 1969.
14. K. von Rabenau, 'Die Entstehung des Buches Ezechiel in formgeschichtlicher Sicht', Wissenschaftliche Zeitschrift der Martin Luther Universitaet Halle-Wittenberg 5, 1955/6, pp.659-694.
15. W.Zimmerli, 'Das Phaenomen der "Fortschreibung" im Buche Ezechiel', Prophecy. Essays presented to Georg Fohrer on his 65th birthday, ed. J.A.Emerton, de Gruyter, Berlin, 1980, pp.174-191. Bernhard Lang, after a survey of the study devoted to the growth of the Book of Ezekiel, comes to the conclusion that redactional activity was on Ezekelian texts and did not insert post-Ezekelian

material. He therefore thinks one should refrain from speaking of a deuteronomistic editor or of 'Fortschreibung' (Ezechiel. Der Prophet und das Buch, Wissenschaftliche Buchgesellschaft, Darmstadt, 1981, pp.29-30).

16. See the short titles at the head of these notes for his two volumes of articles.

17. J.W.Miller, das Verhaeltnis Jeremias und Hesekiels sprachlich und theologisch untersucht, Van Gorcum, Assen, 1955.

18. H.Reventlow, Waechter ueber Israel, Ezechiel und seine Theologie, Toepelmann, Berlin, 1962.

19. S.Herrmann, Die prophetischen Heilserwartungen im Alten Testament, Ursprung und Gestaltwandel, Kohlhammer, Stuttgart, 1965.

20. The editing process of the books Deuteronomy – 2 Kings and of Jeremiah.

21. In the foreword to the second (German) edition of his commentary, 1979, p.ix.

22. H.Schulz, Das Todesrecht im Alten Testament. Studien zur Rechtsform der Mot-Jumat Saetze, Toepelmann, Berlin, 1969.

23. Zimmerli, Theologische Literaturzeitung 95/12, 1970, pp.891-897.

24. Zimmerli, 'Deutero-Ezechiel?', Zeitschrift fuer die altestamentliche Wissenschaft 84/4, 1972, pp.501-516.

25. Lawrence Boadt maintains that the distribution and irregular spacing of the dated oracles as well as the typical early 6th century literary style of writing the dates scotches those hypotheses which suggest a school of disciples adding large amounts of material into the oracles against the nations about a century after Ezekiel (Ezekiel's Oracles Against Egypt. A Literary and Philological study of Ezekiel 29-32, Biblical Institute Press, Rome, 1980, p.11).

26. J.Garscha, Studien zum Ezechielbuch. Eine redaktionskritische Untersuchung von 1-39, Herbert Lang, Bern, 1974.

27. O.Kaiser, Einleitung in das Alte Testament, Mohn, Guetersloh, 4th ed., 1978, p.22.

28. R.Liwak, "Ueberlieferungsgeschichtliche Probleme des Ezechielbuches. Eine Studie zu postezechielischen Interpretationen und Kompositionen", Dissertation Bochum, 1976; W.Thiel, Die deuteronomistische Redaktion von Jeremia 1-25, Neukirchener Verlag, Neukirchen, 1973.

29. Simian, see note 5; F.Hossfeld, Untersuchungen zu Komposition und Theologie des Ezechielbuches, Echter Verlag, Wuerzburg, 1977.

30. See note 8. See also his commentary The Book of the Prophet Ezekiel, The Cambridge Bible Commentary, Cambridge University Press, 1974.

31. T.M.Raitt, A Theology of Exile. Judgement/Deliverance in Jeremiah and Ezekiel, Fortress Press, Philadelphia, 1977.

32. B.S.Childs, Introduction to the Old Testament as Scripture, SCM Press, London, 1979, pp.355-372. R.E.Clements sees the Ezekiel tradition as a form of literary commentary and adaptation of Ezekiel's prophecies emerging not so much from 'disciples' as from among the Babylonian exiles, probably from within the circles of the exiled Zadokite priests, the authors of the Holiness Code and the nascent priestly school. The purpose was to provide a divine sanction for the renewal and revitalizing of worship in Jerusalem after 587 B.C. ('The Ezekiel Tradition: Prophecy in a Time of Crisis', Israel's Prophetic Tradition, ed. by R.J.Coggins et al., Cambridge University Press, Cambridge, 1982, pp.132-133).

I THE SOURCE OF RESPONSIBILITY: 1 - 3

1) What Happens First - God and the Prophet: 1:1-28

1. It was noted before that it has often been thought that 'the 30th year' refers to Ezekiel's age. Another recent and plausible explanation has been given by Anthony D.York. He thinks it referred to the exile and would therefore indicate 567 B.C. He bases this on the theory that the book began originally not only with an inaugural but also with a restoration vision and that it was to the latter that the date referred. This vision was later removed to 43:3ff., but 'the 30th year' was too closely associated with the title of the book to be changed. ('Ezekiel I: Inaugural and Restoration Visions?', Vetus Testamentum XXXVII/1, 1977, pp.82-98). Susumu Higuchi has another application of the 30th year to the exile. He thinks the call-narrative proper was 2:1 - 3:15 and was written soon after Ezekiel's call in 593 B.C., but chapter 1 was a description of a theophany written at the end of Ezekiel's career in 568 - thus interpreting the 30th year - in order to encourage the people in exile ('The Narrative of Ezekiel's Call - Its Tradito-historical Study', Shingaku-Ronshu 26, 1978, pp.84-108; Japanese - my information from Kenichi Kida's abstract in Old Testament Abstracts 2/1, 1979, p.60).

2. On the complicated question of which parts of vv.1-3 are original and which secondary, see Wevers, Ezekiel, p.41, and Garscha, Studien, pp.241-244.

3. See Othmar Keel, Jahwe-Visionen und Siegelkunst. Eine neue Deutung der Majestaetsschilderungen in Jes 6, Ez 1 und 10 und Sach 4, Katholisches Bibelwerk, Stuttgart, 1977, pp.125-273.

4. Keel sees behind these the heaven-bearers known from the 15th century B.C. and which in the 8th to 6th centuries are occasionally given four wings (Jahwe-Visionen, p.246).

5. See Zimmerli, _Ezekiel 1_, pp.101-104.

6. See now on this verse, W.Boyd Barrick, 'The Straight-Legged Cherubim of Ezekiel's Inaugural Vision (Ezekiel 1:7a)', _Catholic Biblical Quarterly_ 44/4, 1982, pp.543-550. He thinks it consistent with both internal literary evidence and external artistic evidence that the legs are straight because the creature did not use them for locomotion.

7. Ernst Vogt thinks, however, that the word pānîm does not mean 'face' here but 'appearance', that they refer to the various partial aspects of the cherub figure, and that this originally had only three appearances, but a fourth was added (that of an ox) because of the importance of the number 'four' here: four creatures, four wings, four wheels, four directions. See also 10-14 and 41:18-19 ('Die vier "Gesichter" der Keruben in Ezechiel', _Biblica_ 60, 1979, pp.327-347). O.Keel thinks the four creatures are 'heaven bearers', the four wings the four cosmic winds, and the four faces the four compass points (_Jahwe-Visionen_, pp.207-216, 235-243, 271).

8. Fohrer, _Ezechiel_, pp.12-13.

9. Zimmerli, _Ezekiel 1_, pp.104-105. Cornelius B.Houk in 'A Statistical Linguistic Study of Ezekiel 1:4 - 3:11' confirms the thesis that the section about wheels is secondary (_ZAW_ 93/1, 1981, p.81).

10. Keel thinks the wheels within wheels may have come from a misunderstanding of thick layers on certain depictions of wheels (_Jahwe-Visionen_, pp.263-267).

11. Zimmerli, _Ezekiel 1_, pp.105-106.

12. The word ḥasmal occurs only here and in 1:4 and 8:2 and its meaning is not exactly clear. Walter Baumgartner gives as the meaning of possible cognate words: Akkadian, (1) 'bluish stone', (2) 'white gold', (3) 'a precious stone gleaming yellow'; Elamite, 'inlay work' (_Hebraeisches und Aramaeisches Lexicon zum Alten Testament_, 3rd edition with the collaboration of Benedikt Hartmann and E.Y.Kutscher, Brill, Leiden, 1967, p.348).

13. H.van Dyke Parunak points out that only the three visions in 1-3; 8-11 and 40-48 are referred to as mar'ôt 'elōhîm, and that this and other matters demonstrate their mutual interrelationships. He sees this first vision as a chiastic adaptation of the prophetic call narrative, e.g. 1:4 and 1:26-28, '...describing the One who rides on the chariot, form a chiastic inclusio for the three paragraphs in between...' ('The Literary Architecture of Ezekiel's mar'ôt 'Elōhîm', _Journal of Biblical Literature_ 99/1, 1980, pp.61-74).

2) The Medium of what Happens and its Goal – the Prophet and the People: 1:28 – 3:15

1. Burke O.Long in fact calls visions in Ezekiel 'dramatic word-visions'. There is a tendency, he thinks, to regard vision as a mere preparation for word. The pattern of the vision is two-fold: 'appearance of kĕbôd Yahweh (1:28b); followed by an artfully constructed divine address, clearly separated from visionary material in chap.1 (2:1-2; cf. Dan 8:15-18), and focusing of course on prophetic vocation' ('Reports of Visions Among Prophets', JBL 95/3, 1976, pp.362-363).
2. Zimmerli, Ezekiel 1, p.131.
3. There is disagreement among scholars whether the vision of Yahweh in chap.1 and the vision of the scroll which follows in chap.2 originally belonged together or not; Zimmerli, Ezekiel 1, pp.97-100, and Wevers, Ezekiel, p.40, think they did; Garscha, Studien, pp.243-244, among a number of others, thinks not. For Houk, application of statistical linguistic tests does not show that 1:4-28 form a unity with 2:1 – 3:11 (ZAW 93/1, 1981, pp.82-83).
4. Zimmerli, Ezekiel 1, p.131.
5. A number of ancient versions including the Septuagint have 'house' rather than 'sons', and this is Ezekiel's usual way of speaking (Zimmerli, Ezekiel 1, p.89). Moshe Greenberg argues however that there is an inner consistency within both the Hebrew and the LXX and that 'sons' should be retained in the former. In general he makes the point that there is a variety of double expressions which permeate the passage ('The Use of the Ancient Versions for Interpreting the Hebrew Text: A Sampling from Ezekiel ii 1 – iii 11', Congress Volume Goettingen 1977. Supplements to Vetus Testamentum XXIX, Brill, Leiden, 1978, pp.135-136). The words 'to nations' do not fit well in the sentence and may have been added to soften an excessively sharp address to Israel (Zimmerli, Ezekiel 1, p.89); 'have transgressed against me' is missing in the LXX and hardly seems necessary after 'rebelled against me'.
6. Parunak points out that though, of the classical elements of the call narrative, Ezekiel lacks the objection, the difficulties of his mission are not ignored and words of reassurance are included which are just as explicit as if Ezekiel had complained of the difficulty of his task ('Ezekiel's mar'ôt 'Elōhîm', JBL 99/1, 1980, p.64). Parunak is basing his claim on the analysis of N.Habel who works out the call structure as applied to Ezekiel: 1. Divine confrontation (1:1-28); 2. Introductory Word (1:29-2:2); 3. Commission (2:3-5); 4. Objection (seen as implied in 2:6 and 2:8); 5. Reassurance (2:6-7); 6. Sign (2:8 – 3:11) ('The Form and Significance of the Call Narratives', ZAW 77/3, 1965, pp.297-323, on Ezekiel pp.313-314). Parunak (p.66) sees Ezekiel 1:1 – 3:15 as an

227

intricately structured (chiastic) adaptation of the
classical call narrative with extreme emphasis on the
transcendence of Yahweh which is the reason for the lack
of specific objection.

7. Robert P.Carroll points out that Ezekiel's only response
is eating the scroll; otherwise he is passive, which
makes a remarkable contrast with other narrators where
prophets respond, argue and demand signs (From Chaos to
Covenant. Uses of Prophecy in the Book of Jeremiah, SCM
Press, London, 1981, p.40).

8. These words are probably a secondary interpretation which
disrupts the parallel statements at the beginning of vv.5
and 6; see Zimmerli, Ezekiel 1, p.93.

9. See the Introduction. Garscha thinks that the centre of
this report is the vision of the scroll in 2:8-10 and 3:2
and that 3:10-15, with its commission to go to the exiles,
is a secondary interpretation (Studien. pp.244-250).
Much of this depends on accepting one argument and then
proceeding to another based on it (there are after all
many references to the exile to be eliminated). For
example, Garscha writes on p.243: 'If our conjecture (my
underlining, 'Vermutung') is correct that the original
beginning of the work was only "In the 30th year, in the
4th month, on the 5th day of the month, the word of Yahweh
came to Ezekiel the son of Buzi the priest", then grave
doubts arise whether the renewed reference to place in v.3
and the whole vision in 1:4-28 (2:2) are original'. But
is this sufficient reason? And though one can imagine
that the reference to place might have been added once,
would it have been done twice?

10. The Hebrew has 'blessed'; 'rose' can be gained by
changing only one letter in the Hebrew word. 'Blessed'
may have arisen from a dogmatic correction or a simple
mistake; see Zimmerli, Ezekiel 1, p.94.

11. Zimmerli, Ezekiel 1, p.94.

12. It seems hardly likely that both this clause and the one
following belonged to the original text. The one in
square brackets, which adds precision by giving a place
name, is most likely to be the expansion.

3) The Medium - the Watchman: 3:16-21

1. See Fohrer, Ezechiel, p.23.

2. Formel des Wortereignisses; see Zimmerli, Ezekiel 1,
pp.144-145. Hossfeld points out that it is used only in
chaps 1-39 (not in 40-48), and since it is always in the
first person, it is an important indication of the
autobiographical stylizing of the Book of Ezekiel
(Untersuchungen, p.26).

3. See Carley, The Book of the Prophet Ezekiel, pp.116-117;
p.221.

4. It is difficult to make sense of this word in this position.

4) The Goal - the People: 3:22-27

1. As Robert R.Wilson writes, however, '...there is no indication that the actions in iii 22-27 are to be considered symbolic' ('An Interpretation of Ezekiel's Dumbness', VT XXII/1, 1972, p.92).
2. On the construction of a renewed commission in 3:22-24, see Garscha, Studien, pp.244-245.
3. R.R.Wilson writes that '...the author of iii 22-27, xxiv 25-27 and xxxiii 21-22 clearly wants the reader to understand that the dumbness continued from the prophetic call to the fall of the city' (VT XXII, p.93). But this applies only to the last two and then only to the fall of the city. Wilson also thinks that Ezekiel is being forbidden here to exercise the office of prophetic mediator between Yahweh and the people (p.101).
4. On this section, see also now C.Sherlock, 'Ezekiel's Dumbness', The Expository Times 94/10, 1983, pp.296-298.

II THE RECIPIENTS OF RESTORATION

1) The Exiles Still Besieged: 4 - 5

1. Since there is a climactic announcement which identifies the besieged city as Jerusalem in 5:5 ('This is Jerusalem!'), it seems likely that all the references to Jerusalem before this are secondary.
2. See, for example, Eichrodt, Ezekiel, p.82.
3. See Zimmerli, Ezekiel 1, pp.163-164.
4. See Zimmerli, 'Zur Vorgeschichte von Jes 53', Studien zur alttestamentlichen Theologie und Prophetie, Gesammelte Aufsaetze II, Kaiser, Munich, 1974, pp.218-220; but see also Garscha, Studien, pp.89-90, notes 259 and 263, and Barbara E.Thiering, 'The Qumran Interpretation of Ezekiel 4:5-6', The Australian Journal of Biblical Archaeology 1/2, 1969, pp.30-34.
5. Zimmerli, Ezekiel 1, p.163.
6. Eichrodt, Ezekiel, pp.83-84.
7. Zimmerli, Ezekiel 1, pp.163-164.
8. Zimmerli, Ezekiel 1, pp.154-157.
9. Zimmerli, Ezekiel 1, p.169.
10. Zimmerli, Ezekiel 1, p.170.
11. 'In contrast to his older contemporary Jeremiah, Ezekiel rarely speaks of himself ... Even though he heard it from God, the proposal was unthinkable' (James Luther Mays, Ezekiel, Second Isaiah, Fortress, Philadelphia, 1978,

p.25).

12. This renders the Hebrew term 'adōnāy; there has been considerable argument as to whether the word is an original part of the text, for very often the oldest Greek translations render the two Hebrew words 'adōnāy yhwh by just one word in Greek. Zimmerli finally came to the conclusion in a long excursus (Ezekiel 1, pp.556-562) that 'adōnāy is most often used with yhwh in certain formulae such as the messenger formula 'Thus says Adonay Yahweh', the divine oracle formula 'says Adonay Yahweh', and (as here) in the lamenting address to Yahweh 'ah Adonay Yahweh'. He concludes then that it was original in these formulas but not elsewhere. See also Lawrence Boadt, 'Textual Problems in Ezekiel and Poetic Analysis of Paired Words' (JBL 97/4, 1978, pp.494-496) who thinks the inconsistencies in the LXX are an internal Greek problem and that this is a poetic pair of which he finds other examples in Ezekiel.

13. Zimmerli, Ezekiel 1, pp.173-174.

14. This is one of a number of examples of what Zimmerli calls 'Fortschreibung', a continuing rewriting of the basic Ezekiel text, here in view of an event which took place among the exiles where some of them were burnt with fire; compare also Jer. 29:22 ('Das Phaenomen der "Fortschreibung" im Buche Ezekiel', Prophecy. Essays Presented to Georg Fohrer on his 65th Birthday, ed. by J.A.Emerton, de Gruyter, Berlin, 1980, p.183).

15. Zimmerli, Ezekiel 1, pp.174-175.

16. Garscha argues that they are dependent on Leviticus 26:23ff. He also thinks that 5:16 - 6:7 were originally a connected unit which was only secondarily disrupted by the address in 6:1-3 (Studien, pp.94-96).

2) The Supports of Religion Removed: 6

1. See Carley, Ezekiel Among the Prophets, pp.40-42; Zimmerli, Ezekiel 1, pp.182-183.

2. Zimmerli, Ezekiel 1, pp.185-186.

3. Volkmar Fritz thinks now that the word ḥammān which used to be translated 'incense altar', means 'a cult place for foreign deities' ('Die Bedeutung von ḥammān im Hebraeischen und von ḥmn' in den palmyrischen Inschriften', Biblische Notizen 15, 1981, pp.9-20).

4. V.5a is repetitive of v.4b; see Simian, Die theologische Nachgeschichte, pp.117-118.

5. Simian points out that a new addressee is introduced (cities and the people connected with them) in v.6 (Die theologische Nachgeschichte, pp.118-119).

6. By Zimmerli; see 'Erkenntnis Gottes nach dem Buche Ezechiel', Gottes Offenbarung. Gesammelte Aufsaetze, pp.41-119; Ezekiel 1, pp.37-40. For some criticism of Zimmerli's understanding, see Lang, Ezechiel, pp.95-97.

7. Herrmann thinks 6:8-10 probably come from the same context
    as 11:14-21 (<u>Heilserwartungen</u>, p.248).

3) Responsibility to Proclaim the End: 7

1. Zimmerli, <u>Ezekiel</u> <u>1</u>, p.201.
2. The Masoretic text has 'one', but a number of manuscripts
    have 'after' (only one consonant difference in Hebrew).
3. This is material lacking in the LXX; see Zimmerli,
    <u>Ezekiel</u> <u>1</u>, p.205.
4. The meaning of the word ṣepirâ is unexplained here.
5. As it stands, the word means 'staff', but by changing the
    vowels the idea of 'warping' (of justice) can be obtained.
6. The sense of the last words of the verse is very obscure;
    see Zimmerli, <u>Ezekiel</u> <u>1</u>, p.197.
7. With reference to the numerous possible additions here and
    elsewhere, one might refer to the remark of Garscha, 'The
    chapter gives evidence of a series of complicated textual
    and literary-critical problems' (<u>Studien</u>, p.98). He
    himself refers to Zimmerli, <u>Ezekiel</u> <u>1</u>, p.193ff.; on
    pp.206-207, Zimmerli sets out the original text as he sees
    it.
8. Hebrew has 'they all groan', but the word for 'groan' is
    similar to that for 'die', and the latter is suggested by
    LXX; see Zimmerli, <u>Ezekiel</u> <u>1</u>, p.199.
9. This word is missing in the LXX and a similar phrase
    occurs in 9:9 without it.
10. It is lacking in the LXX and some other versions, and has
    features peculiar to it both in language and thought
    (Zimmerli, <u>Ezekiel</u> <u>1</u>, p.200).
11. The phrase is missing in the LXX and some other versions.
    Zimmerli maintains that Ezekiel used the following title
    (nāśî') for the king of Judah and the later additor no
    longer understood this and missed the reference to 'king'
    (<u>Ezekiel</u> <u>1</u>, p.200).

4) Jerusalem is the Place Forsaken: 8 - 11

1. Carley concludes that '..."sitting before" Yahweh appears
    to have been a technical expression used of people
    consulting Yahweh, or his priestly or prophetic
    representatives' (<u>Ezekiel</u> <u>Among</u> <u>the</u> <u>Prophets</u>, p.45).
2. On the significance of the expression 'hand of Yahweh',
    see Zimmerli, <u>Ezekiel</u> <u>1</u>, pp.117-118.
3. Hebrew has 'fire', but the LXX has 'man' - just one letter
    difference in Hebrew, and 'man' seems much more likely in
    view of what is related in the following.
4. Zimmerli, <u>Ezekiel</u> <u>1</u>, p.236.
5. Wevers says the words '...are probably an editorial
    expansion for the image of jealousy. Various conjectures
    as to its meaning have been proposed, but none is fully

convincing' (Ezekiel, p.79; see also Zimmerli, Ezekiel 1, p.217).

6. On translocation and the terminology used here, see Carley, Ezekiel Among the Prophets, pp.30-31; 36-37.

7. Herbert G.May, The Book of Ezekiel, The Interpreter's Bible vol.6, Abingdon, New York and Nashville, 1956, p.106.

8. Eichrodt, Ezekiel, p.122.

9. H.Parunak, in addition to thinking that a chiastic pattern is to be found in this vision as well as in chaps 1-3 (e.g. 8:1-4 and 11:22-25), thinks that all the elements of the rib pattern are to be traced in chaps 8-11 ('Ezekiel's mar'ôt 'Ělōhîm', JBL 99/1, 1980, pp.66-69).

10. Childs sees here evidence of Ezekiel's interpretation of other parts of the Bible: to be understood, the cultic abuse has to be seen in the light of the covenant ceremony in Exodus 24:9ff. and the judgement of Korah in Numbers 16:16ff. (Introduction, p.364).

11. The Hebrew actually has 'us'; but the word is missing in the LXX and in the similar statement in 9:9.

12. Eichrodt, Ezekiel, pp.125-126.

13. Eichrodt, Ezekiel, p.127; Zimmerli, Ezekiel 1, p.243, supported by Garscha, Studien, p.257, thinks however that they were priests.

14. Zimmerli, Ezekiel 1, pp.244-245.

15. Ralph W.Klein asks: 'Did Ezekiel base his critique on the sins actually committed in his day, or has he selected sins from various eras of Israel's history to characterize their utter rejection of God? Such a telescoping of Israel's sin history might account for his catalog of sins in chap.6 as well' (Israel in Exile. A Theological Interpretation, Fortress, Philadelphia, 1979, p.78). Moshe Greenberg has a similar view; he considers that 'the point of such a fantasy' in collecting the notorious instances of cultic pollution is to bring home the awful realization that the sanctity of the sanctuary has been hopelessly injured ('The Vision of Jerusalem in Ezekiel 8-11: A Holistic Interpretation', The Divine Helmsman. Studies on God's Control of Human Events, Presented to Lou H.Silberman, ed J.L.Crenshaw & S.Sandmel, Ktav, New York, 1980, p.160). The working assumption underlying this article as a whole (pp.143-163) is that the present composition of chaps 8-11 is an intentional product.

16. Zimmerli, Ezekiel 1, pp.246-247; Eichrodt, Ezekiel, p.130.

17. Zimmerli, Ezekiel 1, p.232.

18. The phrase is probably intended to make 'the city' more specific; Zimmerli, Ezekiel 1, p.224.

19. Eichrodt, Ezekiel, p.131.

20. Zimmerli, Ezekiel 1, p.248.

21. Eichrodt, Ezekiel, p.132.

22. '...added from a wrong assumption that Israel means the Northern kingdom' (Eichrodt, Ezekiel, p.109).

23. Raitt sses this as a striking word pattern which is Ezekiel's expression of God's decision not to forgive. This is an important component of the judgement preaching and part of the developmental sequence in Ezekiel's message which Raitt discerns (mentioned in the Introduction: A Theology of Exile, pp.50-51).

24. On the composition of chap.10, see Zimmerli, Ezekiel 1, pp.231-233; what he considers to be the basic material of chaps 8-11 as a whole is written out on pp.233-234; see also Eichrodt, Ezekiel, pp.112-119. For some criticisms of Zimmerli and another view, see Cornelius B. Houk, 'The Final Redaction of Ezekiel 10', JBL XC/1, 1971, pp.42-54. David J.Halperin thinks 10:9-17 is an exegesis of the wheel passage in 1:15-21 treating the cherubim as a species of angelic being ('The Exegetical Character of Ezek.X 9-17', VT xxvi/2, 1976, pp.129-141). On the relation between chaps 1 and 10, see also Keel, Jahwe-Visionen, pp.125-273; C.H.Sherlock, 'Ezekiel 10: A Prophet Surprised', The Reformed Theological Review XLII/2, 1983, pp.42-44.

25. See, for example, Wevers, Ezekiel, p.87.

26. This is not in the LXX and overloads the sentence.

27. Helmut Lamparter, Zum Waechter Bestellt. Der Prophet Hesekiel, Die Botschaft des Alten Testaments 21, Calwer Verlag, Stuttgart, 1968, p.81; see also Eichrodt, Ezekiel, p.135.

28. 'Have not the houses lately been rebuilt?' 'A definitive interpretation of v.3a has so far not been made' (Zimmerli, Ezekiel 1, p.258; see also Eichrodt, Ezekiel, p.136).

29. Eichrodt, Ezekiel, p.137.

30. Zimmerli, Ezekiel 1, p.258.

31. For the former, Zimmerli, Ezekiel 1, p.259; for the latter, Eichrodt, Ezekiel, p.136 (quoting Eissfeldt).

32. Zimmerli, Ezekiel 1, p.259; Garscha thinks this interpretation very questionable (Studien, p.259).

33. See Eichrodt, Ezekiel, pp.138-142.

34. Garscha points out that, while 11:1-13 is a description of a vision analogous to chap.9, 11:14-21 is a pure 'word-happening' (Wortgeschehen). He still thinks, however, that they are related to each other; for him 11:14-21 belong clearly to the deutero-Ezekielian editing which formed the book into a polemical writing for the conflict between the exiles and the inhabitants of the land (Studien, pp.258-259).

35. This has probably just been written twice by mistake.

36. Norman K.Gottwald thinks the expression means 'rulers of Jerusalem' here (The Tribes of Yahweh, SCM, London, 1980, p.518).

37. Zimmerli, Ezekiel 1, p.261; William H.Brownlee translates 'men of your redemption' and thinks it indicates Ezekiel was in Judah at the time ('The Aftermath of the Fall of Judah According to Ezekiel', JBL LXXXIX/IV, 1970, p.393).

38. Dieter Baltzer thinks that the phrase 'I have become a sanctuary for them' is understandable from the so-called covenant formula ('I will be their God', v.20), and that it shows the inseparable connection of Yahweh with his sanctuary which is typical of Ezekiel (Ezechiel und Deuterojesaja. Beruehrungen in der Heilserwartungen der beiden grossen Exilspropheten, Walter de Gruyter, Berlin, 1971, pp.34-35).

39. Zimmerli, Ezekiel 1, p.263.

40. The Hebrew has 'one', a word which shares two consonants with the word for 'new'; a few manuscripts and the Syriac and Aramaic (Targum) attest to the latter as well as Ezekiel 18:31 and 36:26.

5) The Exiles Faced with still more Exile: 12

1. Berhard Lang thinks that the reason why Ezekiel speaks to the exiles in Babylon of the exiles in Jerusalem is because he is opposed to the exiles indulging in any anti-Babylon politics: such politics lead to exile of the population and the king (Kein Aufstand in Jerusalem. Die Politik des Propheten Ezechiel, Katholisches Bibelwerk, Stuttgart, 2nd ed. 1981, p.24). The implication of this for Lang is that Ezekiel has a definite political intention (not only pedagogical and pastoral) and that he was still hoping for the deliverance of the whole house of Israel (pp.159-160).

2. Houk points out that the form of address with which 12:1 begins ('The word of Yahweh came to me saying, Son of Man...') occurs thirty-eight times in chaps 12-38, not at all afterwards, and only three times before. He concludes from this that 'This collection of judgements and promises within chaps 12-38 was itself a well-defined, completed work before it was expanded into the present book' ('bn-adm Patterns as Literary Criteria in Ezekiel', JBL LXXXVIII/II, 1969, p.185).

3. The passive sense is obtained from the LXX; see below and also Zimmerli, Ezekiel 1, p.267 for references to the land and Zedekiah.

4. Zimmerli, Ezekiel 1, p.271.

5. Zimmerli, 'Die Botschaft des Propheten Ezechiel', Gesammelte Aufsaetze II, p.124.

6. Zimmerli, Ezekiel 1, pp.271-272. The basic text as Zimmerli sees it is on p.268; see also Garscha, who has reservations about the division into an original report and a redactional treatment, and thinks that the former is already a literary construction (Studien, pp.102-111).

7. Zimmerli, *Ezekiel 1*, pp.273-274.
8. Zimmerli, *Ezekiel 1*, pp.276-278. Garscha thinks that the original report in 12:1-14 was the cause of the formation of the second report in 12:17-20 (*Studien*, p.112).
9. Zimmerli, *Ezekiel 1*, p.277.

6) The Prophets out of Touch: 13

1. Zimmerli, *Ezekiel 1*, p.292.
2. Zimmerli, *Ezekiel 1*, p.292.
3. Zimmerli, *Ezekiel 1*, p.293.
4. See Eichrodt, *Ezekiel*, p.163.
5. Eichrodt, *Ezekiel*, p.165.
6. Zimmerli, *Ezekiel 1*, p.294.
7. Zimmerli, *Ezekiel 1*, p.291. It could be said that the whole of Garscha's book is based on a denial of this approach.
8. This uses some anomalous expressions and one not otherwise found in Ezekiel (see Zimmerli, *Ezekiel 1*, p.288).
9. Fritz Dumermuth, 'Zu Ez.XIII 18-21', *VT* XIII/2, 1963, pp.228-229: see also Eichrodt, *Ezekiel*, pp.169-170.

7) The Positive Counterpart of a Negative Reality: 14:1-11

1. Eichrodt, *Ezekiel*, p.180.
2. This reading is taken from v.7; see Zimmerli, *Ezekiel 1*, pp.300-301.
3. By Jacobus Schoneveld, 'Ezekiel 14:1-8', *Oudtestamentische Studien* 15, 1969, pp.193-204.
4. R.Mosis argues that all the elements of form and content in 14:1-11 are co-ordinated with the call to repentance in v.6. The aim is not to announce judgement to the idolaters, but only to call the whole house of Israel to repentance ('Ez 14:1-11 - ein Ruf zur Umkehr', *Biblische Zeitschrift* 19, 1975, p.163). Raitt sees 14:6 as the only suggestion preserved in the book of the possibility of a national repentance (*Theology of Exile*, p.49). This is one of the passages in which Schulz finds the 'sacral-legal declaration' with a protasis, legal explication and apodosis (*Todesrecht*, pp.178-179).

8) The Exiles Given Strange Consolation: 14:12-23

1. See Martin Noth, 'Noah, Daniel und Hiob in Ezechiel 14', *VT* 1, 1951, pp.251-260; also Zimmerli, *Ezekiel 1*, pp.314-315; Fohrer, *Ezechiel*, p.78; H.H.P.Dressler, 'The Identification of the Ugaritic Dnil with the Daniel of Ezekiel', *VT* XXIX, 1979, pp.152-161; J.Day, 'The Daniel of Ugarit and Ezekiel and the Hero in the Book of Daniel',

VT XXX, 1930, pp. 174-184.

2. Herrmann sees vv.21-23 as a piece which subsequently makes the total judgement of vv.12-20 milder, but thinks it is a message of Ezekiel bound to an independent tradition (Heilserwartungen, pp.250-251).

9) The Reality is the Wood, not the Fruit: 15

1. Hossfeld designates them as fables or parabolic speeches and refers to seven of them in Ezekiel: 15:1-7; 16:1-41; 17:1-10; 22:17-22; 23:1-27; 24:1-14; 31:1-14. Their specific structure is in their two-part nature: presentation with an image and its consequences (Untersuchungen, p.91).
2. There are some who think that the interpretation(s) in vv.6-8 is secondary to the parable in vv.1-5; see Garscha, Studien, pp.269-271.

10) Reflective Speechlessness on the State of Jerusalem: 16

1. Zimmerli, Ezekiel 1, p.336. Lang thinks that this view must be expressly contradicted since these images do not represent a distanced world but a striving to address the people (Ezechiel, p.88). I cannot see that the one necessarily contradicts the other.
2. Zimmerli, Ezekiel 1, pp.336-337.
3. Though see Gerhard von Rad, Old Testament Theology. Vol.II The Theology of Israel's Prophetic Traditions, tr. by D.M.G.Stalker, Oliver & Boyd, Edinburgh & London, 1965, p.221.
4. See Wevers, Ezekiel, p.120; Zimmerli, Ezekiel 1, pp.338-339.
5. This is an unintentional repetition; see Zimmerli, Ezekiel 1, pp.323-324 - also for the following secondary addition.
6. These words which seem to be unintelligible and are missing in the LXX and Syriac may have come about in the workings of various additions; see Wevers, Ezekiel, p.123; Zimmerli, Ezekiel 1, p.325.
7. Zimmerli, Ezekiel 1, p.342.
8. On some of the terminology of this verse, see Otto Eissfeldt, 'Hesekiel Kap.16 also Geschichtsquelle', Kleine Schriften, vol.2, Mohr, Tuebingen, 1963, pp.103-104.
9. See Zimmerli, Ezekiel 1, pp.333-336; his basic text, pp.347-348.
10. Garscha sees the influence of chap.23 also in 16:35-41 (Studien, pp.274-279).
11. André Neher sees Ezekiel not only as the one who rehabilitates Sodom within the biblical family, but also as the veritable redeemer (gō'ēl) of Sodom ('Ezéchiel,

Rédempteur de Sodom', Revue d'Histoire et de Philosophie Religieuses 59, 1979, pp.483-490).

12. Zimmerli, Ezekiel 1, p.351.
13. This is correcting what is probably a copyist's error (Wevers, Ezekiel, p.131).
14. Zimmerli, Ezekiel 1, p.349.
15. Zimmerli, Ezekiel 1, p.352.
16. The Hebrew has 'you take', but since the verb seems to belong in sense to the following 'give', which does have 'I', it seems reasonable to read 'I' here as well (with the Syriac); Zimmerli, Ezekiel 1, p.333.
17. See Zimmerli, Ezekiel 1, p.353. Herrmann thinks Sodom and Samaria will not share in the covenant (Heilserwartungen, p.254).

11) A New Chance Rejected: 17

1. Zimmerli, Ezekiel 1, p.359.
2. See Wevers, Ezekiel, p.134.
3. 'Ezekiel is arguably the most important figure in the history of the Old Testament parable. He is a gathering point and a creative imitator for its future' (John Drury, 'Origins of Mark's Parables', Ways of Reading the Bible, ed. Michael Wadsworth, The Harvester Press, Sussex, 1981, p.178).
4. Garscha thinks that it would be possible to construct a preliminary stage of the allegory, consisting of a vine planted in fruitful ground with a water supply for the plant, whose roots and branches turn away and wither from the east wind. This is one of the few pieces of material which can be attributed to Ezekiel himself. He refrains, however, from constructing the text of this, and it seems a curiously vague hypothesis (Studien, pp.30; 40-41). See also Hossfeld, who ascribes the kernel of the whole speech to Ezekiel (Untersuchungen, pp.94-95).
5. Zimmerli, 'Die Botschaft des Propheten Ezechiel', Gesammelte Aufsaetze II, p.124. This factor is also usually seen as a reason for literary separation. For more detail, see Hossfeld, Untersuchungen, pp.60-63.
6. Zimmerli, Ezekiel 1, p.364 - also on importance of treaty below.
7. Garscha argues that this element is secondary (Studien, pp.30-31). Lang maintains that the prophet himself is trying to convince with all possible means, and that the difference between concepts and images is not a sign of subsequent reworking. His remarks are also interesting from the point of view of the function of images (Kein Aufstand, pp.46-49).
8. Zimmerli, Ezekiel 1, p.365.
9. More details about the treaty are given by Lang, Kein Aufstand, pp.54-58.

10. Hossfeld sees the signs of a late (salvation) editor in the theme of 'Yahweh gives new salvation by the re-establishment of the kingship on the temple mountain', as well as in parallels in construction and vocabulary to other passages of the book (Untersuchungen, p.89).

11. These words are missing in various versions; see Zimmerli, Ezekiel 1, pp.358-359.

12. Zimmerli, Ezekiel 1, p.367.

13. This is the LXX's reading and is probably correct because it preserves the parallelism of animals and birds (31:6); Zimmerli, Ezekiel 1, p.359.

14. Herrmann thinks as a matter of fact that vv.22-24 themselves make no direct reference to kingship and are more similar to the ideas of Isaiah 2:2-4. At the very least the promise is ambiguous and leaves the alternative between kingship and temple on the mountain-top open (Heilserwartungen, pp.258-259). Baltzer thinks Herrmann's interpretation is not very plausible since the picture of the cosmic tree (v.23) is also applied to a king in another place (31:1ff.) (Ezechiel und Deuterojesaja, p.137). Garscha also thinks that vv.22-24 derive from the description of the tree in chap.31 (Studien, p.33).

12) Life Possible for Everyone Now: 18

1. Garscha thinks that the fate of the king described in chap.17 serves as an example of the basic principle of guilt and consequence of guilt in chap.18 (Studien, pp.31 and 33).

2. See Zimmerli, Ezekiel 1, pp.374-375. With regard to the quotation of the people's words, see Michael P.O'Connor: 'There are only two voices in Ezekiel's book, the prophet's and God's. Those who consult and oppose Yahweh and Ezekiel never speak. The words of the latter are always doubly framed; Ezekiel quotes Yahweh quoting them in refutation' ('The Weight of God's Name. Ezekiel in Context and Canon', The Bible Today 18, 1980, p.28).

3. Eichrodt, Ezekiel, p.234.

4. Barnabas Lindars sees it as an expression of the hopelessness of the people ('Ezekiel and Individual Responsibility', VT XV/4, 1965, p.458). P.M.Joyce does not believe that it is the 'unit of responsibility' which is the author's concern, '...but rather the urgent need for his audience to accept responsibility as such' ('Individual Responsibility in Ezekiel 18?', Studia Biblica 1978, I Papers on Old Testament and Related Themes, Journal for the Study of the Old Testament Supplement Series, 11, University of Sheffield, 1979, p.187).

5. This is David Green's English term which he uses in his translation of Fohrer's Introduction to the Old Testament, S.P.C.K., London, E.Tr., 1968, p.69. It renders the

German term Beichtspiegel, on which see Zimmerli, Ezekiel
1, pp.375-376 (Clements uses the English term 'confession
of integrity'); Fohrer, Ezechiel, p.98. John B.Geyer
compares Ezekiel 18 with a Hittite treaty and, thinking it
reasonable to suppose the two passages are related in some
way, suggests that in Ezekiel 18 the prophet had in mind a
succession of Judaean kings, addressing himself to the
individual in the context of the state, and that 'life and
death' meant political freedom or disenfranchisement
('Ezekiel 18 and a Hittite treaty of Mursilis II' Journal
for the Study of the Old Testament 12, 1979, pp.31-46).

6. Joyce gives some criticism of this, p.192 (see note 4
   above).
7. An official pronouncement made by a priest, giving a
   judgement on the state of affairs in a cultic situation;
   see von Rad, 'Die Anrechnung des Glaubens zur
   Gerechtigkeit', Gesammelte Studien zum Alten Testament,
   Kaiser, 1958, pp.130-135; also Zimmerli, Ezekiel 1,
   p.376. Schulz gives a detailed analysis of 18:5-9 as a
   'sacral-legal word of declaration' in Todesrecht,
   pp.168-178.
8. Zimmerli, Ezekiel 1, p.383.
9. Hebrew has 'adōnāy, though there are a number of
   manuscripts with 'Yahweh', and the LXX and Targum indicate
   that they were reading the latter. Zimmerli thinks that
   'Adonay' was inserted because it was less offensive in a
   rebellious saying (Ezekiel 1, p.373).
10. This is missing in some versions, is difficult to work
    into the content here, and may have been taken over from
    v.14; Zimmerli, Ezekiel 1, pp.373-374.
11. Herrmann says that vv.30-32 distinguish themselves by
    making 'life' as a future benefit dependent not only on
    God's action, but on expecting a high degree of
    independence and responsibility from members of God's
    people (Heilserwartungen, p.259).

13) The End of the Whole Royal House: 19

1. On this and the identification of the kings, see Zimmerli,
   Ezekiel 1, pp.393-394, though compare Noth, 'Die
   Katastrophe von Jerusalem im Jahre 587 v. Chr. und ihre
   Bedeutung fuer Israel', Gesammelte Studien, 2nd ed., 1960,
   pp.358-371. For more details, see Lang, Kein Aufstand,
   pp.93-108.
2. Hossfeld sees the specific character of this genre (unlike
   the fable) as having only one part (Untersuchungen, p.91).
3. Hebrew has 'knew their widows'. The LXX reading given
   here seems to presuppose similar-looking Hebrew words;
   see Zimmerli, Ezekiel 1, p.389.
4. Garscha thinks that the difficulties arose because of
   presuppositions concerning Ezekiel's authorship and that,
   rather than being an allegory, it is a lament in the form

of a fable on the fate of he Judaean kingship (Studien, pp.35-39).

5. On the meaning of this word, see Harold R.(Chaim) Cohen, Biblical Hapax Legomena in the Light of Akkadian and Ugaritic, Scholar's Press, Missoula, 1978, p.48.

6. 'With hooks' is missing in the Syriac and may have been secondarily added from v.4. The second phrase seems to overload the statement both in content and metre; see Zimmerli, Ezekiel 1, p.390.

7. Zimmerli, Ezekiel 1, p.397.

8. Garscha argues that there are clear correspondences in particular motifs between 19:10-14 and 17:1-10, that the former passage provides the connection between the two chapters, and that there are no less than six stages in the formation of Ezekiel 17-19 (Studien, pp.40; 42; 44-46).

9. Noth points out that here there is a change to masculine terminology which has no correspondence in what comes before this, and it reverts to the feminine in v.12 (Gesammelte Studien, p.363, note 21).

10. This may be a later attempt to link with v.12; see Zimmerli, Ezekiel 1, p.391.

14) **Recognition of Past Evil for the Purpose of Transformation: 20:1-44**

1. See Zimmerli, Ezekiel 1, pp.404-406.

2. Zimmerli, Ezekiel 1, p.406.

3. Zimmerli, Ezekiel 1, p.407.

4. Henning Graf Reventlow puts it this way: that Yahweh's nature is of such a kind that it requires the acknowledgement of the nations and his name may not be 'profaned' in the eyes of the peoples ('Die Voelker als Jahwes Zeugen bei Ezechiel', ZAW 71, 1959, p.41).

5. J.Lust says that possession of the land is lacking because Ezekiel sees the first occupation only as a prolonging of the sinful stay in the desert. The genuine possession of the land is to take place only after exile (Traditie, Redactie en Kerygma bij Ezechiel. Een Analyse van Ez. XX. 1-26, Brussels, 1969, p.154).

6. Baltzer makes the point that this statement shows that for Ezekiel the exile was a theologically relevant event (Ezechiel und Deuterojesaja, p.4).

7. See Zimmerli, Ezekiel 1, p.412.

8. Garscha argues, however, that 20:32-44 is a logical continuation of Yahweh's action for his own sake in vv.5-26, and holds to the unity of chap.20 even though he does not think it can be completely proved (Studien, pp.115-121).

9. Zimmerli, Ezekiel 1, p.404.

10. Herrmann sees this and other features as deuteronomistic. He thinks that vv.33-44 are not without their connections with vv.1-32, but do not grow organically out of them. He believes that the significance of the relationship of Ezekielian salvation words to the commencing sections of a given chapter which are independently formulated is not to be underestimated (Heilserwartungen, pp.263-265).
11. See Zimmerli, 'Der "Neue Exodus" in der Verkuendigung der beiden grossen Exilspropheten', Gesammelte Aufsaetze I, pp.194-195.
12. Zimmerli, Ezekiel 1, pp.415-416.
13. The Hebrew has 'in the bond of the covenant'. The last word is a partial dittography of the next word and 'in the bond of' an error for a similar word in Hebrew, 'by number'; Wevers, Ezekiel, p.159.
14. See Baltzer, Ezechiel und Deuterojesaja, pp.8-9.
15. See Zimmerli, Gesammelte Aufsaetze I, p.197.
16. Zimmerli, Gesammelte Aufsaetze I, p.194.
17. This is not in the Septuagint and other versions, and is probably an explanatory gloss; Zimmerli, Ezekiel 1, p.403.

15) Final Punishment and Total Revolution: 20:45 - 21:32

1. See Zimmerli, Ezekiel 1, p.423.
2. Zimmerli, Ezekiel 1, p.425.
3. Harvey H.Guthrie thinks indeed that the key to the chapter may not be the word 'sword' but rather poetic descriptions of symbolic actions ('Ezekiel 21', ZAW 74/3, 1962, pp.268-281). Garscha thinks that there are too many differences to allow 21:1-10 (Eng. 20:45 - 21:5) to be taken together with other symbolic actions (Studien, p.127).
4. Reading a verb mgr instead of gwr ('live'); see Zimmerli, Ezekiel 1, p.428.
5. Wevers, Ezekiel, p.165.
6. Zimmerli, Ezekiel 1, p.434.
7. See Zimmerli, Ezekiel 1, p.429.
8. A.J.Brawer, Bet Miqra 11/4, 1965/66, p.95 (Hebrew - see ZAW 79/2, 1967, p.240).
9. Changing from a verb 'hd to hdd; see Zimmerli, Ezekiel 1, p.430.
10. Zimmerli, Ezekiel 1, p.441
11. According to Bartdke, W.W.Struwe does seek from two cuneiform texts to demonstrate the existence of the arrow oracle in Babylonian territory ('Der Prophet Ezekiel in moderner Forschung', Theologische Literaturzeitung 99/10, 1971, pp.731-732).
12. Zimmerli, Ezekiel 1, pp.443-444.
13. Probably an addition, anticipating a similar statement later; Zimmerli, Ezekiel 1, p.437.

14. Zimmerli, _Ezekiel 1_, p.445.
15. See Zimmerli, _Ezekiel 1_, pp.447–448; but also Garscha, _Studien_, p.129.
16. Guthrie, _ZAW_ 74, 1962, p.279.

16) The Exiles to Accept Judgement on Jerusalem: 22

1. Garscha thinks that this terms links several units in chaps 22 – 24:14 as a redactional collection (_Studien_, p.47). For Schulz Ezekiel 22:1–16 is one of the key passages for his 'Deutero-Ezekiel', characterized by being rooted exclusively in the traditions of sacral law without any allusion to the preaching situation of a prophet Ezekiel (_Todesrecht_, pp.181–182). See also Hossfeld, _Untersuchungen_, pp.99–101.
2. Zimmerli, _Ezekiel 1_, p.455.
3. Eichrodt, _Ezekiel_, p.311.
4. Zimmerli, _Ezekiel 1_, pp.463–464.
5. But see Moshé Anbar, 'Une Nouvelle Allusion à une Tradition Babylonienne dans Ezéchiel (XXII 24)', _VT_ XXIX/3, 1979, p.352.
6. This is a reading from the LXX rather than a second 'oppressed' which the Hebrew has; Zimmerli, _Ezekiel 1_, p.466.
7. See Zimmerli, _Ezekiel 1_, p.469; but see also Garscha, _Studien_, p.52.

17) Do the Exiles Still Wish to Put their Trust in Jerusalem?: 23

1. Zimmerli, _Ezekiel 1_, p.481.
2. Zimmerli, _Ezekiel 1_, pp.482–483. Bernhard Lang in an analysis of 12:1–55; 17; 19; 21:23–27 sees a much stronger political interest in Ezekiel than has usually been thought. (One might refer, for example, to Joseph Blenkinsopp: 'In Ezekiel this rootedness in present historical realities is already much less apparent' – _Prophecy and Canon. A Contribution to the Study of Jewish Origins_, University of Notre Dame Press, 1977, p.73). But Lang thinks that, in his early period, Ezekiel wanted to persuade the exiles not to take any part in Jerusalem's rebellion against Babylon (_Kein Aufstand in Jerusalem. Die Politik des Propheten Ezechiel_, Katholisches Bibelwerk, Stuttgart, 1978).
3. This is probably anticipating the interpretation; Eichrodt, _Ezekiel_, p.319.
4. See Zimmerli, _Ezekiel 1_, pp.483–484.
5. Literally, 'Oholah had illicit intercourse instead of with me'.

6. Zimmerli, <u>Ezekiel</u> <u>1</u>, p.486.
7. Zimmerli, <u>Ezekiel</u> <u>1</u>, p.488.
8. Zimmerli, <u>Ezekiel</u> <u>1</u>, p.489.
9. Zimmerli, <u>Ezekiel</u> <u>1</u>, p.491.
10. Garscha thinks, however, that with Oholah and Oholibah the author is already no longer intending Samaria and Jerusalem, but individual 'females' as a cautionary example for the marital and social behaviour of individual women (<u>Studien</u>, pp.54-55).
11. Zimmerli, <u>Ezekiel</u> <u>1</u>, p.492.
12. It seems to me that this point would have to be kept in mind against Childs' wish to do justice to the versatility of the image (<u>Introduction</u>, p.369).

18) The People Must Respond: 24:1-14

1. See Zimmerli, <u>Ezekiel</u> <u>1</u>, pp.496-497.
2. For the first, Hebrew has 'bones', which hardly seems to fit the sense; one letter less in Hebrew gives 'wood'. A similar change gives 'pieces' for 'boilings'; see Zimmerli, <u>Ezekiel</u> <u>1</u>, pp.493-494.
3. Eichrodt, <u>Ezekiel</u>, pp.337-338.
4. Zimmerli, <u>Ezekiel</u> <u>1</u>, p.497.
5. On the translation of vv.7-8, see H.J.van Dijk, 'A Neglected Connotation of Three Hebrew Verbs', <u>VT</u> XVIII/1, 1968, pp.21-22.

19) The People's Reaction to Jerusalem's Destruction: 24:15-27

1. Eichrodt, <u>Ezekiel</u>, p.342.
2. See Eichrodt, <u>Ezekiel</u>, pp.342-343.
3. Zimmerli, <u>Ezekiel</u> <u>1</u>, p.506. In connection with the mourning customs, Garscha thinks that the report is at the most a subsequent reflection on an event in the life of the prophet (<u>Studien</u>, p.81).
4. Zimmerli, <u>Ezekiel</u> <u>1</u>, p.507.
5. Zimmerli, <u>Ezekiel</u> <u>1</u>, p.507.
6. Zimmerli, <u>Ezekiel</u> <u>1</u>, p.508.
7. The Hebrew does not have the word 'to'; Wevers thinks it likely that this was a marginal notation indicating the theme of the passage, and that therefore it should be omitted (<u>Ezekiel</u>, p.195). Garscha believes that the addition has the aim of characterizing Ezekiel as a prophet of the exile (<u>Studien</u>, p.85).

1) A Reaction Concerning Yahweh's Reputation: 25

1. By Zimmerli; see 'Das Wort des goettlichen Selbsterweises
   (Erweiswort), eine prophetische Gattung', Gesammelte
   Aufsaetze I, pp.120-132. This form has also been used
   previously, for example in chap.13; see Zimmerli, Ezekiel
   1, p.290 (Clements uses the English term 'proof oracle').
   On chap.25, see Zimmerli, Ezekiel 2, pp.10-11.
2. Eichrodt, Ezekiel, p.358.
3. This is not to be found in the LXX and other ancient
   versions, and anticipates the later saying on Edom
   (Zimmerli, Ezekiel 2, p.8).
4. On 25:10, see Lang, 'A Neglected Method in Ezekiel
   Research. Editorial Criticism', VT XXIX/1, 1979,
   pp.39-44.
5. See Zimmerli, Ezekiel 2, p.13f.
6. On this and other matters concerning revenge in the Old
   Testament, see Walter Dietrich, 'Rache. Erwaegungen zu
   einem alttestamentlichen Thema', Evangelische Theologie
   36/5, 1976, pp.450-472; see also George E.Mendenhall, The
   Tenth Generation. The Origins of the Biblical Tradition,
   John Hopkins U.P., Baltimore & London, 1973, pp.69-104.

2) A Reaction to Tyre's Pride: 26 - 28

1. Zimmerli, Ezekiel 2, p.24.
2. Hebrew has 'I am becoming full'; the change of one
   consonant achieves the reading given.
3. Eichrodt, Ezekiel, p.369.
4. But see Garscha, Studien, pp.152-153.
5. Zimmerli, Ezekiel 2, p.37.
6. The Hebrew has 'at sea entrances', but various ancient
   versions suggest a reading with the singular and an
   article; see Zimmerli, Ezekiel 2, p.42.
7. Zimmerli, Ezekiel 2, p.57.
8. Zimmerli, Ezekiel 2, p.53.
9. Zimmerli, Ezekiel 2, pp.70-71. Moshe Elat finds that
   Ezekiel 27:19 reflects the geographical condition of the
   first half of the first millenium when territories of the
   Ionians and the Danneans were located south of the
   iron-rich region of 'ūzāl in the Anatolian mountains, on
   the trade routes leading to Phoenicia ('The Iron Export
   from Uzal (Ezekiel XXVII 19)', VT XXXIII/3, 1983,
   pp.323-330).
10. Zimmerli, Ezekiel 2, p.61
11. 'Like silence' hardly seems correct here; see Zimmerli,
    Ezekiel 2, p.52; Wevers, Ezekiel, p.212.

12. Changing a word for 'time' by one consonant to 'now'.
13. Zimmerli, Ezekiel 2, p.69.
14. Fohrer, Ezechiel, p.156.
15. Zimmerli, Ezekiel 2, p.75.
16. Zimmerli, Ezekiel 2, p.79. Bruno Pennacchini, Temi Mitici in Ezechiele 28:1-19, Studio Teologico "Porziuncola", Assisi, 1973, pp.116-117.
17. See Donald E.Gowan, When Man Becomes God. Humanism and Hybris in the Old Testament, The Pickwick Press, Pittsburgh, 1975, pp.78-81.
18. See Pennacchini, Temi Mitici, pp.125-147; Gowan, When Man Becomes God, pp.83-84.
19. See Zimmerli, Ezekiel 2, pp.82-85; Wevers, Ezekiel, pp.217-218.
20. See Pennacchini, Temi Mitici, pp.65-98: Gowan, When Man Becomes God, pp.81-82.
21. See Gowan, When Man Becomes God, pp.75-78.
22. Zimmerli, Ezekiel 2, p.90; Eichrodt, Ezekiel, p.392.
23. By Anthony J.Williams; on this and the following, see his 'The Mythological Background of Ezekiel 28:12-19?', Biblical Theology Bulletin VI/1, 1976, pp.49-61.
24. Zimmerli, Ezekiel 2, p.93; Wevers, Ezekiel, p.218.
25. Zimmerli, Ezekiel 2, p.98.
26. Zimmerli, Ezekiel 2, p.99.

3) A Reaction to Egypt's Power: 29 - 32

1. Eichrodt, Ezekiel, p.399. Boadt concludes that the Egyptian oracles are dated from the time of the prophet himself, are in historical order (except for 29:17-21; 30:1-19), and were composed as occasional speeches (Ezekiel's Oracles, pp.11-12).
2. Boadt thinks that '...Ezekiel's fondness for traditional paired words and reduplicated commands obviates any need for emendation of dabbēr in Ezekiel 29:3' ('Textual Problems in Ezekiel and Poetic Analysis of Paired Words', JBL 97/4, 1978, pp.496-498).
3. Boadt argues for the meaning 'chaos-monster' (Ezekiel's Oracles, pp.27-28).
4. Hebrew has a curious 'I made myself'; it is probably just a mistake in writing; Zimmerli, Ezekiel 2, pp.106-107.
5. Zimmerli, Ezekiel 2, p.111.
6. Wevers thinks that the original poem referred only to Pharaoh and the reference to the fish is a later expansion (Ezekiel, pp.221-222; see also Garscha, Studien, p.168).
7. Hebrew has 'shoulder', the LXX and Syriac 'hand'; see Zimmerli, Ezekiel 2, p.107.
8. See Zimmerli, Ezekiel 2, p.114.
9. See Zimmerli, Ezekiel 2, p.118.
10. Robert P.Carroll's characterization of this prophecy as explanation by means of adaptation does not seem to me to take enough account of this (When Prophecy Failed, SCM

Press, 1979, pp.174-176).
11. Zimmerli, Ezekiel 2, p.120.
12. For a survey of various views on the composition of 30:1-19, see Hossfeld, Untersuchungen, pp.184-185.
13. Zimmerli, Ezekiel 2, p.131.
14. Fohrer thinks there are three strophes at the basis of which lie short lists of names which indicated the extent of Egypt or described particular districts (Ezechiel, pp.172-173; but see Garscha, Studien, p.178, and Hossfeld, Untersuchungen, p.198; pp.209-216).
15. Eichrodt, Ezekiel, pp.420-421.
16. Zimmerli, Ezekiel 2, p.148.
17. On the cosmic tree, see Gowan, When Man Becomes God, pp.93-116; the sacred tree, Boadt, Ezekiel's Oracles, pp.99-103.
18. This is missing in the Septuagint; it is also the only time in the poem that God is introduced in the first person; Zimmerli, Ezekiel 2, p.143.
19. The meaning of the Hebrew word rāmût is unclear; see Wevers, Ezekiel, pp.241-242.
20. The Hebrew is active; the LXX suggests passive; see Zimmerli, Ezekiel 2, p.155.
21. The Hebrew has 'destruction'; change of one letter gives 'captivity', also suggested by the LXX; Zimmerli, Ezekiel 2, p.156.
22. See Zimmerli, Ezekiel 2, pp.65-66; Garscha, however, does not think any particular historical memories are presupposed (Studien, p.193).

IV RESPONSIBILITY AND RESTORATION: 33 - 39

1) Responsibility for Restoration: 33

1. See Eichrodt, Ezekiel, pp.442-443.
2. G. del Olmo Lete sees a perfect formal correlation between vv.2-6 and 7-9 ('Estructura literaria de Ez. 33, 1-20', Estudios Bíblicos 22, 1963, p.17).
3. Zimmerli, Ezekiel 2, p.183.
4. Zimmerli, Ezekiel 2, p.185.
5. See Eichrodt, Ezekiel, p.75; Zimmerli, Ezekiel 2, p.189.
6. But see Schulz, Todesrecht, p.180, note 58.
7. William H.Brownlee claims that the parable of the watchman serves triple duty by dividing Ezekiel's career into three periods of watchman's service: in chap.3, watchman for Israel; in chaps 25-32, watchman for the nations; and in chap.33, once more watchman for Israel ('Ezekiel's Parable of the Watchman and the Editing of Ezekiel', VT XXVIII/4, 1978, p.399).

8. Zimmerli, Ezekiel 2, p.187.
9. Rolf Knierim, Die Hauptbegriffe fuer Suende im Alten Testament, Guetersloher Verlagshaus Gerd Mohn, Guetersloh, 2nd ed., 1967, p.234.
10. See Zimmerli, '"Leben" und "Tod" im Buche des Propheten Ezechiel', Gesammelte Aufsaetze I, pp.178-179; see also von Rad, '"Gerechtigkeit" und "Leben" in der Kultsprache der Psalmen', Gesammelte Studien, pp.225-247.
11. Zimmerli, Ezekiel 2, p.187. Herrmann thinks the parallels between chap.33 and chap.18 are so clear that it is sufficient to list them; see Heilserwartungen, p.268.
12. Herrmann, for example, sees a complicated composition of casuistry which did not belong originally to the picture of the watchman (Heilserwartungen, p.268). Garscha, however, does not think it can be proved conclusively that the individual parts of vv.1-20 were brought together as a unity only secondarily (Studien, p.197).
13. Eichrodt, Ezekiel, p.455.
14. Zimmerli argues that the clause after this one, the last in the verse, is probably secondary, because there is a word in it which has no specific antecedent, and it disturbs the parallelism of the pair of cases continued in 33:13-16 (Ezekiel 2, p.181).
15. See Zimmerli, Gesammelte Aufsaetze I, p.181.
16. Zimmerli, Gesammelte Aufsaetze I, p.182.
17. Zimmerli, Ezekiel 2, p.189.
18. The Hebrew has 'twelfth' - see below.
19. See Zimmerli, Ezekiel 2, p.192. Garscha, however, thinks that 33:21-22 come from his Deutero-Ezekiel, who, wanting to characterize Ezekiel as a prophet of the exile, invented the messenger and accordingly shifted the date of the fall of the city (Studien, pp.84-85; p.198). But see also Ernst Vogt, 'Die Laehmung und Stummheit des Propheten Ezechiel', Wort-Gebot-Glaube. Walter Eichrodt zum 80. Geburtstag, Zwingli, Zurich, 1970, p.95, note 18. The whole article (pp.87-100) discusses the relation between the various passages on Ezekiel's dumbness in chaps 3, 24 and now 33:22.
20. Zimmerli, Ezekiel 2, p.191.
21. Zimmerli, Ezekiel 2, p.193.
22. Zimmerli, Ezekiel 1, p.190.
23. Zimmerli, Ezekiel 2, p.199.
24. Zimmerli, Ezekiel 2, p.201.
25. Von Rad, Old Testament Theology 2, p.223, note 8.

2) The Responsibility of Leaders: 34

1. See Eichrodt, Ezekiel, p.469; Zimmerli, Ezekiel 2, pp.213-214.
2. Zimmerli, Ezekiel 2, p.216.

3. Zimmerli, Ezekiel 2, p.217.
4. Eichrodt, Ezekiel, p.472.
5. See C.K.Barrett, The Gospel According to St. John. An Introduction with Commentary and Notes on the Greek Text, S.P.C.K., London, 1958, p.310.
6. See Zimmerli, Ezekiel 2, pp.212-213.
7. See Eichrodt, Ezekiel, p.473.
8. Eichrodt, Ezekiel, p.478.
9. Zimmerli, Ezekiel 2, p.218.
10. Zimmerli, Ezekiel 2, p.219.
11. Mentioned in Eichrodt, Ezekiel, p.475.
12. Mentioned in Zimmerli, Ezekiel 2, p.219.
13. Zimmerli, Ezekiel 2, p.218.
14. Eichrodt, Ezekiel, pp.476-477.
15. See Noth, 'Gebrauch und Bedeutung des Worts nāśî'', Das System der zwoelf Staemme Israels (1930), reprint Wissenschaftliche Buchgesellschaft, Darmstadt, 1966, pp.151-162.
16. Garscha thinks that the break in thought with vv.25ff. can be explained by the dependence of the text on Leviticus 26:4-13, and that Ezekiel 34:1-3, 9-10, 11-15 and 25-30 should be understood as a unified complex (Studien, pp.204-205). Karl Elliger gives an analysis of the relationship between Leviticus 26 and Ezekiel 34:25-30, and thinks both passages depend on a common source, the liturgy of the Harvest Festival (Leviticus, Handbuch zum Alten Testament 4, Mohr, Tuebingen, 1966, p.366). Baltzer presents a synopsis of the Hebrew text of the two passages and thinks Ezekiel 34 is directly dependent on Leviticus 26 (Ezechiel und Deuterojesaja, pp.156-160).
17. Zimmerli, Ezekiel 2, pp.220-221.
18. Lothar Perlitt, Bundestheologie im Alten Testament, Neukirchener Verlag, Neukirchen, 1969, p.145.

3) Responsibility for Another Nation and One's Own: 35:1 - 36:15

1. See Zimmerli, Ezekiel 2, pp.232-234.
2. Zimmerli, Ezekiel 2, p.234.
3. In a comparison of Ezekiel 35:1-4 with the oracle against the nations (especially 28:20-23), Simian actually comes to the conclusion that the principal interest already of 35:1-4 is not the punishment of Seir but a theological statement. Edom is the personification of all the enemies of Israel (Die theologische Nachgeschichte, pp.185-189).
4. See Zimmerli, Gesammelte Aufsaetze I, pp.90-91.
5. See Zimmerli, Gesammelte Aufsaetze I, pp.127-128.
6. The words in square brackets are missing in the LXX and some other versions, and interrupt the introduction and consequence of the oath clause 'as I live, you are guilty'. For 'guilty' Hebrew has 'hate', which lacks

sense in the context. 'You are guilty of blood' is the reading of the LXX (Zimmerli, Ezekiel 2, pp.224-225).

7. See Klaus Koch, 'Gibt es ein Vergeltungsdogma im Alten Testament?', Um das Prinzip der Vergeltung in Religion und Recht des Alten Testaments, ed. by K.Koch, Wissenschaftliche Buchgesellschaft, Darmstadt, 1972, pp.130-180.

8. Von Rad, Old Testament Theology 2, p.224.

9. Zimmerli, Ezekiel 2, pp.233-234; p.236. Simian finds the relation between chap.6 and chaps 35-36 difficult to define (Die theologische Nachgeschichte, p.354).

10. Zimmerli, Ezekiel 2, p.233.

11. Simian points out that it is now quite clear that the main interest is not in the enemies of Israel, but in Israel herself (Die theologische Nachgeschichte, p.74).

12. Zimmerli, Ezekiel 2, p.234; see also Simian, Die theologische Nachgeschichte, pp.154-155.

13. These words are missing in the LXX and interrupt the direct address to the mountains; Zimmerli, Ezekiel 2, p.230.

14. Zimmerli, Ezekiel 2, p.233.

15. These words become an address in the 2nd person masculine singular; Zimmerli, Ezekiel 2, p.231.

16. Hebrew has 'stumble', a similar word to 'bereave' in that language; Zimmerli, Ezekiel 2, p.231.

17. Zimmerli thinks these words (lacking in the LXX) have been mistakenly written again from v.14 (Zimmerli, Ezekiel 2, p.231).

4) Responsibility for God and the Renewal of People: 36:16-38

1. Eichrodt, Ezekiel, p.495.

2. Zimmerli, Ezekiel 2, p.247.

3. Zimmerli, Gesammelte Aufsaetze I, p.191. Herrmann puts more emphasis on Yahweh's own honour (Heilserwartungen, p.272).

4. Zimmerli, Ezekiel 2, p.249.

5. See Eichrodt, Ezekiel, p.499.

6. Zimmerli, Ezekiel 2, p.248. Herrmann points out that this section draws consequences which also involve the individual (Heilserwartungen, p.271).

7. Zimmerli, Ezekiel 2, p.249.

8. Herrmann sees the use of deuteronomistic formulations in vv.26ff. crowned with this (Heilserwartungen, p.272).

9. See Eichrodt, Ezekiel, p.504.

10. On the other hand, there may be at least something deliberate about this. Fohrer points out that 36:16-38 is made up of 20 strophes in 5 parts and that each of these decreases by one strophe, i.e. from six to two (Ezekiel, p.202). Herrmann comments that this could be a deliberate principle of form: that of decreasing quantity

(<u>Heilserwartungen</u>, p.273). J.Lust thinks, however, that
the whole of 36:23c-38, which is missing in Pap.967 and
the Codex Wirceburgensis, was composed as a transtion from
chaps 36 to 37 after an original order of chaps 36; 38;
39; 40-48 was altered ('De Samenhang van Ez. 36-40.
Theologische relevantie van het ontbreken van Ez. 36,
23c-38 in enkele handschriften', <u>Tijdschrift</u> <u>voor</u>
<u>Theologie</u> 20, 1980, pp.26-39). In a later article he
concludes that '...Ezekiel 36:23c-38 is most probably a
late redactional addition. Both in the Hebrew text and in
the traditional Greek version, the style and the
vocabulary betray a hand different from the one in the
surrounding parts of the book. The redactor appears to
have been inspired by the Book of Jeremiah in its final
form...' ('Ezekiel 36-40 in the Oldest Greek Manuscript',
<u>Catholic</u> <u>Biblical</u> <u>Quarterly</u> 43/4, 1981, pp.517- 533). But
see Lang, <u>Ezechiel</u>, p.31.
11. Zimmerli, <u>Ezekiel</u> <u>2</u>, p.243.

5) **Responsibility for Life:** 37:1-14

1. See Zimmerli, <u>Ezekiel</u> <u>2</u>, p.259; also Michael V.Fox, 'The
   Rhetoric of Ezekiel's Vision of the Valley of the Bones',
   <u>Hebrew</u> <u>Union</u> <u>College</u> <u>Annual</u> LI, 1980, pp.1-15.
2. Zimmerli, <u>Ezekiel</u> <u>1</u>, pp.117-118.
3. Zimmerli thinks the expression was a fixed technical term
   which was retained even in this context (<u>Ezekiel</u> <u>2</u>,
   p.259); but see also Hossfeld who argues that the
   expression does not belong to the basic text
   (<u>Untersuchungen</u>, pp.345-347).
4. Zimmerli, <u>Ezekiel</u> <u>1</u>, p.157.
5. Zimmerli, <u>Ezekiel</u> <u>2</u>, p.260.
6. See Eichrodt, <u>Ezekiel</u>, p.508; Zimmerli, <u>Ezekiel</u> <u>2</u>, p.260.
7. Eichrodt, <u>Ezekiel</u>, p.508.
8. See Zimmerli, <u>Ezekiel</u> <u>2</u>, p.261; Eichrodt, <u>Ezekiel</u>,
   pp.508-509.
9. For example Fohrer, <u>Ezechiel</u>, pp.206-210; Wevers,
   <u>Ezekiel</u>, pp.277-279. But see also Eichrodt, <u>Ezekiel</u>,
   pp.509-511; Zimmerli, <u>Ezekiel</u> <u>2</u>, pp.257-258. Hossfeld
   gives a survey of various views (<u>Untersuchungen</u>,
   pp.341-344). Baltzer thinks that vv.1-10 are unified in
   themselves and do not need an interpretation, and that
   only the words 'our bones are dried up' (v.11) refer
   directly to the vision and that they were inserted
   secondarily into v.11, which was originally independent.
   He thinks further that the vision has a quality of
   proclamation for new creation not matched by any of the
   additions in vv.11-14 (<u>Ezechiel</u> <u>und</u> <u>Deuterojesaja</u>,
   pp.100-118). Garscha thinks, however, that the change
   from the idea of a field of bones to a grave is to be
   explained by the different setting of the two; for the
   first there was the plain, but for the second, the place

from which the people were to be led, it was more
appropriate to speak of graves. He does not believe
either that Baltzer gives sufficient explanation of how
the present state of the text came into being (Studien,
pp.219-223). See also Peter Hoeffken, 'Beobachtungen zu
Ezechiel XXXVII 1-10', VT XXXI/3, 1981, pp.305-317, though
this has mainly to do with the literary growth of vv.1-10.
10. These words (also in v.13) are not in the LXX and Syriac
(see Zimmerli, Ezekiel 2, p.256).

6) Responsibility for Separated Brethren: 37:15-28

1. Christoph Barth thinks indeed that the whole of chap.37
can be seen as a unity. He finds various themes of
vv.1-14 recurring in vv.15-28: leading out, bringing
home, the whole house of Israel in v.11, the prophet as
mediator. There are new features in vv.15-28 which stem
however from giving vv.1-14 a new interpretation
proceeding from the announcement that Yahweh will give the
whole house of Israel his spirit ('Ezechiel 37 als
Einheit', Beitraege zur alttestamentlichen Theologie.
Festschrift fuer Walther Zimmerli zum 70. Geburtstag, ed.
by Herbert Donner et al., Vandenhoeck & Ruprecht,
Goettingen, 1977, pp.37-52).
2. See Zimmerli, Ezekiel 2, p.273.
3. Zimmerli, Ezekiel 2, p.274.
4. Robert Martin-Achard, 'Quelques remarques sur la
réunification du peuple de Dieu d'après Ezéchiel 37, 15
ss' Wort-Gebot-Glaube. Beitraege zur Theologie des Alten
Testaments. Walther Eichrodt zum 80. Geburtstag, ed. by
H.J.Stoebe et al., 1970, pp.67-85.
5. 'Them' is probably a secondary reference to the 'tribes of
Israel'; Zimmerli, Ezekiel 2, p.269.
6. Zimmerli, Ezekiel 2, p.278.
7. Zimmerli, Ezekiel 2, p.279.
8. Johannes Herrmann thought these words might have been a
note in the margin subsequently transferred to the text;
see Zimmerli, Ezekiel 2, pp.270-271.
9. Avi Hurvitz thinks that in the light of the agreement
between Leviticus 26:11-12 and Ezekiel 37:26-27, the
absence of God + hithallek in Ezekiel can be explained by
the later Ezekiel avoiding this uncomfortable expression.
As with many other expressions, Hurvitz seeks to show that
Ezekiel is later than P (A Linguistic Study of the
Relationship Between the Priestly Source and the Book of
Ezekiel, Gabalda, Paris, 1982, p.103). Many of his
examples are taken, however, from Ezekiel 40-48 and other
passages which many scholars believe to be later than the
exilic Ezekiel.

Appendix: The Restoration of Ultimate Reality: 38 - 39

1. Zimmerli, Ezechiel. Gestalt und Botschaft, Neukirchener
   Verlag, Neukirchen, 1972, p.129.
2. See Zimmerli, Ezekiel 2, pp.300-302; Eichrodt, Ezekiel,
   p.522; Michael C.Astour, 'Ezekiel's Prophecy of Gog and
   the Cuthean Legend of Naram-Sin', JBL 95/4, 1976,
   pp.569-572. Astour seeks to demonstrate '...that the
   basic conception of the Gog prophecy goes back to a
   Babylonian didactic poem known as the Cuthean Legend of
   Naram-Sin'.
3. Zimmerli, Ezekiel 2, p.305.
4. Zimmerli finds the basic text in 38:1-9; 39:1-51, 17-20
   (Ezekiel 2, pp.296-299). Hossfeld gives a survey of
   various opinions (Untersuchungen, pp.402-405), finds the
   basic text himself in 38:1-3a; 39:1b-5, and discovers no
   reason to see in Gog anything else but a historical entity
   (p.498).
5. Zimmerli, Ezekiel 2, p.310.
6. Zimmerli, Ezekiel 2, p.312.
7. See Reventlow, 'Die Voelker als Jahwes Zeugen bei
   Ezechiel', ZAW 71, 1959, pp.33-43.
8. Hossfeld, Untersuchungen, pp.450-451.
9. In speaking of exegetical activity within the Bible,
   Childs sees here an explicit attempt within the canonical
   process to link Ezekiel's message to previous prophecies.
   Ezekiel's prophecy against Gog is seen as fulfilling
   earlier prophecies which foretold the coming of the enemy
   from the north (Introduction, pp.367-368).

V THE RESTORATION OF THE MEDIUM OF LIFE: 40 - 48

1) The Place: 40 - 42

1. Menahem Haran sees a series of three in 40-44:3;
   44:4-46:24; 47-48; i.e. the temple's layout, temple
   procedures, the land. He regards this code in 40-48 as
   merely a late and epigonic outgrowth of the P school, i.e.
   it is another expression of Haran's well-known early
   dating of P ('The Law Code of Ezekiel and the Priestly
   School', Hebrew Union College Annual L, 1979, pp.53-54).
2. Zimmerli, Ezekiel 2, p.361.
3. Zimmerli, Ezekiel 2, p.327. Parunak points out that the
   prologue in 40:1-4 parallels some of the themes of 8:1-4
   ('Ezekiel's mar'ōt 'Ělōhîm', JBL 99/1, 1980, p.70).
   Childs sees 40-48 portraying a community which
   demonstrates the proper worship of God as a conscious
   contrast to 8-11 (Introduction, p.367).

4. Raitt speaks of Ezekiel's preoccupation with the temple and quotes D.N.Freedman as making the point well: 'The theme of the Temple runs through the entire book, and is the key to its unity. In a sentence, it is the story of the departure of the glory of God from the Temple, and its return' (Raitt, A Theology of Exile, pp.67-68).

5. See Rudolf Smend, Die Bundesformel, EVZ Verlag, Zurich, 1963.

6. G.Ch. Macholz says that it is something peculiar to this passage in the whole Old Testament that hope is expressed in the form of a plan ('Noch Einmal: Planungen fuer den Wiederaufbau nach der Katastrophe von 587. Erwaegungen zum Schlussteil des sog. "Verfassungsentwurf des Hesekiel"', VT XIX/3, 1969, p.322).

7. Jon Douglas Levenson argues that the unnamed mountain is literally Mount Zion, though at the same time typologically identical to Sinai (Theology of the Program of Restoration of Ezekiel 40-48, Scholars Press, Missoula, 1976, pp.7-24).

8. Hartmut Gese, Der Verfassungsentwurf des Ezechiel (Kap.40-48) traditionsgeschichtlich untersucht, Mohr, Tuebingen, 1957, p.2 (this book is basic for the history of the tradition in 40-48). Levenson sees the tour of Zion as a way to grow in the knowledge of God (Theology of the Program of Restoration, p.16).

9. Zimmerli, Ezekiel 2, p.343.

10. The fact is one of conviction. In fact, the temple was never restored as described in 40-48. On the other hand, there was a restoration of the temple which was crucial in the future development of Israel; and Zimmerli maintains that the plan set out here was not simply invented but contains memories of the pre-exilic city of Solomon, as well as being influenced by the second temple which was actually built. Gese has shown that 40-48 is the result of a process of literary growth, Zimmerli adds ('Ezechieltempel und Salomostadt', Gesammelte Aufsaetze II, pp.148-149).

11. Gese, Verfassungsentwurf, pp.12-13.

12. Eichrodt, Ezekiel, p.545.

13. Zimmerli finds the basic text of 40-42 in 40:1-37, 47-49; 41:1-4 (Ezekiel 2, p.329).

14. Eichrodt, Ezekiel, p.546.

15. See Gese, Verfassungsentwurf, p.22.

16. Zimmerli, Ezekiel 2, p.381.

17. Zimmerli, Ezekiel 2, p.386.

18. Zimmerli, Ezekiel 2, pp.398, 401.

2) What Happens in the Place: 43 - 46

1. See Zimmerli, _Ezekiel 2_, p.413.
2. See Zimmerli, _Ezekiel 2_, pp.414–415.
3. See Zimmerli, _Ezekiel 2_, p.415.
4. Baltzer writes that the salvation of the return of Yahweh to the temple and his promise to dwell there forever, as well as the turning away from the sinful past of the people, are brought together here with great concentration (_Ezechiel und Deuterojesaja_, pp.56–57).
5. Zimmerli, _Ezekiel 2_, p.416.
6. An alteration in vocalization changes this from a word meaning 'high place'; see Zimmerli, _Ezekiel 2_, p.409.
7. Zimmerli, _Ezekiel 2_, p.418.
8. Zimmerli, _Ezekiel 2_, p.418.
9. Zimmerli, _Ezekiel 2_, p.418.
10. This is one of the examples which Herrmann gives of the traditional links which he sees between 40-48 and 1-39 – in this case with 17:23 and 20:40 (_Heilserwartungen_, p.277).
11. Zimmerli, _Ezekiel 2_, p.427.
12. Eichrodt, _Ezekiel_, p.558.
13. Zimmerli, _Ezekiel 2_, p.440.
14. Paul D.Hanson presents 40-48 as serving the purpose of the Zadokite priests along the official lines of a hierocratic tradition in contrast to the visionary followers of the Second Isaiah (_The Dawn of Apocalyptic_, Fortress Press, Philadelphia, 1975, pp.228-240).
15. Zimmerli, _Ezekiel 2_, p.445.
16. Zimmerli, _Ezekiel 2_, p.463.
17. Zimmerli, _Ezekiel 2_, p.453.
18. See Zimmerli, _Ezekiel 2_, p.454; also Raymond Abba, 'Priests and Levites in Ezekiel', _VT_ XXVIII/1, 1978, p.3.
19. See Abba, 'Priests and Levites in Ezekiel', _VT_ XXVIII, 1978, pp.1-9, who thinks that the polemic here may not be directed against the deposed priests of the Judaean high places, but against those who had taken part in Jeroboam I's calf-worship in Northern Israel (1 Kings 12:28-32). Levenson notes the possibility of an intra-Aaronite struggle, rejects the theory that the apostate priests were the Gibeonites, and also seems attracted to the idea of polemic against those taking part in calf-worship (_Theology of the Program of Restoration_, pp.132-137). R.E.Clements remarks that it is clear that it was the restoration of full sacrificial worship in the rebuilt Jerusalem temple in 516 B.C. that necessitated a satisfactory resolution of the priesthood issue. He sees therefore good reason for regarding the regulation governing the priesthood in Ezekiel 44:15ff. (Zadokites rather than sons of Aaron) as having been compiled before 516 B.C. (_Israel's Prophetic Tradition_, p.131).

20. For other remarks on this matter, see Levenson, _Theology of the Program of Restoration_, pp.144-151.
21. Gese argues that 45:1ff. is excerpted from 48:9ff. but newly formulated on the basis of 44:6ff. (_Verfassungsentwurf_, pp.106-107).
22. The term used is nāśî', and Levenson has a survey of the discussion concerning its meaning (_Theology of the Program of Restoration_, pp.57-62). Like Baltzer (_Ezechiel und Deuterojesaja_, pp.136-141), Levenson himself thinks the term is messianic (pp.62-69). He also discusses earlier passages in Ezekiel (17; 34; 37) and concludes that 'Ezekiel hoped for a new David who would stand in a new relationship to YHWH as Zedekiah stood in relationship to Nebuchnezzar - as a vassal...' He thinks that the Davidic office was depoliticized during the exile and the messianic figure absorbed into the divine personality (pp.75-101).
23. Eichrodt, _Ezekiel_, pp.571-572.
24. Eichrodt, _Ezekiel_, pp.572-573.
25. Eichrodt, _Ezekiel_, p.574.
26. Menahem Haran thinks that, in Ezekiel's code, the distinctive character of the first day as the ḥag day has become obscured. The wording is an indication of the secondary character of Ezekiel's code (_Temples and Temple Service in Ancient Israel_, Clarendon Press, Oxford, 1978, p.296, note 13).
27. See Zimmerli, _Ezekiel 2_, p.500.

3) The Land Surrounding the Place: 47 - 48

1. Eichrodt, _Ezekiel_, pp.581-582.
2. Macholz thinks the succession of describing the land and distributing the land may go back to a procedure of land distribution in the framework of the local community (_VT_ XIX/3, 1969, p.329).
3. Eichrodt, _Ezekiel_, pp.590-591.
4. Eichrodt, _Ezekiel_, p.592.
5. See Levenson, _Theology of the Program of Restoration_, p.123.
6. See Levenson, _Theology of the Program of Restoration_, pp.116-121.
7. Zimmerli, _Ezekiel 2_, pp.540-541.
8. Zimmerli, _Ezekiel 2_, p.545.
9. Zimmerli, _Ezekiel 2_, p.547.